Ernst & Young's Profit from the New Tax Law

Ernst & Young's Profit from the New Tax Law

Martin Nissenbaum
Jeffrey Bolson
Marc Myers

John Wiley & Sons, Inc.
New York • Chichester • Weinheim • Brisbane • Singapore • Toronto

Published by John Wiley & Sons, Inc.
Published simultaneously in Canada.

This publication is designed to provide accurate and authoritative information in regard to the subject matter covered. It is sold with the understanding that the publisher is not engaged in rendering professional services. If professional advice or other expert assistance is required, the services of a competent professional person should be sought.

Library of Congress Cataloging-in-Publication Data:

ISBN 0-471-08302-X

Printed in the United States of America.

10 9 8 7 6 5 4 3 2 1

Contents

Austin-American
Statesman

GIFT

10-06-01

About the Authors

Martin Nissenbaum is Ernst & Young's director of Personal Income Tax Planning, specializing in individual income tax and personal financial planning. He is an attorney and a Certified Public Accountant (CPA) and holds an LL.M. in tax; he is a Certified Financial Planner (CFP) and holds the Personal Financial Specialist (PFS) accreditation from the American Institute of Certified Public Accounts. Based in New York, Mr. Nissenbaum is a speaker on compensation, and personal financial and tax planning to professional organizations, including the New York State Society of CPAs, the National Association of Accountants, the International Association of Financial Planners, the New York University Tax Society, and the Tax Executives Institute. He is frequently quoted and was named by *PR Week* as one of the top 10 quoted people in the business press.

E-mail address: martin.nissenbaum@ey.com.

Jeffrey Bolson is a tax partner with 28 years of diversified experience in the Metro New York and London offices of Ernst & Young. He has served multi-national clients in the fields of insurance, manufacturing, entertainment, importing, distribution, high technology and life sciences. Jeff is in charge of Personal Financial Counseling Program to the partners of the firm.

A graduate of New York University, Jeff received his MBA in accounting in 1973. He is a member of the American Institute of Certified Public Accountants and of the Institute's Personal Financial Planning Division. He served as President, Director and Chairman of the Tax Committee of the Bergen Chapter of the New Jersey Society of Certified Public Accounts and Vice President of the New Jersey Society of Certified Public Accountants and is currently President of the Bergen County YMHA and a Trustee of New Jersey Society of Certified Public Accountants Political Action Committee.

He has appeared frequently on the CNBC *Money Talk* series and CNN *Moneyline* as well as other cable and national television programs. He has written a number of articles for professional

periodicals and has lectured and provided financial planning semi-
nars for various organizations and corporations.
    E-mail address: jeffrey.bolson@ey.com.

Marc Myers is one of the country's leading personal finance writers
and editors specializing in tax planning, investing, estate planning,
and retirement savings. Mr. Myers was editor-in-chief of *Bottom
Line/Personal*, the country's largest financial newsletter, and is the
former editorial director/vice president of Netfolio Inc., a financial advisory investment firm. He has served as business editor of several
major magazines, and his articles have appeared on the Op-Ed page
of *The New York Times* as well as in other national publications. He is
author of *How to Make Luck: 7 Secrets Lucky People Use to Succeed*.
    E-mail address: myersmarc@aol.com.

Introduction

Unless it's repealed or modified by future legislation, the $1.35 trillion tax cut signed into law by President George W. Bush on June 7, 2001 will touch almost every aspect of your personal tax bill through 2010.

Each year over the next 10 years, the new tax law will phase out old rates, phases in new ones, and establishes a range of tax breaks and benefits. The most significant changes include lower income tax rates, a reduction and repeal of the estate tax, higher retirement-plan contribution levels, tax-free withdrawals from education-savings plans, and some short-term alternative minimum tax (AMT) relief.

What makes the new law so unusual and challenging for individuals is how often its rules keep changing from year to year. In fact, the new law made 441 changes to the old law, and many of them pop in and out at different times like a jack-in-the-box. And the biggest pop of all is that the entire law disappears in 2011! Keeping track of these changes will be challenging while the rules themselves are sure to create confusion for taxpayers.

That's why we wrote this book. Our intention is to clarify the new tax law in terms you can understand. You'll find that the book is organized in a way that tells you what rules are changing, whether or not they affect you, and how to profit from them..

THE BIG CHANGES

Known officially as the Economic Growth and Tax Relief Reconciliation Act of 2001, the new law represents the biggest tax reduction in 20 years and provides the first drop in individual income-tax rates since 1987.

The tax law took effect on July 1, 2001, when the top four income tax rates were cut by a point. In reality, these rates will drop only a half point in 2001. Congress decided that it's easier this way, to average your old 2001 rate and your new one. Then, in 2002, the top four rates will drop another half point—giving you the full-point drop mandated by the new law.

These income tax rates will drop again in 2004 and in 2006, at which point the very top rate will have come down almost five percentage points while the other three will have dropped three percentage points. The 15% rate remains unchanged, but a new bottom rate of 10% was created.

As you probably know by now, "advance payment" checks of up to $600 began arriving in taxpayers' mailboxes in the late summer. While many have referred to the check as a "rebate," it's really an advance payment based on the taxes you'll pay next April on the income you earned in 2001. Congress doesn't want you to invest the advance payment check or use it to pay off credit cards. The government wants you to spend the money at the mall to help stimulate economic growth.

Another significant change created by the new tax law is the slow death of the estate tax. Starting in 2002, the amount an individual can pass on to heirs tax-free will gradually rise each year, while the top estate-tax rate starts to decline. For example, the current $675,000 individual exemption will jump to $1 million in 2002 and rise to $3.5 million between 2004 and 2009. The current top estate-tax rate of 55% will fall to 50% in 2002, slipping to 45% over the same period. In 2010, the estate tax is due to be repealed.

There is also a higher tax credit for families with children under age 17. This credit will rise to $600 per child in 2001, $700 in 2005, $800 in 2009, and $1,000 in 2010 and beyond.

Annual maximum contribution levels for 401(k)s and other retirement plans will start to rise in 2002, and higher deductions for married couples will begin in 2006. People who are age 50 or older will be allowed to contribute even more.

In 2002 you also will be able to withdraw assets from Education IRAs tax-free. The new law allows you to use those assets for tuition and selected costs at elementary and secondary schools as well as at colleges.

WHAT YOU NEED TO KNOW

As the income tax rates drop, you should wind up with more money in your pocket. But with more take-home pay, rising retirement-plan contribution levels, and new estate-tax rules, careful financial planning and flexibility will be essential.

For example, favorable changes in the estate-tax law mean you should review existing estate plans with your estate planner. You also will want to encourage your parents to do the same so that their inheritance wishes are in harmony with the new rules. Some trusts will still make sense. Others may not. Still others will need fine-tuning.

But don't expect all aspects of the current tax law to remain unchanged for the full 10 years. Historically, Congress has never met a tax law it liked for very long. Following the Reagan tax cut of 1981, Congress passed legislation in 1982, 1983, and 1984 that erased nearly a third of the original legislation. Then the Tax Reform Act of 1986 eliminated other tax breaks but lowered income tax rates. Between 1996 and 2001 alone, there were 1,916 changes to the federal tax code.

How significant the changes to the new tax law will be will depend on the political party that controls Congress and the overall health of the economy. For example, when the current tax cuts were first being discussed in 1999, the government expected to be sitting on a huge budget surplus. By the time the law was signed in June, the anticipated surplus looked like it might be much smaller. And don't rule out the wild card of election years, when politicians make promises that can be kept only by proposing tax law revisions.

No one knows what the future hold for the new tax law. For now, however, the law creates many opportunities for individuals, if you know how to take advantage of them. I hope you find this book easy to understand and that it becomes a quick reference guide for you in the future.

Martin Nissenbaum
Director of Personal Income Tax Planning
Ernst & Young LLP

Tax Law Changes: Year at a Glance

2001

- **Advance payment checks.** Arrive in mailboxes.
- **Income tax.** Top four rates drop by a half point.
- **Child credit.** Rises to $600.
- **AMT exemption.** Rises to $49,000 (married) and $35,750 (single).

2002

- **Income tax.** Top four rates drop by another half point. New 10% rate takes effect.
- **Earned income tax credit.** Eligibility level starts to rise.
- **"529" college-savings plan.** Withdrawals are tax-free.
- **Education IRA.** Top annual contribution rises to $2,000. Tax-free withdrawals can be used for nearly all types of education. Eligibility level rises for married couples.
- **Estate.** Estate and GST tax exemption rises to $1 million. Top estate tax rate drops to 50%. State death-tax credit is reduced by 25%.
- **Traditional and Roth IRAs.** Top annual contribution rises to $3,000. For 50+ savers, top contribution is $3,500.
- **401(k) and similar plans.** Top annual contribution rises to $11,000. For 50+ savers, top contribution is $12,000.
- **Adoption.** One-time credit rises to $10,000.

2003

- **Child care credit.** Maximum rises to $2,100.
- **Estate.** Top tax rate drops to 49%. State death-tax credit is reduced by 50%.
- **401(k) and similar plans.** Top annual contribution rises to $12,000. For 50+ savers, top contribution rises to $14,000.

2004

- *Income tax.* Top four rates drop by one point.
- *Estate.* Estate and GST tax exemption level rises to $1.5 million. Top estate tax rate drops to 48%. State death-tax credit is reduced by 75%.
- *401(k) and similar plans.* Top annual contribution rises to $13,000. For 50+ savers, top contribution rises to $16,000.

2005

- *Income tax.* Top end of 15% bracket rises for married couples.
- *AMT exemption.* Returns to pre-law level unless relief is extended by Congress.
- *Married standard deduction.* Rises to level that is 174% of single taxpayers.
- *Child credit.* Rises to $700.
- *Estate.* Top tax rate drops to 47%. State death-tax credit is repealed.
- *Traditional and Roth IRAs.* Top annual contribution rises to $4,000. For 50+ savers, top contribution is $4,500.
- *401(k) and similar plans.* Top annual contribution rises to $14,000. For 50+ savers, top contribution rises to $18,000.

2006

- *Income tax.* Three rates below the top rate drop by another point; top rate drops by 2.6 points to 35%. Top end of 15% bracket rises again for married couples.
- *Married standard deduction.* Rises to level that is 184% of single taxpayers.
- *Personal exemptions.* Restrictions start to ease.
- *Itemized deductions.* Limitations start to ease.
- *Estate.* Estate and GST tax exemption levels rise to $2 million. Top tax rate drops to 46%.
- *Traditional and Roth IRAs.* Top annual contribution for 50+ savers rises to $5,000.
- *401(k) and similar plans.* Top annual contribution rises to $15,000. For 50+ savers, top contribution rises to $20,000.

2007

- *Married standard deduction.* Rises to level that is 187% of single taxpayers.
- *Estate.* Top tax rate drops to 45%.
- *Income tax.* Top end of 15% bracket rises again for married couples.

2008

- *Married standard deduction.* Rises to level that is 190% of single taxpayers.
- **Estate:** Estate and GST tax exemption level rises to $2 million.
- *Traditional and Roth IRAs.* Top annual contribution rises to $5,000. Top contribution for 50+ savers rises to $6,000.
- *Income tax.* Top end of 15% bracket rises again for married couples.

2009

- *Married standard deduction.* Rises to level that is 200% or twice that of single taxpayers.
- *Child credit.* Rises to $800.
- *Estate.* Estate and GST tax exemption level rises to $3.5 million.

2010

- *Child credit.* Rises to $1,000.
- *Estate.* Estate tax is repealed.

2011

- *Sunset provision.* Every provision of the new law disappears and the old law returns—unless Congress extends it.

Tax Law Changes:
Topics at a Glance

ADVANCE PAYMENT CHECKS

Married taxpayers who earned at least $12,000 in 2000 will receive $600 in 2001

Head of a household who earned at least $10,000 in 2000 will receive $500 in 2001

Single taxpayers who earned at least $6,000 in 2000 will receive $300 in 2001

INCOME TAX RATES

How the top four income tax rates stack up in:

2001	39.1%
	35.5
	30.5
	27.5
2002–2003	38.6%
	35
	30
	27
2004–2005	37.6%
	34
	29
	26
2006 and beyond	35%
	33
	28
	25

ALTERNATIVE MINIMUM TAX EXEMPTION

The standard exemption under the AMT (2001–2004):

$49,000 (married), $35,750 (single) and, $24,500 (married filing separately)

MARRIED COUPLES

The Standard deduction for joint returns will be the following percentage of the deduction allowed for single returns:

2005	174%
2006	184
2007	187
2008	190
2009	200

The top end of the 15% tax bracket for joint returns will rise by the following percentage of the 15% bracket income for single returns:

2005	180%
2006	187
2007	193
2008	200

CHILD CREDIT

The maximum tax *credit per child*:

2001–2004	$ 600
2005–2008	700
2009	800
2010 and beyond	1,000

INDIVIDUAL RETIREMENT ACCOUNTS

The maximum annual contribution to a *Traditional IRA* and *Roth IRA*:

2001	$2,000
2002–2004	3,000
2005–2007	4,000
2008	5,000

After 2008, the maximum annual contribution ($5,000) will be indexed for inflation in $500 steps.

The maximum annual contribution to a *Traditional IRA* and *Roth IRA* for taxpayers age 50 or older:

2001	$2,000
2002–2004	3,500
2005	4,500
2006–2007	5,000
2008	6,000

QUALIFIED RETIREMENT PLANS

The maximum annual contribution to *401(k)* and *403(b)* plans:

2001	$10,500
2002	11,000
2003	12,000
2004	13,000
2005	14,000
2006	15,000

After 2006, the maximum annual contribution ($15,000) will be indexed for inflation in $500 steps.

The maximum annual contribution that a taxpayer age 50 or older can make to *401(k)* and *403(b)* plans, and SEP plans will be:

2001	$10,500
2002	12,000
2003	14,000
2004	16,000
2005	18,000
2006	20,000

After 2006, this amount will be indexed for inflation in $500 steps.

EDUCATION

The maximum annual contribution *to an Education IRA* per beneficiary:

2001	$ 500
2002 and beyond	2,000

ESTATE AND GIFT TAX

The maximum *estate tax exclusion*:

2001	$ 675,000
2002–2003	1 million
2004–2005	1.5 million
2006–2008	2 million
2009	3.5 million
2010	Unlimited (estate tax repealed)

The maximum lifetime *gift-tax exclusion*:

2001	$ 675,000
2002–2010	1 million

The top *estate tax* rate:

2001	55%
2002	50
2003	49
2004	48
2005	47
2006	46
2007–2009	45
2010	0

The top *gift tax* rate:

2001	55%
2002	50
2003	49
2004	48
2005	47
2006	46
2007–2009	45
2010	35

How the New Tax Law Was Won

Date	Action	Vote
Dec. 1999	Presidential candidate George W. Bush proposes a $500 billion tax cut	
Feb. 8, 2001	President Bush submits $1.6 trillion tax-cut plan to Congress	
March 8	House Republican caucus approves income-tax rate cut	219–0
March 8	Full House passes income-tax rate-cut resolution	230–198
March 29	House Republican caucus approves married couple tax cut	217–0
March 29	Full House passes married couple tax-cut resolution	282–144
April 4	House Republican caucus approves estate-tax repeal	217–0
April 4	Full House passes estate tax-repeal resolution	274–154
May 2	House Republican caucus approves retirement savings increase	219–1
May 2	Full House passes retirement savings increase resolution	407–24
May 9	House Republican caucus approves revised budget	214–3
May 9	Full House passes revised budget	221–207
May 11	Senate approves budget plan	53–47
May 15	Senate begins debating its version of tax bill	
May 16	House passes repackaged version of income tax rate cut bill	230–197
May 23	Senate passes its version of income tax rate cut	62–38
May 26	Joint Congressional Committee approves $1.35 trillion tax bill	
May 26	Full House votes and approves final joint tax bill	240–154
May 26	Senate passes final joint tax bill	58–33
June 7	President Bush signs tax relief bill into law	

New Tax Rates and Income Brackets

On the next page is a table that will help you figure out what you will owe in 2001—before subtracting your tax credits. The table includes the new tax rates for 2001, depending on your marital status and income tax bracket. Remember, in 2001 you'll receive the benefit of the new 10% tax rate through an advance payment check.

For comparison, the second table provides an estimate of how the tax rates and brackets will appear in 2006, when all of the income-tax rate cuts are in place.

Tax Brackets for 2001

Married Filing Jointly

If taxable income is:	But not over:	Then your regular income tax equals:
0	$ 45,200	15% of taxable income
$ 45,200	$109,250	$ 6,780.00, plus 27.5% of the amount over $ 45,200
$109,250	$166,500	$24,393.75, plus 30.5% of the amount over $109,250
$166,500	$297,350	$41,855.00, plus 35.5% of the amount over $166,500
$297,350	—	$88,306.75, plus 39.1% of the amount over $297,350

Single Taxpayer

If taxable income is:	But not over:	Then your regular income tax equals:
0	$ 27,050	15% of taxable income
$ 27,050	$ 65,550	$ 4,057.50, plus 27.5% of the amount over $ 27,050
$ 65,550	$136,750	$14,645.00, plus 30.5% of the amount over $ 65,550
$136,750	$297,350	$36,361.00, plus 35.5% of the amount over $136,750
$297,350	—	$93,374.00, plus 39.1% of the amount over $297,350

Head of Household

If taxable income is:	But not over:	Then your regular income tax equals:
0	$ 36,250	15% of taxable income
$ 36,250	$ 93,650	$ 5,437.50, plus 27.5% of the amount over $ 36,250
$ 93,650	$151,650	$21,222.50, plus 30.5% of the amount over $ 93,650
$151,650	$297,350	$38,912.50, plus 35.5% of the amount over $151,650
$297,350	—	$90,636.00, plus 39.1% of the amount over $297,350

Projected Tax Brackets for 2006
(When rate cuts are complete)

If taxable income is:	But not over:	Then your regular income tax equals:
		For single individuals
0	$ 6,000	10% of taxable income
$ 6,000	$ 30,950	$600, plus 15% of amount over $6,000
$ 30,950	$ 74,950	$4,342.50, plus 25% of amount over $30,950
$ 74,950	$156,300	$15,342.50, plus 28% of amount over $74,950
$156,300	$339,850	$38,120.50, plus 33% of amount over $156,300
Over $339,850		$98,692, plus 35% of amount over $339,850
		For heads of households
0	$ 10,000	10% of taxable income
$ 10,000	$ 41,450	$1,000, plus 15% of amount over $10,000
$ 41,450	$107,000	$5,717.50, plus 25% of amount over $41,450
$107,000	$173,300	$22,105, plus 28% of amount over $107,000
$173,300	$339,850	$40,669, plus 33% of amount over $173,300
Over $339,850		$95,630.50, plus 35% of amount over $339,850
		For married couples filing joint returns
0	$ 12,000	10% of taxable income
$ 12,000	$ 57,850	$1,200, plus 15% of amount over $12,000
$ 57,850	$124,900	$8,077.50, plus 25% of amount over $57,850
$124,900	$190,300	$24,840, plus 28% of amount over $124,900
$190,300	$339,850	$43,152, plus 33% of amount over $190,300
Over $339,850		$92,503.50, plus 35% of amount over $339,850

Brief History of the U.S. Income Tax

The income tax is a relatively new way for the U.S. government to raise money to pay its bills. Back in 1791, when the country began, the federal government taxed Americans only on the sale of alcohol, sugar, tobacco, carriages, bonds, and property sold at auction. The sales tax was expanded during the War of 1812 to include gold, silverware, jewelry, and watches. But by 1817, with imports from Europe rising, Congress eliminated all taxes on American goods and instead charged just tariffs on the sale of foreign products.

This virtually tax-free period ended in 1862, during the Civil War, when the North needed to raise enormous amounts of cash without the South's help. In that year, Congress passed the first graduated income tax. A person living in the North who earned $600 to $10,000 a year paid a 3% tax, while those with incomes of more than $10,000 paid taxes at a higher rate. Sales and excise taxes were added along with the first "inheritance" tax. By 1866, a year after the war's end, the annual amount collected through taxes reached a high—more than $310 million.

Two years later, with the war over, Congress shifted its taxation efforts to tobacco and alcohol, eliminating the income tax in 1872. The income tax was revived briefly in 1894 but was declared unconstitutional a year later by the U.S. Supreme Court, which said it wasn't apportioned evenly among the states as mandated by the Constitution.

But by the turn of the century, the lack of an income tax at the turn of the century aggravated a class struggle. Fortunes amassed by industrialists who had profited handsomely during the advent of the railroad, machinery and assembly lines were safe from taxation. Instead, the government was relying on revenue almost entirely from sales taxes, which fell most heavily on the lower and middle classes. So in 1909, Congress passed legislation that established a 2% corporate tax and also agreed to pass a constitutional amendment authorizing a personal income tax.

Over the next four years, progressive Democrats and Republicans joined to support ratification of the 16th Amendment. It was passed on February 25, 1913, and made the income tax a permanent fixture of the U.S. tax system. In fiscal year 1918, annual internal revenue collections for the first time passed the billion-dollar mark, rising to $5.4 billion by 1920.

The withholding tax on wages began in 1943 and was instrumental in increasing the number of taxpayers to 60 million and tax collections to $43 billion by 1945.

The next big change came in 1981, when Congress enacted the largest tax cut in U.S. history up to that point—about $750 billion over six years. But that tax reduction was partially offset by tax acts in 1982 and 1984 that attempted to raise approximately $265 billion in revenue.

So on October 22, 1986, President Reagan signed into law The Tax Reform Act of 1986, one of the most far-reaching reforms of the U.S. tax system since the adoption of the income tax. The act called for a $120 billion increase in business taxation and a corresponding decrease in individual taxation over a five-year period.

Following what seemed to be a yearly tradition of new tax acts that began in 1986, the Revenue Reconciliation Act was signed into law on November 5, 1990. As with the 1987, 1988, and 1989 acts, the 1990 act provided a number of key provisions. But it also increased taxes on the wealthy.

On August 10, 1993, President Clinton signed the Revenue Reconciliation Act. Its purpose was to reduce by about $496 billion the federal deficit that would otherwise accumulate in fiscal years 1994 through 1998. Approximately $241 billion of the deficit reduction was to be accomplished through tax increases.

Four years later, on August 5, 1997, President Clinton signed the Taxpayer Relief Act, which included $152 billion in tax cuts. The bill included a reduction in capital gains tax for individuals, a $500 per child tax credit, estate tax relief, tax incentives for education, and a host of revenue-raising and tax-simplification provisions.

Anticipating a revenue surplus and insisting that the excess be returned to the American taxpayers rather than be used for government programs, President George W. Bush asked Congress in 2001 for a $1.6 trillion tax cut over 11 years. In the end, Congress approved and President Bush signed into law a $1.35 trillion tax cut over 10 years. The law's most significant changes include a gradual lowering of the top four income-tax rates over five years and a phase-out of estate tax by 2010.

Federal Income Tax Rates (1913–2001)

Year	Lowest Bracket Rate (%)	Lowest Bracket Taxable Income up to	Highest Bracket Rate (%)	Highest Bracket Taxable Income over
1913–1915	1	$20,000	7	$500,000
1916	2	20,000	15	2M
1917	2	2,000	67	2M
1918	6	4,000	77	1M
1919–1920	4	4,000	73	1M
1921	4	4,000	73	1M
1922	4	4,000	56	200,000
1923	3	4,000	56	200,000
1924	1.5	4,000	46	500,000
1925–1928	1	4,000	25	100,000
1929	4	4,000	24	100,000
1930–1931	1	4,000	25	100,000
1932–1933	4	4,000	63	1M
1934–1935	4	4,000	63	1M
1936–1939	4	4,000	79	5M
1940	4.4	4,000	81.1	5M
1941	10	2,000	81	5M
1942–1943	19	2,000	88	200,000
1944–1945	23	2,000	94	200,000
1946–1947	19	2,000	86.45	200,000
1948–1949	16.6	4,000	82.13	400,000
1950	17.4	4,000	91	400,000
1951	20.4	4,000	91	400,000
1952–1953	22.2	4,000	92	400,000
1954–1963	20	4,000	91	400,000
1964	16	1,000	77	400,000
1965–1967	14	1,000	70	200,000
1968	14	1,000	75.25	200,000
1969	14	1,000	77	200,000
1970	14	1,000	71.75	200,000

| Year | Lowest Bracket | | Highest Bracket | |
	Rate (%)	Taxable Income up to	Rate (%)	Taxable Income over
1971	14	1,000	70	200,000
1972–1978	14	1,000	70	200,000
1979–1980	14	2,100	70	212,000
1981	13.825	2,100	69.125	212,000
1982	12	2,100	50	106,000
1983	11	2,100	50	106,000
1984	11	2,100	50	159,000
1985	11	2,180	50	165,480
1986	11	2,270	50	171,580
1987	11	3,000	38.5	90,000
1988	15	29,750	28	29,750
1989	15	30,950	28	30,950
1990	15	32,450	28	32,450
1991	15	34,000	31	82,150
1992	15	35,800	31	86,500
1993	15	36,900	39.6	250,000
1994	15	38,000	39.6	250,000
1995	15	39,000	39.6	256,500
1996	15	40,100	39.6	263,750
1997	15	41,200	39.6	271,050
1998	15	42,350	39.6	278,450
1999	15	43,050	39.6	283,150
2000	15	43,850	39.6	288,350
2001	15	45,200	39.1	297,350

I

What You Need to Know Now

QUESTIONS ABOUT THE NEW TAX LAW

Over the coming months and years, the new tax law will affect nearly all areas of your financial life. Income tax rates will decline through 2006. The amount that can be inherited and passed along to heirs free of estate tax will rise through 2010. The maximum annual contribution levels to IRAs and 401(k), 403(b), and other retirement plans will increase. There even will be new tax breaks for married couples, families, and people who invest in educational savings plans.

Naturally, you have many questions. Below, Martin Nissenbaum, Ernst & Young's Director of Personal Income Tax Planning, answers the big ones:

Q. What can I do to minimize my income tax before the end of 2001?

Try to take more tax-deductible expenses this year if your income-tax rate is higher than it will be next year. The same rule holds true in 2003 and 2005, the years that precede the next tax cuts.

Such deductions will help offset your steeper tax bill. For example, in 2001 your income will be taxed at a rate that's halfway

1

between the January 1st rate and the lower July 1st rate. In 2002, the rate for the whole year falls to the one that took effect on July 1, 2001. So if you're in the highest tax bracket, your tax rate for 2001 is 39.1%. In 2002, your rate will be 38.6%.

As a result, it's more beneficial to have allowable deductions in 2001, 2003, and 2005, when your tax rate will be higher than in the following years. So, buying a computer for your home office or giving to charity in those years will produce deductions that are more beneficial from a tax standpoint than if they were made in the years immediately afterward. Paying points on a new mortgage in any of these years also is more beneficial than waiting until the following year.

Even though the new law didn't change the tax treatment of capital gains, you still should consider offsetting capital gains with capital losses. You can only deduct losses up to the amount of your gains, plus $3,000 (or $1,500 for married individuals filing a separate return).

You also may want to adjust your withholding at work so more of your total tax bill comes out of this year's remaining paychecks rather than having to pay a large balance next April.

Lastly, further reduce your bill this year by deferring income when possible to next year. If you're owed a check for consulting or you're due a bonus at year-end, ask to be paid next year. This advice holds true in 2003 and 2005, when you should defer income to the following year, when the tax rate drops. The rules for effectively deferring income for tax purposes are complex, so start the process as soon as possible.

Q. As I prepare my tax return next spring, what deductions can I take?

Most of the deductions that existed in the past remain in place. Here are the big ones that most taxpayers overlook:
- *Air conditioners and other home improvements that ease allergies and other health problems or disabilities.* The home-renovation's cost must exceed the property-value increase created by the improvement. Then you can only deduct the excess. You also need to have a doctor state in writing that the equipment and renovations were necessary.

■ *Job-search expenses.* Deduct the costs of looking for a new job in your present occupation. Costs include fees paid for resume preparation and outplacement agencies. You cannot deduct networking lunches and clothes purchased for the job search. But you can deduct travel to job interviews.

■ *Medical insurance.* 60% of medical insurance premiums are deductible by self-employed people who pay for their own health coverage. (A proposal to increase this deduction did not make it into the final law.) 70% is deductible in 2002, 100% afterwards.

■ *Unreimbursed expenses for certain health treatments.* They include contact lenses, laser surgery, eyeglasses, hearing devices, birth control pills, vasectomies and tubal ligation, and hospital service fees.

■ *Treatment for alcoholism, smoking, and drug abuse.*

■ *Lamaze class fees*, if the childbirth-preparation classes included instruction for obstetrical care, such as breathing exercises and your partner's role in the birth.

■ *Investment advisory fees.* Also deductible are IRA trustee's administrative fees—as long as they are billed and paid separately from your annual IRA contribution—and margin account interest expenses.

■ *Points paid on a mortgage.* Points can be deducted in the year your mortgage is obtained.

■ *Safe-deposit box rental fees*, only when the box is used to hold savings bonds, stock certificates, or other investments.

■ *Home-office expenses.* Your home office no longer needs to be the primary place of business. You can deduct the cost if you have no other place for management or record-keeping. You also can deduct cell phones and computers if they are required in your employment.

■ *Casualty losses.* This includes damage caused by storms, vandalism, lightning, theft, or floods. Deduct casualty losses that exceed 10% of your adjusted gross income, minus a $100 "deductible."

■ *Labor union dues*, protective clothing required at work, and education expenses for courses that are needed to maintain or improve your occupational skills.

■ *Subscriptions* to publications used for work purposes.

■ *Home computers* used to track investments. When you use a home computer to manage your finances, deduct a percentage of

the cost equal to the percentage of time you spend on your investment portfolio.
- *Penalties* on early withdrawal of savings from CDs.
- *Real estate taxes* related to the sale or purchase of property.
- *Half of your federal self-employment tax* is deductible.
- *Your state's personal property taxes* on cars and boats.
- *Property donated to a charity that had appreciated.* When you donate stocks or other appreciated property that you've owned for more than a year, you can deduct the full fair-market value of the asset—not just the amount that you paid. But you cannot deduct the full appreciated value of tangible personal property, like jewels or artwork, if the charity does not use the property in its operation.
- *Legal fees used to obtain or collect alimony.* Attorneys' fees for tax advice related to a divorce are deductible only when the bill specifies the amount charged for tax counsel.
- *Hobby expenses*, up to the amount of income you earn from that hobby.

Q. How does the new tax law affect my stocks and other investments?

The new tax law doesn't address the issue of capital gains directly. However, the new law will indirectly affect your investments in several ways.

As you know, gains on investments held for a year or less are taxed at the same rate as ordinary income. The government does that to encourage you to hold on to your investments and avoid the temptation to time the market. So if you're preparing to sell stock you've held for 12 months or less before the end of the year, hold off until January 1 and you'll owe a lower capital gains tax when your income tax rate drops.

This rule holds true for the end of 2003 and 2005—the years that precede the next rate cuts. For example, if you buy a stock in June 2005 and want to sell it in December of that year and will reap a $10,000 gain, you will owe federal tax of $3,760 if you are in the 37.6% tax bracket. Sell the same stock in January of 2006, when your tax bracket drops to 35%, and you'll owe just $3,500 instead.

The new law also indirectly affects retirement plan assets. Starting in 2002, the maximum limit on annual contributions to a traditional

IRA and Roth IRA, and 401(k) and similar types of plans will rise. Prior to the new law, the most people could invest each year to a 401(k) was $10,500. But with the top level increasing steadily over the next 10 years, you will be able to invest more and watch the larger amount compound tax-deferred.

There's a big difference between the results. For example, contribute $10,000 to a 401(k) plan that compounds at 10% for 20 years and you'll have $67,275. Contribute $12,000 in 2003 and, after the same 20-year time period and at the same rate of return, you will wind up with $80,730. Big difference.

Q. What are the other big retirement plan changes?

In addition to increasing the maximum annual contributions to IRAs and retirement plans, new breaks were created for individuals over age 49. This part of the tax law was designed to enable women who were out of the workplace for years raising children to save more now.

But the law allows anyone age 50 and older to take advantage of the "catch up" rule. The rule for this age group affects 401(k)-type plans and IRAs.

Coming to a place where you work in 2006 and beyond, companies will be able to offer a Roth 401(k). All employees will be eligible to participate—even those whose income prevents them from qualifying for a Roth IRA.

Q. Should I change my estate plans?

The estate tax starts to phase out in 2002 and is repealed in 2010. The phase-out occurs two different ways. First, the limit on the amount individuals can pass along to heirs free of estate tax will rise. Second, the tax rate on the amount that exceeds the limit will decline. So heirs will be able to keep more of the estate while the amount of estate taxes they owe on the rest will decline.

Do your estate plans need a major overhaul? The answer is "maybe." Everyone should have at least a will so that their heirs aren't hamstrung by the "laws of intestacy." That is a fancy way of saying that the state decides who inherits the assets and who manages the estate.

With the new tax law now in place, trusts already set up should probably remain in place. That's because, in essence, a trust is an entity that not only may keep your estate from owing more taxes than legally necessary but also ensures that the right people receive your assets and in the way you feel is best.

As for setting up new trusts, that depends on your net worth and whether your estate is unnecessarily exposed to estate tax risk. It also depends on whether your heirs can handle what they'll receive from your estate or whether it makes more sense to qualify how your assets are distributed and paid out.

In addition to the estate-tax changes, the credit individuals received from the federal government for paying state estate taxes will phase out starting in 2002. That's bad news. Why? As your credit for paying state estate taxes fades away, your state could raise its estate-tax rates to make up the difference in lost revenue.

That's because the estate tax changed by many states is directly tied to the amount of the federal credit. So as the federal credit goes down, so does the state estate tax. The estate tax in other states, such as New York, is not tied to the new credit. So if you live in one of those states, the total estate tax may be higher than it was before!

Estate planning is still critical, and consulting a qualified estate planner is key if your financial situation improves and asset values rise. Even if your savings and property value remain relatively flat, you may own a large life insurance policy. Life insurance payouts are viewed as part of an estate's total value. The only exception is if the decedent gave away the policy while he or she was alive.

So while the value of investments and real estate at the time of death may escape estate tax, a large life insurance payout could bump an estate into taxable territory—even under the new law.

With all of the nuances to the new tax law in the coming years, your estate plans need to be flexible so heirs don't wind up in a tax trap in an off year or wind up with more than you intended to give them.

At the very least, review your estate plans with a qualified estate planner.

Q. How should my parents adjust their estate?

While it's important to review your estate with an estate planner, it's equally important that your parents do the same.

All of the attention surrounding the phase-out of the "death tax" has convinced many people that further estate planning is unnecessary. Why bother with additional estate planning when the amount of assets you can pass along to heirs tax-free will rise each year?

For example, if you inherit assets before 2010, those assets will be valued at their current market value, which will be your cost basis for tax purposes. This is known as the "stepped up" basis. But under the new tax law, if you inherit assets in 2010 and sell them that year, you will have to determine how much those assets have grown in value from the time they were originally purchased. Only then will you be able to determine the capital gains taxes owed.

In addition, in 2010, the new tax law will allow a spouse to obtain a stepped-up basis in inherited property of up to $4.3 million to avoid future capital gains. However, the stepped-up basis for property inherited by someone other than a spouse will be limited to $1.3 million starting in 2010. Gains above these amounts will be taxed at the 20% long-term rate. If the assets were held for five years or longer, the capital gains rate will be 18%.

If your parents own a small business, other considerations need to be applied to be sure that the business will pass to heirs as intact as possible under the new law.

All that said, your parents should organize their papers carefully so that the price they originally paid for assets is clear and in one place for the surviving spouse and other heirs. The key going forward is to enhance or modify estate plans so they take into account all of the law's annual variations.

Q. How does the new law affect my college funding and credits?

The big news is that under the new law, withdrawals from Qualified Tuition Programs—known as "529" college savings plans—are tax-free. Under the old law, they weren't. In the past, only states could offer these tax-friendly plans. Now colleges can offer them as well.

There are changes to the Education IRA as well. (Technically, the Education IRA is known as the Coverdell Education Savings Account. On July 26, 2001, President Bush signed a law that made this change in honor of Paul Coverdell, a well-respected Senator who had died in office in July 2000.) Under the old law, you could contribute $500 a year to an Education IRA for each child. The savings could be withdrawn tax-free only for college expenses. Starting in 2002, the annual contribution ceiling is raised to $2,000, and the types of schools where the money can be spent on tuition will be widened to include elementary and secondary schools.

The Education IRA still has income limits. In the past, you could not contribute to such a plan if you and your spouse had joint income of more than $160,000 or you were a single taxpayer with income of more than $110,000. The new law increases the phase-out range for married taxpayers filing jointly. The new range is $190,000 to $220,000 of income. The single taxpayer's range remains the same.

In addition, the new law allows a taxpayer an interesting double play. You can claim a HOPE credit or Lifetime Learning credit for a taxable year and still withdraw assets tax-free from an Education IRA for the same student. The only catch is that the Education IRA distribution cannot be used for the exact same educational expenses the credit was used for. So you're safe if you use Education IRA assets for tuition and a HOPE credit for a laptop computer.

Also under the new law, an annual Education IRA contribution can be made up until the following April 15 to qualify for the prior year. As for special needs students, there is no longer an age restriction for Education IRA contributions. All other students must be under age 18 for contributions to qualify.

Q. Am I going to be hit by the alternative minimum tax?

The alternative minimum tax (AMT) was unleashed on taxpayers as part of the Revenue Act of 1978. Its original purpose was to ensure that wealthy individuals who could avoid paying income taxes using their many deductions and credits paid at least some taxes.

Think of the AMT as a separate taxation system. To determine whether you're subject to it, you must calculate your taxes two ways—using the regular income tax table and the AMT table. Then you must pay whichever result is higher.

In general, AMT rates are lower than regular income tax rates. But because you won't receive many of the deductions and benefits you would with the regular income tax, the AMT may end up being higher.

Who is likely to face the AMT? Anyone with large capital gains, a large number of exemptions, significant income from exercised incentive stock options, and residents of a state with a high state tax, among others.

Under the old tax law, only about 1 million taxpayers had to pay the AMT each year. But the number of Americans likely to be snagged by the AMT is likely to skyrocket to more than 30 million after 2004 unless Congress takes steps before then to amend the tax law.

What's all the fuss? Most taxpayers have been shielded from the AMT by their relatively low level of preferential income and deductions.

The reason so many more people will be swept up by the AMT now is that the AMT bracket and exemption levels were never indexed for inflation over the years. Meanwhile, the incomes of millions of taxpayers have been climbing, making them subject to the AMT. And by lowering ordinary tax rates, the law now makes exposure to the AMT even more likely.

The new law's attempt to deal with this looming problem was half-hearted at best. Instead of indexing the AMT income bracket and exemption levels for inflation so that they correspond to today's wealthiest taxpayers, the new law merely raises the exemption amount. The other problem is that while the hike in the exemption amount starts in 2001, it lasts only through tax year 2004. Then we go back to the old painful rules.

Until Congress overhauls the AMT, you'll need to carefully monitor your exposure to it by properly timing those items that create the most AMT risk.

Q. Can the new tax law be reversed down the road?

Though the new law is scheduled to last until 2010 and then disappear in its entirety, history has proven that tax laws are meant to be amended. For example, the last time we had a tax law this significant was in 1981. That law was changed in 1982, 1983, and 1984. The fact is that the tax law will most likely be altered should the government need money or if it's politically expedient to change it.

As a result, you need to consider the new law's benefits on a year-by-year basis. The odds of the law remaining in its current state aren't likely, and it's impossible to identify now those destined for the scrap heap. That's why strategic but flexible financial planning is so important in the wake of the new tax law.

How to Profit from the New Tax Law in 2001

Many of the new tax law's changes don't begin until 2002. But there are steps you can take, before the end of 2001 that can help you lower your taxable income, boost your deductions, and minimize your tax bill in April.

- **Size up your income tax due for 2001.** In order to avoid a penalty, the amount of tax withheld from your check this year plus any quarterly estimated tax payments must add up to 90% of your total tax bill for 2001—or 100% of your final tax bill for 2000 (110% if your adjusted gross income was more than $150,000), whichever is less.
  - *Did you pay too much tax this year?* Reduce your withholding and estimated tax payments for the rest of the year.
  - *Did you fail to pay enough?* Increase your withholding before the end of the year to make up the difference. Otherwise, you will owe a penalty.
- **Reduce your adjusted gross income.** Under the new law, if you have one or more children under age 17 and your adjusted gross income (AGI) does not exceed $110,000 (married filing jointly), $75,000 (single), and $55,000 (married filing separately), you can claim the full $600 child credit.

  As your AGI exceeds these thresholds, the amount of your credit will start to decline and eventually disappear.

  So if your AGI is on the border, take advantage of income-reduction strategies to qualify for the child credit.
- **Wait until January to make a "529" plan withdrawal.** Delay taking a withdrawal from your "529" college savings plan until January 2002, when the withdrawal will be tax-free.

  Withdraw assets from the plan in 2001 and the earnings on the amount withdrawn will be taxed at your child's income-tax bracket.
- **Offset capital gains with capital losses.** If you sold securities such as stocks or bonds, you will owe taxes if you realized a

profit. The amount of tax depends on how long you owned the security.

If you held the security for a year or less, you'll owe federal taxes at your regular rate—up to 39.1% this year. If you held the security for more than 12 months, you'll owe the lower long-term rate of 20%.

Minimize your tax by offsetting short-term gains with long-term losses. Net losses can offset up to $3,000 of ordinary income.

■ ***Otherwise, hold off selling securities until January.*** If the stocks you're about to sell were held for less than 12 months, you will owe taxes at your regular rate rather than the lower long-term 20% rate.

If you wait to sell until January, you will owe the tax when you complete your returns in 2003—and at a slightly lower rate. Under the new tax law, most regular income tax rates will decline another half point in 2002.

■ ***Donate equipment, clothes, and cars to charity.*** Most people own things that they no longer use. Give what you no longer need to a charity by year-end and you'll receive a deduction for their value.

■ ***Raise your number of qualified deductions.*** The key here is to take all of the deductions you're entitled to in 2001 without triggering the alternative minimum tax (AMT) or an IRS audit. Even though under the new tax law some AMT relief begins in 2001, talk to your tax planner about whether it's worth deducting the following:

— Amounts owed for alimony, business expenses, and interest on mortgage debts.

— State and local taxes in 2001. If you pay your state and local taxes by December 31, 2001 rather than in January or April 2002, the payment is deductible on your 2001 federal return.

■ ***Carefully examine your expenses.*** The IRS lets you deduct different types of expenses when those expenses exceed specific percentages of your income. Just be sure taking them doesn't force you to use the alternative minimum tax rules when calculating your taxes next year.

These include:

— *Medical expenses* that weren't reimbursed by your health plan are deductible if they exceed 7.5% of your adjusted gross income (AGI).

— *Miscellaneous expenses* such as employee business expenses, investment fees and legal fees are deductible if they exceed 2% of your AGI.

If your expenses in these areas look like they won't be above their thresholds, shift some of them into 2002 and reduce your level this year. If your expenses seem as if they'll be above the thresholds, take more of them this year instead of next year to maximize your deduction.

■ **Cut your taxable income.** Don't overlook ways to hold down additional income this year by taking the following steps:

— Don't bill for work done this year until 2002 if you own your own business or you're a consultant.

— Request that payments owed you be put off until 2002.

— Ask that your bonus be paid in January rather than in December.

— Put off receiving taxable income from cash accounts by investing the assets in Treasury bills that mature early next year. Treasury bill interest isn't taxable until the bill matures.

— Maximize your 401(k) and deductible IRA contributions.

How to Profit from the New Tax Law in 2002

The new tax law changes that take effect in 2002 offer many tax-saving opportunities. Here are the big ones:

■ **Take the $600 child credit—if you qualify.** If you have one or more children and your adjusted gross income (AGI) does not exceed $110,000 (married filing jointly), $75,000 (single), and $55,000 (married filing separately), you can take the full $600 credit for each child under age 17. Under the old law, the credit was $500.

As your AGI exceeds these income thresholds, the amount of your credit will start to decline and eventually disappear.

- *Make tax-free withdrawals from a "529" college plan.* Starting in 2002, withdrawals from these savings plans are tax-free when they're used to pay for college costs. Under the old law, withdrawals for college costs were taxed at your child's tax bracket.
- *Use Education IRA assets for almost any grade.* Under the old law, assets in an Education IRA could be used only for college costs.

   Starting in 2002, they can be used to pay for costs associated with nearly all levels of education, including primary and secondary school.

   And if you qualify for Hope and Lifetime Learning credits, you can claim them even when Education IRA assets are withdrawn—provided the credits and the IRA assets are used for different costs.
- *Contribute the max to an Education IRA.* If you qualify to make a contribution to an Education IRA, you can deposit up to $2,000 a year—up from $500 last year.

   You qualify to make an Education IRA contribution if your AGI is under $220,000 (married) and under $110,000 (single).
- *Pass along up to $1 million to heirs estate-tax-free.* Under the old law, the most a decedent could pass to heirs without causing them to face the estate tax was $675,000.

   Under the new law, that amount rises to $1 million in 2002.

   In addition, the top estate-tax rate drops to 50%—down from 55% under the old law. This means if you die next year, your estate will owe less on the assets in your estate that exceed the amount subject to the top bracket!
- *Make the new maximum IRA contribution.* The maximum you can contribute to a Traditional IRA or Roth IRA in 2002 is $3,000—up from $2,000 last year.

   Make the contribution early in the year so that the assets have more time to compound tax-free. You can own both a Traditional IRA and a Roth IRA—if you qualify—but the combined contribution cannot exceed $3,000 in 2002.
- *Contribute the max to your 401(k) or other plan.* In 2002, you can contribute up to $11,000 of pre-tax income to your company-sponsored plan—up from $10,500 last year.
- *If you're age 50 or older, enjoy the new rules.* If you're in this age group (50 years old by the end of 2002), the new tax law

allows you to make a top annual contribution to a Traditional IRA or Roth IRA of $3,500 in 2002. Last year, the max was $2,000.

And you can contribute an extra $1,000 to a 401(k) plan or other company-sponsored plan in 2002—in addition to the regular $11,000 contribution.

The new rules for taxpayers age 50 and older were intended for women who left the workplace years ago to raise children and could not save for retirement. The new higher level allows them to catch up.

But to be fair, the new law applies to both men and women in this age group—regardless of whether or not they spent time at home raising children.

How to Reduce Your Adjusted Gross Income

Under the new tax law, the size of your adjusted gross income (AGI) plays a big role in determining how much gain or pain you experience over the next 10 years.

At stake are your eligibility for tax credits, certain retirement accounts, ability to deduct certain itemized deductions, and significant rate and rule changes. The size of your AGI determines whether or not you qualify for many of the new tax breaks.

Under the new tax law, your AGI determines your:
- Roth IRA eligibility and size of your contribution
- Education IRA eligibility and size of your deposit
- The size of your child credit
- Your personal exemption restriction
- Itemized deduction limitations including limitations for unreimbursed medical expenses, casualty losses, and miscellaneous itemized deductions
- Ability to claim student loan interest and deduction for qualified higher education expenses

How your AGI is calculated

Your AGI is calculated by reducing your gross income by specific expenses—if you qualify for them. These expenses include:
- An IRA deduction
- Alimony payments

- Keogh plan contributions
- Any penalty paid on early withdrawals of assets from a savings account or CD

But don't make the mistake of going too far. You arrive at your AGI *before* you start subtracting your personal exemptions and itemized deductions or the standard deduction.

How to reduce your AGI

The size of your AGI depends on your gross income and how many qualified adjustments you are able to make to it.

The following strategies can help you reduce your AGI. They will come in especially handy if you find that your AGI is a little too high and is preventing you from qualifying for some or all of the new tax law's rules:

- *Contribute to your company-sponsored retirement plan.* Contributions to these plans are made with your pre-tax dollars. These dollars do not turn up in your paycheck, so they are not considered part of your annual gross income.
- *Offset capital gains with capital losses.* You're allowed to offset your capital gains with capital losses each year. If your losses exceed your capital gains, you can claim up to a $3,000 of your capital loss against your other income.
- *Invest in tax-exempt and tax-deferred securities.* Municipal bonds and municipal bond funds and tax-deferred annuities do not produce taxable income. Shifting assets out of income-producing securities and into these tax-favored investments will reduce your income.
- *Defer income to a future year.* By asking the people who owe you money to pay you in January rather than December, you can limit how much income you take in, thereby reducing your AGI. Of course, this strategy makes sense only if you can afford to wait for the money.
- *Avoid selling securities for a gain.* If you sell securities at a gain, the gains will be considered income. Defer the sale until a later year.
- *Take the IRA deduction.* If you qualify for this deduction, you'll be able to use it to reduce your AGI.
- *Make your alimony payments.* You can use them to reduce your AGI.

- *Consider shifting invested assets to children who are 14 or older.* This may subject the investment income to a potentially lower tax and at the same time reduce your AGI.
- *Establish a Keogh or SEP.* If you are self-employed, consider establishing a Keogh retirement plan or SEP before year-end and making the maximum contribution allowed.

TAX-RETURN MISTAKES THAT RAISE IRS RED FLAGS

As you complete your 2001 tax returns in February and March of 2002, be careful not to misread the new tax law or go too far when taking your deductions.

Here are the errors that most often raise IRS red flags:

- **Reducing your tax rate by a full point in 2001.** Many taxpayers think that under the new law they owe regular income tax at a rate that's a full point lower than their old one. While the new tax law did call for a one-point reduction starting July 1, 2001, the IRS decide that doing so from a practical standpoint would create a processing nightmare.

  So the IRS used a blended rate for 2001—the average of your old rate and your new rate, which works out to a *half-point* reduction for most taxpayers.

  While the 2001 IRS tax tables will show clearly the rates allowed for 2001, many taxpayers could miscalculate their tax liability.

  Here's how to protect yourself:
  — Know your new tax rate before you begin.
  — Use the proper rate for all taxable income.

- **Not calculating the alternative minimum tax.** The alternative minimum tax (AMT) used to be the rich-person's tax. No more. Now, a growing number of taxpayers are finding that they owe taxes under the AMT rules.

  Here's how to protect yourself:
  — The only way to know if you fall into AMT territory is by calculating your tax liability both ways—under the regular tax rules and the AMT rules. You owe whichever result is higher.

- **Failing to reconcile your advance payment check.** If you paid income taxes in 2000, you received or will shortly receive a check from the Treasury Department. This is an advance payment that the government wants you to spend immediately to stimulate the economy. Because it's an advance payment, you must reflect it on your 2001 return.

Here's how to protect yourself:

— The amount of the check must be reconciled on a worksheet with the credit allowed for the new 10% rate most taxpayers are subject to.

■ *Overstating your home-office deductions.* To be deducted, your home office does not have to be your primary business location. You can use the office solely for management or record-keeping if you have no other place to perform these functions.

The IRS looks hard at this area because many taxpayers overstate their home-office deduction.

Here's how to protect yourself:

— Allocate home expenses to your home office based on some reasonable method, such as square footage or a per room basis.

— Make sure your office is used only for business purposes. A kitchen or TV room can't double as a home office for tax-return purposes. Dedicate an entire room to the office. Or if space is tight, partition part of the room with bookcases or filing cabinets.

— Start-up and part-time businesses cannot deduct home office expenses that exceed the income they earn from their ventures.

■ *Claiming a huge tax refund.* The IRS grows suspicious of any tax refund that is large relative to the amount of income you report. A large refund often means unusually hefty deductions. Such returns often are flagged and pulled from the general pool at the IRS. They then pass through a separate level of IRS review.

Here's how to protect yourself:

— If you work full time for a company, ask your employer to reduce your tax withholding based on a new Form W-4.

— If you're self-employed, review and decrease quarterly estimated tax payments. Be careful not to take too much of a reduction so that you don't subject yourself to estimated tax penalties.

■ *Deducting cars given to charity.* The IRS is cracking down on perceived abuses in contributions of cars to charity. The general rule is that when donations exceed $500 in value, you must report those donations in detail on Form 8283 to deduct them. You can only deduct the real value of the used car.

Here's how to protect yourself:

— Ask the charity to document the condition of your old car in its receipt.

— Provide independent valuation of the vehicle's worth by referring to the *Kelly Blue Book* or a similar source for used car values.

■ *Claiming huge investment expenses.* Many people had big losses in 2001. To use those losses, some people try to claim that they've done enough trading to qualify as the owner of a trading business.

If you do qualify, the status makes the depreciation of the cost of your computer, investment periodicals, and other expenses fully deductible. By comparison, if you're not a trader, "miscellaneous expenses" such as these are deductible only if they exceed 2% of your adjusted gross income—and if you itemize.

Here's the step to take:

— If you claim this status, be sure you can document your trading activities to prove to the IRS that you are a trader, not simply an aggressive investor. Computer printouts, brokerage confirmations, and record books will justify trading activity.

■ *Deducting excessive business expenses.* The costs of personal organizers, cell phones, and laptop computers are deductible when they are purchased for the convenience of your employer and are required as a condition of employment.

Here's how to protect yourself:

— Ask your employer to reimburse such expenses instead of paying them yourself and deducting the cost.

— Or keep careful records of your purchases and the business reasons for buying them.

■ *Deducting IRA contributions.* If you are an employee and participate in your employer's company-sponsored retirement plan, you may not be able to deduct an IRA contribution.

If you are single and earn between $33,000 and $43,000, or you and your spouse file a joint return and earn between $53,000 and $63,000, part of the IRA contribution will be deductible. A special limit between $150,000 and $160,000 of income applies when only one spouse is covered by a retirement plan at work.

Here's how to protect yourself:

— Don't take the IRA deduction unless you really qualify for it. Otherwise you will owe income taxes and penalties.

— If you qualify, file Form 8606, which documents your non-deductible contributions.

— Remember, the IRS keeps close tabs on retirement-plan contributions because employers are required to report that information on your Form W-2.

■ *Forgetting to include key information.* Missing Social Security numbers or miscalculations will cause your return to pop out of the IRS computer and into the in-box of an IRS employee. Once the return is pulled, there's always the possibility that the IRS will look at it carefully.

Here's how to protect yourself:

— Be neat. When the computer can't read your return's data, an IRS employee will do it.

— Securely attach your W-2 and all other forms or schedules to your return.

— Follow IRS printed instructions carefully.

— Use the correct tax tables.

■ *Misreporting 1099 income.* Businesses that pay you income are required to mail you a Form 1099 and file a copy with the IRS. This includes interest, dividends, and investment sales, as well as income from freelance work and sales of real estate.

Report these amounts on your tax return exactly as they appear on the 1099. Otherwise, the computer that crosschecks your return with the copies filed by the payor will flag your return for closer scrutiny.

Here's how to protect yourself:

— When you receive an incorrect Form 1099, contact the payor and ask for a corrected Form 1099 before you file your return.

— If you can't get a corrected form in time, carefully attach a detailed explanation of the discrepancy to your return.

II

Profiting From the New Tax Law

1

Advance Payment

THE BIG NEWS

Most taxpayers will receive a check in the mail by late summer or early fall of 2001. The amount is up to $600, $500, or $300—depending on your marital status.

Do You Qualify for This?

Yes. *If you filed a 2000 federal tax return in April 2001 and weren't eligible to be claimed as a dependent on someone else's return. If you asked for an extension in April and have paid your taxes, your check will be delayed.*

BACKGROUND

In January 2000, just a few days before the New Hampshire presidential primary, candidate George W. Bush explained in a media interview why he was calling for a $500 billion tax cut over 10 years. The government, he said, was expecting a huge budget surplus. The money should be returned to the American people, not kept by the government to pay for existing and new federal programs.

At the time, the national economy was booming, and there was no end in sight to its historic double-digit annual growth rate.

But when President Bush officially submitted his $1.6 trillion tax-cut plan to Congress more than a year later, on February 8, 2001, the economy and its future were hanging by a thread. Economic growth had slowed to near zero and many experts feared that the country was inching toward recession.

What happened? The Internet sector collapsed in the spring of 2000, taking the Nasdaq down with it. Irrational investor exuberance had perilously inflated the value of most Internet and related technology companies. When investors suddenly decided to stop pumping cash into companies that weren't showing a profit and had no clue about when they would, the sector started to tank.

On its way down during the spring, summer, and fall of 2000, the Internet sector hurt many larger companies in other industries that had made expensive investments in the new over-hyped technology. By the start of 2001, the New Economy and much of the old one were facing hard times.

Fearing a prolonged economic downturn, the Federal Reserve moved aggressively to stimulate growth. It cut interest rates five times between January and the end of May 2001. It dropped the key federal funds rate from 6.5% to 4%, thereby making it easier for companies to borrow. But the initial rate cuts had little immediate or sustained impact on the economy. Unemployment was still rising, consumer confidence was falling, and the stock market was flat.

Many legislators in Congress who were debating the tax-cut proposal during this period grew increasingly worried. The benefits produced by interest-rate cuts and a sweeping tax law would probably not be felt by the economy for at least 8 to 12 months. The monetary and fiscal moves, though noble, could come too late.

As a result, Congress voted to send taxpayers a check with hopes that it would be spent quickly. Consumer spending is healthy for the economy because it increases corporate profits, creates new jobs, and ultimately lifts the stock markets. While some in Congress bristled at the thought of sending taxpayers what they said amounted to a "welfare check," most legislators agreed that an advance payment would help buy the economy some time before the interest rate cuts and tax cuts would begin to make a difference.

So an amendment authorizing the U.S. Treasury to mail out checks was worked into the final $1.35 trillion tax package approved by Congress and signed into law by President Bush on June 7.

THE NEW LAW

- *Married couples* with taxable income of at least $12,000 in 2000 will receive a check up to $600.
- *Heads of households* with taxable income of at least $10,000 in 2000 will receive a check up to $500.
- *Single taxpayers* with taxable income of at least $6,000 in 2000 will receive a check up to $300. This does not include dependents who earned this amount.

The U.S. Treasury said it expected the checks to reach most tax-payers by September 30, 2001. But a backlog of other Treasury mailings and extra time needed to create and print letters explaining the rebate could delay some checks' arrival until later in the fall.

WHAT YOU NEED TO KNOW

The government wants you to spend the money

The government would prefer that you spend the money on TV sets, tires for your car, clothing, or other goods and services. The U.S. Treasury sent the money in the form of a check rather than a non-refundable tax credit because it expects you to get out there immediately and help the economy grow.

Although you are free to spend the money any way you wish, Congress prefers that you not invest or save the amount. It also doesn't want you to use it to pay down credit-card balances or other forms of debt. Such uses for this money would not have a direct and immediate impact on the economy and would defeat the check's purpose.

You need to figure the check into your 2001 tax return

In early 2002, as you complete your 2001 tax return, you will be required to reconcile the amount of the credit with the check you receive. You'll have to complete a worksheet calculating the amount of the credit based on your 2001 return. That's why the IRS calls it an "advance payment."

Q&A

Q. If the economy recovers before I get my check, do I have to return it?

A. No. The government cannot cancel the checks unless Congress does so by law, which isn't likely. The money is yours to keep. Such an economic turnaround did occur in 1975 during the Ford Administration, just after checks were sent out. The money remained in taxpayers' hands, but the government took a lot of heat for being out of touch with the economy.

Q. How exactly must I account for the advance payment on my 2001 tax return?

A. The amount of the check must be reconciled on a worksheet with the credit allowed for the new 10% rate most taxpayers are subject to. The amount then is subtracted from the credit. For most taxpayers, the amount and the credit will be identical. But if the credit is higher than the amount you received in your check, the difference can be claimed as a credit on the 2001 return. If the check exceeds the credit, it's the government's goof and no repayment is required.

Q. Will I receive a check if I requested an extension in April 2001?

A. Yes, but only if you've already filed your return. If you requested an extension and filed a return, you'll receive your check later than those who filed in April. However, if you did not file a return yet, you may be out of luck. The IRS says that no checks will be issued after December 31, 2001.

Q. If I owe back taxes, will I get a check?

A. The amount of your advance payment will be applied first to any federal income tax you owe. If the amount is larger than the debt, you will get a check for the difference. If the full amount is applied to the taxes, you will not receive a check.

Q. Will college students with a part-time job who paid income taxes but live at home get a check?

A. If the student could be claimed as a dependent on someone else's return in 2000, the student will not be eligible for the advance payment.

Q. If I filed jointly in tax year 2001 but won't be doing so for 2002, how should I reconcile my check on my return?

A. The U.S. Treasury treats the advance payment to married couples as half for one and half for the other. For example, if you filed jointly and received a check for $600, treat your advance payment as $300 when completing a single return for tax year 2001.

Q. How long should I wait for my advance payment before checking on it?

A. The last checks for those who filed by April were to be mailed the week of September 24, 2001. If you did not receive a check by the following Friday, October 5, consult the Web site of the IRS (*www.irs.gov*).

The Advance Payment Lottery

How did the U.S. Treasury decide who would receive rebate checks first? The order in which the 91.6 million checks were sent out was based on the last two numbers of your Social Security number. For married taxpayers, the U.S. Treasury used the Social Security number of the first spouse shown on the return. For example, taxpayers whose last two digits are 00 through 09 received their check in July (see Table 1.1).

Table 1.1   Your Check's in the Mail

If the last two numbers of your Social Security number are:	You should have received your check the week of:
00–09	July 23
10–19	July 30
20–29	August 6
30–39	August 13
40–49	August 20
50–59	August 27
60–69	September 3
70–79	September 20
80–89	September 17
90–99	September 24

2

Tax Rates

THE BIG NEWS

- The top four income-tax rates drop in 2001, 2002, 2004, and 2006.
- A new 10% tax bracket is created in 2001, affecting most taxpayers.
- Personal exemption deduction limits start to ease in 2006.
- Itemized deduction limits start to ease in 2006.

THE FIRST CHANGE

The top four income-tax rates drop in 2001, 2002, 2004, and 2006.

Do You Qualify for This?

Yes. If your taxable income qualifies for one of the four top tax brackets.

BACKGROUND

One of the fastest ways to gain public support for proposed changes to the tax law is to call for lower regular income tax rates.

Most other types of tax breaks are narrow. They may relate to you or they may not, depending on your income, marital status, and other standards of eligibility. For example, many retirement-plan and education benefits are available only if your income does not exceed a certain level. Other credits take effect only if you and your spouse have children.

But the income tax rate schedule is a different story. It affects everyone who works, and everyone gets excited when they hear that they're going to pay less and hopefully keep more.

How the tax system works

The amount you owe each year in taxes is determined using a series of calculations:

Step 1. Add up your all of your gross income earned over the year.

Step 2. Reduce the amount by certain allowable expenses, which include student loan interest and any alimony paid. The result is known as your adjusted gross income or "AGI."

Step 3. Reduce your AGI by your standard or itemized deductions and by the amount of your personal exemptions. These exemptions are calculated taking into account a spouse and children.

Step 4. The result is known as your "taxable income."

To see what you owe, you match your taxable income to the appropriate tax bracket in the IRS tax tables. Each tax bracket has a corresponding tax rate.

When the Bush tax plan was debated in Congress in early 2001, the Senate and the House differed on the amount of the tax-rate cut. The Senate wanted to cut the 39.6% rate to 33%, the 36% rate to 33%, the 31% rate to 25%, and the 28% rate to 25% incrementally through 2007. But the House thought the Senate's proposed cuts for taxpayers in the upper brackets were excessive and accelerated too quickly.

So a compromise was reached that allowed for a smaller break for top-income taxpayers but allowed the rate cuts to be phased in completely in 2006 rather than in 2007.

When is a tax cut larger than it seems?

Actually, taxpayers in the top tax bracket will receive a bigger tax cut than the 4.6% called for by the new law.

After 2006, high-income taxpayers will be able to claim a higher share of itemized deductions and personal exemptions.

These tax breaks mean that the overall cut for taxpayers in the top tax bracket will actually be more like 6% rather than 4.6% by 2010.

THE NEW LAW

Lower tax rates. The new tax law reduces the top four income tax rates incrementally through 2006 (see Table 2.1).

Why your rate dropped by only a half point in 2001

If you're in the top four tax brackets, your tax rate drops by only a half point in 2001. What happened to the full-point drop starting July 1, 2001?

It would have been a tax nightmare for you to have to calculate half your income in 2001 at your old rate and the other half at the new one. So Congress is allowing for a "blended" rate—the average of the higher one and the new lower one. In 2002, the rates will come down another half point, bringing your rate into full compliance with the full point drop.

Table 2.1   The Tax Rates Decline

If your old rate was 39.6%, your new rate will be:

39.1% in 2001
38.6% in 2002
37.6% in 2004
35% in 2006+

If your old rate was 36%, your new rate will be:

35.5% in 2001
35% in 2002
34% in 2004
33% in 2006+

If your old rate was 31%, your new rate will be:

30.5% in 2001
30% in 2002
29% in 2004
28% in 2006+

If your old rate was 28%, your new rate will be:

27.5% in 2001
27% in 2002
26% in 2004
25% in 2006+

Table 2.2 What You Owe in Tax Year 2001

Married Filing Jointly

If taxable income is:	But not over:	Then your regular income tax equals:	
0	$ 45,200	15%	0
$ 45,200	$109,250	$ 6,780.00, plus 27.5% of the amount over	$ 45,200
$109,250	$166,500	$24,393.75, plus 30.5% of the amount over	$109,250
$166,500	$297,350	$41,855.00, plus 35.5% of the amount over	$166,500
$297,350	—	$88,306.75, plus 39.1% of the amount over	$297,350

Single Taxpayer

If taxable income is:	But not over:	Then your regular income tax equals:	
0	$ 27,050	15%	0
$ 27,050	$ 65,550	$4,057.50, plus 27.5% of the amount over	$ 27,050
$ 65,550	$136,750	$14,645.00, plus 30.5% of the amount over	$ 65,550
$136,750	$297,350	$36,361.00, plus 35.5% of the amount over	$136,750
$297,350	—	$93,374.00, plus 39.1% of the amount over	$297,350

Head of Household

If taxable income is:	But not over:	Then your regular income tax equals:	
0	$ 36,250	15%	0
$ 36,250	$ 93,650	$ 5,437.50, plus 27.5% of the amount over	$ 36,250
$ 93,650	$151,650	$21,222.50, plus 30.5% of the amount over	$ 93,650
$151,650	$297,350	$38,912.50, plus 35.5% of the amount over	$151,650
$297,350		$90,636.00, plus 39.1% of the amount over	$297,350

Married Filing Separately

If taxable income is:	But not over:	Your regular income tax equals:	
0	$ 22,600	15%	0
$ 22,600	$ 54,625	$ 3,390.00, plus 27.5% of the amount over	$ 22,600
$ 54,625	$ 83,250	$12,196.88, plus 30.5% of the amount over	$ 54,625
$ 83,250	$148,675	$20,927.50, plus 35.5% of the amount over	$ 83,250
$148,670	—	$44,153.38, plus 39.1% of the amount over	$148,675

WHAT YOU NEED TO KNOW

The long-term capital gains rate remains the same

The new tax law changed many things. But one tax it did not touch was the long-term capital gains rate. Profits on assets held longer than a year remain taxed at 20%—or at 18% if it's held longer than five years and was purchased after 2000. If you're in the 10% or 15% tax bracket, five-year gains are taxed at 8%—regardless of when the property was purchased.

The lower long-term capital gains rate is the government's way of encouraging you to hold onto your stocks and other investment assets for the long term rather than trying to time the market and expose your portfolio to greater risk.

Profits on stocks, bonds, and other securities held for 12 months or less are known as short-term capital gains and are taxed at your higher, ordinary income-tax rate.

Under the new law, you will benefit if the stocks you feel you must sell within 12 months are sold in a year when your income tax rate drops. This can happen if you bought stocks in June 2001 and want to sell them at a profit before June 2002. If you sell them in 2001, you will suffer a slightly higher tax hit than if you had waited to sell them in early 2002, when rates drop.

Short-term capital gains may be taxed at the same rate as ordinary income, but you're better off being taxed at a lower income tax rate if you can manage it.

The new rates affect bonuses and income from stock-option exercises

Under the new law, bonuses and income from exercised nonqualified stock options are still treated as compensation income and taxed at your ordinary income tax rate. That's why it makes sense whenever possible to exercise stock options and receive bonuses in years when your income-tax rate is lower. It's also beneficial to postpone such events if the extra income will bump you up into a higher tax bracket.

Action: Before exercising stock options, calculate the impact on your total annual income. Also consult your tax advisor, in case your taxable income will exceed last year's level, forcing you to make estimated tax payments this year.

If you're due to receive a bonus in December, ask if it can be deferred until January. For this to happen, you need to ask your employer for the delayed payment before your employer has determined your bonus. Otherwise it's too late.

> **Caution:** Just because you ask that a bonus be given to you in January doesn't mean it will escape being counted as income in the previous year. For the bonus to be counted as next year's income, the bonus check needs to be part of the following year's payroll. A bonus check that's merely held until the new year and then handed to you is simply a late bonus.

By deferring income until 2002, your income will be taxed at the new rate, which is a half point lower than the one in 2001. That means you will get to keep more of your money.

Maximize deductions in years that precede rate drops

The IRS allows for many different types of itemized deductions. As the tax rates drop, consider buying that air conditioner your doctor says you need for allergies or paying for investment advice in years when your tax rate is higher. By doing so, you'll be able to reduce your higher tax bill and not squander it in a year when your tax bill is coming down anyway.

Pay state and local taxes in December instead of waiting until April

State and local income taxes you pay are deductible on your federal return. Pay those state and local taxes in December and you can deduct them in a year when the tax rate is higher rather than in January or April, when your rate may be lower anyway.

Pay property taxes in December

Real estate taxes also are deductible on your federal return. The deduction is more valuable to you if you can take it in a year when your federal rate is higher than the following year.

Prepay a year's worth of expenses

The tax law allows you to "prepay" certain expenses and then deduct them in the year they are paid. For example, in 2001, you can pay for subscriptions to investment periodicals through the end of 2002. You also can prepay your accountant's fee for 2002 and deduct those payments in 2001.

Q&A

Q. Are my state income taxes affected by the new federal law?
A. Yes—in states that calculate your tax based on your federal taxable income. The other important issue to remember is that you owe state and local taxes on gains that are taxed as income.

   So, if you're in the top federal income tax bracket, under the new law your tax rate will decline to 38.6% in 2002. But you still may owe a total of nearly 50% on your income after you add up your federal, state and local taxes.

Q. Will I have to make estimated tax payments?
A. The federal government doesn't like being shortchanged. So it imposes a penalty on taxpayers who do not pay in enough tax during the year through withholdings or estimated tax payments.

   The penalty is actually an interest charge based on the IRS interest rates throughout the year. The rates may change each quarter based on changes in commercial interest rates. For 2001 the rates were 9% from January 1 through March 31, 8% from April 1 through June 30, and 7% from July 1 through September 30.

   To avoid this penalty:

- Pay 90% of the current year's taxes likely to be owed little by little throughout the year. This method requires you to estimate what your liability will be for the current year.
- Pay an amount equal to 100% of the prior year's tax bill. If your adjusted gross income for the prior year was greater than $150,000, the percentage of the prior year's tax you must pay during the current year is:
  — 110% in 2001
  — 112% in 2002
  — 110% in 2003 and beyond

This method is useful where you have a substantially higher tax liability during the current year. It is not useful when your liability is expected to go down.

■ Pay 90% of an amount calculated on an annualized basis each period based on your taxable items for that period.

For example, if your taxable income as of March 31, 2002 is $30,000, you would calculate the tax on $120,000 of taxable income ($30,000 × 4), divide the result by 4 and multiply it by 90%.

You would then determine how much tax had been withheld as of March 31 and pay the difference as an estimated tax payment.

This method works best when income is earned unequally throughout the year.

THE SECOND CHANGE

A new 10% tax bracket created in 2001 will affect most taxpayers.

Do You Qualify for This?

Yes. *Nearly everyone qualifies for this one based on our progressive tax system.*

BACKGROUND

In an effort to cut everyone's taxes, the new law created a new 10% tax rate. The rate will be used to tax a portion of your income.

This isn't a new tax. Under the old law, part of every taxpayer's income was taxed at 15%. So the 10% rate represents something of a tax break.

Example: If you're married, the government now taxes your first $12,000 of income at 10% rather than the 15% used in the past. Then the rest of your income is taxed at the rate that applies to someone in your income bracket.

The last time the lowest tax rate for individuals was below 10% was in 1986. Believe it or not, back then part of your income wasn't taxed at all.

Although the 10% tax rate technically won't be used to calculate your tax returns until 2002, you received the benefit of the new rate in 2001 in a roundabout way. For 2001, a portion of your income will be taxed at the old 15% rate. The 5% difference arrived in the mail in the form of an advance payment check.

THE NEW LAW

A new 10% tax rate. The new 10% rate officially starts in 2001, but it won't be used to tax part of your income until 2002. How much of your income will be taxed at the new 10% rate? (See Table 2.3.)

Table 2.3   How You Will Be Taxed Under the New 10% Rate

	(2002–2007)	
If you are:	*Your first:*	*Is taxed at:*
Married filing jointly	$12,000 in income	10%
Head of household	$10,000 in income	10%
Single	$ 6,000 in income	10%
	(2008 and Beyond)	
If you are:	*Your first:*	*Is taxed at:*
Married filing jointly	$14,000 in income	10%
Head of household	$12,000 in income	10%
Single	$ 7,000 in income	10%

Table 2.4 shows the tax rates for the rest of your income, depending on your taxable income and corresponding tax bracket.

Table 2.4   The New Tax Rates (2001–2010)

2001	*2002*	*2003*	*2004*	*2005*	*2006*	*2007*	*2008*	*2009*	*2010*
39.1	38.6	38.6	37.6	37.6	35	35	35	35	35
35.5	35	35	34	34	33	33	33	33	33
30.5	30	30	29	29	28	28	28	28	28
27.5	27	27	26	26	25	25	25	25	25
15	15	15	15	15	15	15	15	15	15
	10	10	10	10	10	10	10	10	10

WHAT YOU NEED TO KNOW

Everyone is subject to the 10% rate

The new 10% rate is most beneficial for anyone with an extremely low level of income. This includes students and retirees with part-time jobs. But taxpayers in every income bracket will feel relief.

Why? Because under our tax system, the first portion of your taxable income up to the amount set by the law will be taxed at this lower rate. In the past, the first part of your taxable income had been taxed at 15%.

Before explaining how the break works, you need to have a clear understanding of how our tax system works.

Let's make it simple. Imagine your taxable income is a layer cake. The greater your taxable income, the taller the cake and the more layers in the cake. Now imagine there is a different tax rate for each income "layer." The greater your taxable income, the more rates that apply.

So, as your income rises, the more rates are needed to calculate the tax owed on each layer of income.

Example: If you are single and had taxable income of $125,000 in 2000, you owed 15% on the income "layer" up to $26,250, 28% on the layer between $26,250 and $63,550, and 31% on the layer between $63,550 and $125,000—for a total tax of $33,431.

The new 10% rate also eases the "marriage penalty"

Now that you're a tax expert, let's introduce another concept known as the "marriage penalty."

In general, married couples who work and file jointly pay more in taxes than they would if they were two individuals filing as single taxpayers.

Too bad for them, you say? Well, it really isn't fair.

Example: Let's say a couple has $250,000 in taxable income. They both work hard, so let's assume that each spouse is responsible for an equal share—$125,000 each.

Here's where the penalty part comes in: Based on the current tax law, the couple will pay more in taxes than if each were allowed to use the same tax bracket as the single person.

Put a different way, think of them all as individuals. The two individuals who are married pay a higher rate on their individual shares than the single taxpayer who earned the same amount. That's because married couples are "penalized" by being subjected to rates that correspond to higher brackets.

So instead of the couple paying $66,862—twice what our single taxpayer owed—they pay $73,049 of tax.

The married couple paid $6,187 more than the two single persons would have—despite the fact all three people produced the exact same amount of taxable income in 2000.

Now you know why so many married couples scream about the marriage penalty and why it pays for some people to live together rather than get married.

The new 10% rate and rules ease the marriage penalty slightly. Under the new law, a married couple with $250,000 in taxable income in 2002 will pay a rate of 10% on their first $12,000 of taxable income. That works out to $1,200—or $600 each. Meanwhile, the single taxpayer who earned $125,000 will pay 10% of the first $6,000—or $600. Now that's fair.

Get married this year or hold off until next year?

While love and taxes are two very separate matters, it may pay to wait until January 2002 to take the plunge—if your future spouse's in-laws will let you.

Next year, most married couples will face a lower income tax rate and a much more marriage-friendly 10% rate. And by delaying your nuptials, you push the marriage penalty off by a year.

Of course, if only one of you works, marrying this year may make sense because of the "marriage benefit." In this case, a married couple with only one spouse working will pay less in taxes than a single person.

Example: Assume that only one spouse earned $250,000 of taxable income in 2000. The couple would pay tax of $73,049. A single taxpayer with $250,000 of taxable income pays $78,051. So the couple gets a marriage *benefit* of $5,002!

Unfortunately for married couples filing jointly, the same type of equality that exists in the 10% bracket does not occur among all the tax "layers."

Last word: One bad feature of the new law is that the income brackets exposed to 10% won't change with the inflation rate. So as you earn more money, a smaller and smaller piece will face this low, more favorable rate.

The income brackets are scheduled to remain the same until 2008, when they will rise by $1,000 across the board.

THE THIRD CHANGE

Limitations on the personal exemption deduction for higher income taxpayers start to ease in 2006.

Do You Qualify for This?

Yes. If your adjusted gross income is high starting in 2006, you will be able to claim a larger part of your personal exemptions.

BACKGROUND

You already know that to calculate your income taxes, you add up your gross income for the year. Then you subtract the allowable adjustments, such as a deduction for an IRA, Keogh plan contributions, alimony payments, and any penalty paid on early withdrawals from a savings account or CD.

What remains is known as your adjusted gross income (AGI).

Then the IRS cuts you a few breaks under the regular tax rules. It allows you to subtract your "personal exemptions." This is a fancy way of saying that you can subtract a specific amount from your AGI for every person in your household. The law figures that the more people under your roof, the bigger your break—provided your AGI isn't too high. If it is high, the law figures, the size of your exemption should be limited since you don't really need the break.

You can claim an "exemption" for you, your spouse, and each of your dependents. According to the IRS, a dependent is a relative or member of your household. The person must be a U.S. citizen, resident alien, or a resident of Canada or Mexico for whom you provided more than half of his or her support for the year.

You can only claim an exemption for someone in your care who had less than $2,900 of income in 2001. The exceptions are children under age 19 or children under age 24 who are students living at home.

Once you know the number of people at home that you can qualify as dependents, you have to do a little math: Count up the number of people who qualify to be exempt and multiply that number by a benchmark amount set by the tax law.

In 2001, the maximum benchmark is $2,900, which is adjusted upward each year for inflation. After you do this calculation, the result will be the amount you can subtract from your AGI.

Example: Let's say a married couple who files jointly has an AGI of $150,000. They have two children, and the couple supports a 70-year-old parent, who has less than $2,900 of income. They would have five personal exemptions and could reduce their AGI by $14,500 ($2,900 × 5).

But wait. In the world of personal exemptions, there's a price to pay for earning too much money. Under the law, the size of your maximum exemption starts to shrink if your AGI rises above a certain level. The IRS isn't about to give you too big a break if you're doing well.

In 2001, the $2,900 maximum exemption starts to get smaller when your AGI rises above:

- $199,450 for married couples filing jointly
- $166,200 for heads of households
- $132,950 for single taxpayers
- $99,725 for married couples filing separate returns

These levels also are adjusted upward for inflation each year.

But if your AGI exceeds these thresholds, the $2,900 maximum exemption starts to get smaller. Your maximum exemption will be reduced by 2%—or by $58—for each $2,500 of AGI above the threshold. The only exception is married couples filing separate returns. The reduction in their case is 2% for every $1,250 that exceeds the threshold.

Well, it doesn't take a rocket scientist to realize that, at some point, your AGI could be so large that you're no longer eligible for the personal exemption at all.

In 2001, you no longer can claim any personal exemption if you are:

- Married filing jointly or a surviving spouse with AGI of $321,950 or more.
- Single head of household with AGI of $288,700 or more.
- Single taxpayer with AGI $255,450 or more.
- Married couples filing separately with AGI of $160,975 or more.

Example: Let's say a married couple filing jointly has three kids. If the family could qualify for the full exemption amount, they could deduct $14,500 (5 × $2,900). But they can't because the couple's AGI is $223,000.

In 2001, this level of AGI doesn't disqualify them from taking the exemption but it does reduce the size of it. That's because their AGI is $23,550 above the $199,450 limit for married couples filing joint returns who qualify for the maximum exemption.

So they divide the excess—$23,550—by $2,500, which as you recall is the amount that determines the reduced exemption. The result is 10, rounded upward. Since they will lose 2% for each $2,500 of AGI above their threshold, that comes to 2 × 10 or 20%. So they would lose 20% of $14,500 (the amount if their AGI hadn't been over the line)—or $2,900. As a result, the couple's personal exemptions that can be deducted on their tax return total $11,600.

THE NEW LAW

Higher-income taxpayers catch a break. Starting in 2006, higher-income taxpayers will be able to claim a larger piece of the personal exemption than they could under the old law.

Under the old law, the most that taxpayers could deduct for each person in their household was $2,900. Taxpayers who had adjusted gross income (AGI) that exceeded certain levels could claim only a piece of that total. The thinking was that the more you made, the less you needed a full personal exemption.

Under the new law, the most taxpayers can deduct for each member of their household remains the same ($2,900 adjusted upward each year for inflation). The levels of AGI also remain the same (also adjusted upward each year for inflation).

The big change: Higher-income taxpayers who qualified only for a smaller percentage of the full amount will now be able to claim a larger percentage. How does that work out? Once you finish using the inflation-adjusted formula to find out the number you need to subtract from the maximum exemption, you will be able to multiply that number by 2/3 beginning in 2006.

Upshot: Higher-income taxpayers won't have to reduce the maximum exemption by as much starting in 2006. The result is that they will be able to claim more of the maximum exemption than they could in the past.

Then in 2008 and 2009, higher income taxpayers will be able to multiply their reduction number by 1/3, allowing them to claim more of the maximum exemption.

In 2010, there will be no more reductions on personal exemptions. All taxpayers—regardless of your AGI—will use the same calculation adjusted annually for inflation to determine your personal exemptions.

WHAT YOU NEED TO KNOW

Don't expect fireworks immediately. The truth is that high-income taxpayers will not start to see a change until 2006—and even then relief will be slight. Remember, the restriction isn't removed completely until 2010. It's also likely that the tax law will be changed many times between now and then. Whether this part of the law remains untouched is yet to be seen. Hence, there isn't much tax planning you can do now other than arranging to have more children.

Q&A

Q. **If I get divorced in the next five years, who gets to claim our child as a personal exemption?**

A. The parent who has custody of the child generally claims the child as a personal exemption. But that parent can release the claim to the other parent using IRS Form 8332.

If it's a friendly divorce, the spouse with the lower adjusted gross income will benefit most if he or she can claim the exemption, because that person is more likely to be able to take the full amount allowed.

But this rule isn't set in stone. Starting in 2006, the personal exemption restrictions will start to disappear, making the exemption attractive to either parent. On the other hand, if the other parent can use the full deduction and is in a higher tax bracket, the exemption deduction would be more valuable to him or her.

THE FOURTH CHANGE

Limitations on itemized deductions for higher income taxpayers start to ease in 2006.

Do You Qualify for This?

Yes. *If your adjusted gross income is high in 2006–2009, you will be able to claim more of your total itemized deductions. In 2010, the limitation will be repealed and you will be able to claim all of your total itemized deductions.*

BACKGROUND

Income taxes are determined by first adding up your gross income. Then you subtract the adjustments that the government allows. The result is your adjusted gross income (AGI).

The next step is to subtract your personal exemptions and itemized deductions to arrive at your taxable income—or the amount that will be taxed according to the brackets and rates set by the IRS's tax table.

A deduction is a personal expense that the government allows you to subtract from your AGI when calculating your tax hit. You can itemize your deductions—meaning you list them one by one. Or, if you don't have too many, you can use the government's "standard deduction."

There are hundreds of personal expenses that the tax law lets you deduct from your AGI. Certain expenses are subject to separate limitations. They include state and local taxes, and mortgage interest payments. Some have limits. For example, your medical expenses can be deducted only if they exceed 7.5% of your AGI and your miscellaneous itemized deductions, such as employee business expenses and tax return preparation costs can only be deducted to the extent they're more than 2% of your AGI. Once you add up all of these deductions, you have your *total itemized deduction*.

But not so fast. The government believes that if you make a lot of money, you shouldn't be able to deduct too much. As a result, if you have a higher level of AGI, you will likely have to reduce the size of your total itemized deduction.

In 2001, if your AGI exceeds $132,950 ($66,475 for married couples filing separately), your total itemized deduction starts to decline. This "threshold" level inches up each year as it is adjusted for inflation.

How do you determine how your total itemized deduction is reduced if your AGI breaks that threshold? There's a formula.

In 2001, if your AGI is over $132,950, the total itemized deduction must be reduced using one of the two following formulas, whichever one produces the lower number:

- 3% of the AGI that exceeds $132,950 (or $66,475 for married couples filing separately).
- Or 80% of the total itemized deduction that is allowed for the tax year.

But hold on. The second formula does not include medical expenses, investment interest, casualty losses, and gambling losses. You're entitled to those in full. (So, if you want to maximize your deductions, be sure to become ill in your broker's office after losing money at the casino during a hurricane.)

> **Example:** Let's say that a couple in 2001 has a combined AGI of $750,000 and $60,000 of itemized deductions. These deductions consist of $18,000 in state taxes, $4,000 in contributions, and $38,000 in investment interest. Because the couple's AGI broke the threshold, their total itemized deduction will be reduced by $17,600, leaving an allowable deduction of $42,400. How did they arrive at $17,600? It's the smaller of the two results produced by using the following two formulas:
> - 3% of the excess AGI of $617,050 ($750,000–$132,950), or $18,512.
> - Or 80% of the sum of the contributions and taxes, or $17,600.

THE NEW LAW

- *Starting in 2006*, higher income taxpayers will be able to claim more of their total itemized deduction.
- They still will have to perform the same calculation to come up with the reduction number. But once they arrive at this number, they will be able to shrink it by 2/3.

Example: A couple in 2006 determines after the first round of calculations that they have to reduce their total itemized deduction by $17,600. They then multiply this number by 66%. As a result, they would have to reduce their total itemized deduction by only $11,733.

- *In 2008 and 2009*, higher income taxpayers will be able to claim even more of their itemized deductions. In these years, they will be able to shrink their initial reduction number by 1/3.

Example: Our couple calculates after the first round that they have to reduce their total itemized deduction by $17,600 in 2008 or 2009. After they multiply this number by 33%, they will discover that they have to reduce their total itemized deduction by just $5,867.

- *In 2010 and beyond*, the so-called "deduction reduction" is repealed. Higher income taxpayers no longer will have to reduce their total itemized deduction based on their AGI.

WHAT YOU NEED TO KNOW

Get ready to perform two calculations

Once the limitations on itemized deductions start to ease in 2006, taxpayers in the higher tax brackets will have to do two calculations.

- First, they will have to determine the regular limitation on their itemized deductions, using the 3% and 80% formulas.
- Second, they'll have to determine the new amount they can subtract from the AGI in that particular tax year.

As a result, taxpayers should ask their tax planners in 2005 whether they will be affected by the rules in 2006, even as the limitations are being eased.

If you do expect to have a high level of AGI in 2006

It may be smart in 2005 to delay deductible expenses until 2006 once you reach the AGI threshold. That's because you'll be able to claim a higher total amount of itemized deductions in 2006. Conduct this same planning exercise in 2006 for 2007 and for every year until 2010, when the limitation on high-income taxpayers is repealed.

> *Reality check:* Keep in mind, however, that the limitations don't start lightening up until 2006 and the limitations aren't repealed until 2010. A lot can happen in 10 years. The limitations could be made tougher—or they could be completely repealed sooner. The key is to plan and remain flexible.

Q&A

Q. Does repeal mean I'll be able to take an unlimited number of deductions in 2010?

A. No. In 2010, you still will be restricted to a partial amount of the itemized deductions you can claim—depending on what type of deduction it is.

The law's "repeal" in 2010 simply means that previous restrictions on high-income taxpayers will no longer be in place, allowing them to subtract all of their qualified deductions.

3

Alternative Minimum Tax

THE BIG NEWS

The alternative minimum tax exemption rises in 2001 and remains at that level through 2004.

Do You Qualify for This?

Yes. Almost everyone runs the risk of having to pay the alternative minimum tax (AMT) instead of the regular income tax. The key question is whether or not you qualify for the full AMT exemption.

BACKGROUND

Understanding how the dreaded AMT works isn't as hard as it seems. Let's start with a simple analogy:

Imagine you're driving along Interstate IRS and that it's customary to be pulled over by the police once a year. For the sake of this analogy, let's assume that your speed is your annual gross income and the faster you are driving, the higher your income when you're pulled over.

You look in the rear-view mirror and watch as two officers get out of their car and head toward yours. The patrolman who walks over to your side is Officer Regular Tax. He's a relatively sympathetic guy who is fair and generous if you are a productive citizen. The other patrolman is Officer AMT. He's standing on the other side of your car and he isn't as tolerant or understanding.

Officer Regular Tax begins by asking you a bunch of questions about your personal life before adding up your fine. Your answers are important because, on this highway, your responses can reduce the size of your ticket. And the questions can get mighty personal.

Officer Regular Tax asks if you are married, whether you have kids, do you have any interest on a home loan, etc. He considers each answer and uses your answers to reduce the size of your ticket—provided your speed (income) didn't exceed certain limits. Little by little, the size of your penalty shrinks as he recognizes that you're an upstanding citizen who deserves a few breaks.

Listening to all of this from the other side of the car is Officer AMT. At some point—depending on whether those breaks are a little too cushy compared to how fast you were driving—Officer AMT gets fed up. Personally, he thinks all of the breaks that Officer Regular Tax hands out are for weenies.

Officer AMT usually takes over when it looks as if Officer Regular Tax is giving away the store. Officer AMT's job is to make sure his partner doesn't bill you much less than he should.

So when the breaks start to add up, Officer AMT cuts in. Leaning down next to the passenger side, he asks you a completely different set of questions to determine what your fine should be. He isn't nearly as nice about giving you breaks for your personal and professional life. In fact, he has a completely different set of rules than his partner. Unlike Officer Regular Tax, who bills you using six different rates, Officer AMT uses only two.

When he's done, Officer AMT adds up what he thinks you owe. Officer Regular Tax does the same. Then they both show you what they think you should pay. You have to pay the higher amount.

While our turnpike drama is an oversimplification, it does give you a feel for how the AMT works. Put simply, the AMT is a separate set of tax rules that is used to calculate your income tax bill. The only way to tell if you owe the AMT is by doing your taxes both ways—using the regular tax rules and the AMT rules.

In general, you are more likely to owe the AMT if you have a large number of personal exemptions, high state and local taxes, deduct interest on home-equity loans, and exercise incentive stock options. The odds of falling into the AMT's clutches rise when all of the adjustments to your income tax return increased faster than your income.

So even if your income does not rise from one year to the next, you still may face the AMT if your preferences and adjustments jumped significantly.

To calculate your AMT liability, you complete IRS Form 6251, which can be downloaded at *www.irs.gov*. As you work through the form, you're in for a shocker. You'll notice that you can't claim some of those fat personal exemptions that were allowed under the regular tax rules. Also lost is your deduction for interest paid on a home-equity loan—unless the loan was used to purchase or build a new home, or to renovate your existing home.

Also, under the AMT rules, say goodbye to the deduction for paying state and local taxes, as well as the standard deduction if you didn't itemize. If you did itemize deductions, the AMT does not allow you to claim a range of them, including some business, investment, and medical expenses.

Deductions not allowed under the AMT

- State and local taxes
- Unreimbursed medical and dental expenses except to the extent they exceed 10% of your AGI (rather than the 7.5% limit used for regular tax purposes)
- Interest on home-equity loans not used to improve your home
- Employment-related expenses, such as dues, subscriptions, uniforms, tools and supplies, educational, unreimbursed meals, entertainment, home office, etc.
- Safe-deposit box fees
- Tax-preparation and counsel fees
- Investment expenses
- IRA custodian fees
- Accelerated depreciation

What do incentive stock options have to do with the AMT? Nothing—unless you exercise them. Employers grant incentive stock options for two big reasons. First, they want to keep valuable employees from leaving the company. Second, granting incentive stock options is a way to encourage valuable employees to improve the company's bottom line. That's why they're called "incentive" stock options. To exercise a stock option doesn't mean to sell it. It just means that a certain amount is paid to own it in your portfolio. The next step would be to sell it.

If it turns out you will owe taxes under the AMT rules, the incentive stock options that you exercised are taxed in a way that you wouldn't face under the regular tax rules. Under the AMT, you owe tax on the difference between the price of the stock options when they were granted to you and the market price when you exercised them.

This gap is called the "spread."

Example: You work as an executive at a *Fortune* 500 company. You're super smart and instrumental to the company's future. So five years ago, your company granted you 5,000 incentive stock options at $25 each.

Now, you believe that a new product the company has launched is going to be highly successful. You believe that, in a year, the price of the company's stock could double.

However, you don't want to face a huge "spread." So you want to take steps to ensure that the appreciation on your options will be taxed at the lower, long-term capital gains rate rather than at the ordinary income tax rate.

So you exercise your stock options now, at the current price of $60 each. Then you hold the shares for at least a year before selling them in order to ensure long-term capital gains treatment.

Hence, the spread of $35 per share will be treated as a tax adjustment item for AMT purposes.

Under the AMT, the difference between the grant price of your stock option and the price you paid to exercise it is considered taxable income.

The AMT does cut you some slack. Any tax refund you received from your state or city during the year is not taxable. And some expenses that you incur if you own your own business are deductible.

The AMT exemption: The biggest AMT break is its standard exemption. Under the old law, the AMT's exemption was $45,000 for married couples filing jointly, $33,750 for single taxpayers, and $22,500 for married couples filing separately.

Under the new law, those levels are higher.

But qualifying for the exemption is not that easy. You have to meet certain criteria. For example, the size of your standard exemption under the AMT declines if your taxable income rises above a certain level.

Formula: Under the old law—and under the new one—your standard exemption is reduced by 25 cents for every dollar of taxable income above $150,000 (married couples filing jointly), $112,500 (single taxpayers), and $75,000 (married taxpayers filing separately).

After you've taken the exemption, the result is your alternative minimum taxable income (AMTI).

How to calculate your AMTI

- Take your regular taxable income.
- Add your disallowed deductions, such as state and local taxes, personal exemptions, etc.
- Add your income that's taxable only for the AMT but not regular tax purposes, such as tax-exempt interest from "private activity bonds" and incentive stock option "spread."
- Add or subtract other adjustments.
- Subtract your AMT exemption amount.
- The result is your alternative minimum taxable income.

Now it's time to apply the AMT tax rates to this number to see what you owe. As you know, the regular income tax next year and in following years has six different rates. Each one is applied to a different level of your taxable income. You will pay 10% on your first level of income, 15% on the next level and so on, depending on the size of your taxable income.

But the angry old AMT can't be bothered with all of those tax rates. Instead, the AMT uses just two. Whether you're married filing jointly or you're single, your first $175,000 is taxed at 26%. If you're married but filing separate returns, your first $87,500 is taxed at 26%.

Any amount above those levels for all taxpayers is charged at the 28% rate.

At first glance, it may seem that because these rates are lower than the rates high-income taxpayers face under the regular income tax rules that your tax hit will be less. But don't let those AMT tax rates fool you. Remember, under the AMT, you cannot reduce your tax liability using many of your fancy exemptions and deductions. Hence, the AMT tax bite may actually be deeper.

But wait, there's an even bigger problem. If you become one of the AMT's victims, you won't be able to lower your tax bill by many of the tax breaks created by the new law. As a result, your tax liability under the AMT could be even more painful—despite the 26% and 28% tax rates. Sort of like not being allowed to go to the new tax-law party with everyone else.

Congress does feel a little bit bad about all of this. So it lets you take a new tax credit for paying the AMT in future years. But you can only claim this credit in years when your regular tax is higher than your AMT and only for AMT that you paid that was attributable to "deferral" adjustments, like incentive stock options, and not for AMT that resulted from "exclusion" adjustments, such as state and local taxes and miscellaneous itemized deductions. To find out the size of the credit you'll receive, you have to fill out IRS Form 8801 or talk to your tax planner.

Why will so many more people be affected by the AMT in future years? Because the AMT rules have not kept up with the times. The AMT's standard exemption, the exemption's phase-out levels, and the AMT's tax brackets have not been adjusted for inflation since 1970, when the AMT was first unleashed on taxpayers.

To understand how constricting this is, ask yourself whether you would fit comfortably into clothes worn when the Beatles' *Let It Be* was No. 1 on the pop charts and the Carpenters were singing *Close to You*.

Because the AMT net has not been adjusted each year for inflation, incomes that were considered flush 30 years ago are much more common today. For example, only 19,000 wealthy people paid the AMT back in 1970. Today, the AMT snags about 1.5 million tax-payers. That number will climb rapidly if the AMT relief provided by the new law isn't extended by the end of 2004, when the higher standard AMT exemption will disappear.

And the AMT's victims won't all be wealthy. Many middle-income taxpayers also can be subjected to the AMT if their exemptions and deductions rise faster than their adjusted gross income (AGI). In fact, someone with just $28,000 in AGI could be forced to pay taxes under the AMT—if the person has two or more children (a lots of personal exemptions) and has paid their state and local taxes (a big deduction) in a state where taxes are high.

Even Congress has acknowledged that the AMT's original intent wasn't to tax the little people. For example, the Treasury Department estimates that those taxpayers affected by the AMT will soon shift from higher-income people with many dependents to middle-income taxpayers with moderately sized families.

> **Bottom line:** If your taxable income is between $50,000 and $75,000 and you have four personal exemptions, there's a good chance you'll be tagged by the AMT in coming years.

Fortunately there are ways to reduce your AMT risk and reduce the pain if you fall into its trap. But first, let's be clear on the new law.

THE NEW LAW

The AMT's standard exemption rises in 2001 and remains at that level through 2004

The exemption is the amount the IRS will let you subtract from your AMT income before calculating your AMT tax. But the amount of that exemption starts to decline as your AMT income increases.

Table 3.1   The New AMT Exemption (2001–2004)

Marital Status	Old Exemption	New Exemption
Married filing jointly	$45,000	$49,000
Single	33,750	35,750
Married filing separately	22,500	24,500

When the full exemption starts to fade: The amount of your exemption is reduced by 25% for every $1 of AMT income over:

- $150,000 if you are married filing jointly or are a qualifying widow(er)
- $112,500 if you are single or head of household
- $75,000 if you are married filing separately

Here's where it gets painful. Because the new law raised the AMT exemption level, the point at which you will lose your AMT exemption completely has increased as well.

Table 3.2   When Your AMT Exemption Disappears*

Marital Status	Old Law (1970–2000)	New Law (2001–2004)**
Married filing jointly or qualifying widow(er)	$330,000	$346,000
Single or head of household	$247,500	$255,500
Married filing separately	$165,000	$173,000

*Dollar amounts reflect taxable income under the AMT.
**In 2005, the AMT exemption reverts back to the old law unless the new law is extended or amended.

Special rule for married taxpayers filing separately

Under the old law, married taxpayers who filed separate returns were required to undergo a separate step to determine the cutoff point for the AMT exemption. The purpose of this step was to put their cutoff point on par with the one for married couples.

Under the new law, if you are married filing separately, the point at which you lose your AMT exemption is determined by multiplying the amount over the cutoff point by 25%. Your exemption is fully phased out at $173,000 of AMTI. If your exemption is phased out, you must to add to your AMTI the result of 25% multiplied by the excess amount that exceeds $173,000. This result is capped at $24,500.

Now the child credit can be claimed under the AMT

Taxpayers who qualify can claim a credit of $600 for each dependent child under age 17 for tax years 2001–2004. In the years that follow, the value of the full credit will rise gradually to $1,000 by 2010.

Under prior law, the child credit was scheduled not to be available under the AMT after 2001. Under the new law, the child credit can be deducted under the AMT if you qualify for it.

> *Caution:* Do not confuse the child credit with the personal exemption, which allows you to multiply the number of people in your household by a dollar amount to determine how much you can deduct from your adjusted gross income. Under the AMT, the personal exemption is not allowed.

Refundable child credit escapes the AMT

Starting in 2001, part of the child credit may be refundable for all taxpayers with children, regardless of your regular tax or AMT liability and regardless of the number of qualifying children. Refundable means the government will send you a check for the amount even if you owe no tax that would otherwise be offset by the credit.

The refundable credit will be equal to 10% of your earned income in excess of $10,000 (15% after 2004).

WHAT YOU NEED TO KNOW

Check whether you'll have to pay the AMT

To determine whether you owe taxes under the AMT or the regular tax rules, you must complete both forms. Then you owe the higher amount.

As a result, it's smart to do the AMT math before year-end. Even better is to do the estimate at mid-year, in order to leave yourself enough time to plan around your AMT liability. If you wait until January 2002, it will be too late to take steps to limit your risk for 2001.

In 2001, a couple with taxable income of $100,000 that claims adjustments that exceed $33,041 will likely owe taxes under the AMT rules.

If you're a borderline case . . .

There are two steps to consider taking before year-end to limit your risk.

Step 1. Consider not pre-paying state and local taxes. Many people prepay these taxes instead of paying them when they're due in April of the following year. They prepay them so that they can deduct the payment on their federal taxes for the current year.

But this deduction could push you over the line and into AMT territory. Whether or not you're subject to the AMT depends on the amount of your deductions, exemptions, and other adjustments under the regular tax rules and how they relate to the growth of your adjusted gross income. Too many deductions can trigger the AMT.

What's more, the deduction you receive for prepaying state and local taxes under the regular tax rules does not exist under the AMT.

> *What to do:* If you discover after doing the math that you aren't likely to owe taxes under the AMT in 2001 but may in 2002, prepay state and local taxes in 2001 and take the deduction under the regular tax rules.

When looking to deduct state and local taxes, don't forget to review your annual checkbook entries. You're looking for any prepayment of state and local taxes, including withholding and property taxes, which can be deducted.

However, if you live in a high-tax state and are close to the AMT threshold, don't try to double up on prepaying state and local taxes in one year. Some aggressive taxpayers in December like to prepay that year's taxes and prepay part of the following year's taxes to deduct them both on the federal return due in April. The large deduction created by the move could trigger the AMT.

Step 2. Boost your level of regular income. The other way to dodge the AMT if you're close to being subject to it is to increase your regular income. Remember, the AMT often is triggered when the adjustments to your taxable income increase disproportionately to your income.

One way to increase your level of regular income is to sell securities that you've held short term this year that you had planned to sell next year (long-term gains don't work because the maximum tax rate for those gains is the same for both regular tax and AMT purposes—20%).

You also generate income by asking that your bonus and consulting fees be paid this year instead of next year.

Or you could exercise nonqualified stock options or sell stock that you got on the exercise of incentive stock options (within 12 months from exercise or two years from grant) to generate the extra income. Gains realized on the sale of ISO stock within a year of exercise are taxed at regular income tax rates to the extent of the original spread. (By contrast, incentive stock options are not taxed when you exercise them, only when the stock is sold.)

If you are self-employed, create billings or speed up invoice collections before year-end.

All of these strategies can be tricky, so consult your tax planner. The last thing you want to do is miscalculate your AMT liability and sell securities to generate income only to find that you weren't even close to falling under the AMT and now have taxes to pay on gains you could have deferred until next year.

If you definitely will owe the AMT tax . . .

Take advantage of the few benefits that the AMT provides:

- Try to shift more income into this tax year that would have come in 2002. Your goal here is to have more of your income taxed at the lower AMT rates of 26% and 28%.
- Limit expenses in 2001 that can't be deducted under the AMT. Instead, spend the money in 2002, when you may be back to paying taxes under the regular tax rules. Such deductions include unreimbursed business expenses, which are considered a miscellaneous itemized deduction and aren't permitted under the AMT.

- Take the credits you are due under the AMT. Under the new tax law, there are a number of credits now available under the AMT that weren't available under the old law. Ask your tax planner about those in the following list:
  - Alternative minimum tax foreign tax credit
  - Empowerment-zone credit
  - Refundable child tax credit
  - Earned income credit
  - Excess social security tax withheld
  - Railroad retirement tax withheld
  - Gasoline and special fuels credit

If you won't owe the AMT as of now—but could . . .

Avoid making moves that will trigger the AMT.

- *Deducting certain home-loan interest.* Not all home-loan interest is alike. The IRS allows you to deduct interest paid on a primary mortgage up to $1 million for most taxpayers or on a home-equity loan of up to $100,000. The purpose of the loan comes into question with the AMT.

  > *Example:* On a return filed using the regular tax rules, all of the interest you pay on a home-equity loan of up to $100,000 is deductible. But under the AMT, you can deduct the interest only if the loan is being used to buy, build, or improve your home.

  So, before taking out a home-equity loan to consolidate credit card debt or buy a car, be aware that the deduction on the interest can trigger the AMT and the interest won't be deductible under the AMT's rules.

  > *What to do:* When it looks as if you're going to be subject to the AMT, pay down a home-equity loan if the money isn't being used to fix up your house.

- *Selling your home.* Selling a home may result in state and local taxes (if the gain is taxable). These taxes are deductible under the regular tax rules but could trigger the AMT, and the taxes paid aren't deductible under the AMT's rules.

■ *Exercising stock options.* If exercising incentive stock options will likely cause you to pay taxes under the AMT, exercise them next year. Remember, under the AMT, the "spread"—the amount between the grant price and exercise price—is taxed as income.

Under the regular tax rules, you're only taxed on the gain when you sell the stock you acquired exercising incentive stock options, not when you exercise them. And remember, exercising a stock option merely puts it in your portfolio. It doesn't put cash in your pocket until you sell the stock at a profit.

Always talk to your tax planner before exercising incentive stock options. If you fail to discuss such a move first with a tax planner, you could find yourself in a bind, especially if the stock you got on the exercise of the stock options plummets in value.

> **Example:** Let's say you exercised incentive stock options and you're subject to the AMT. How much tax will you owe on the options? Let's do a little math: Assume the price at which you were granted the stock was $75 and you exercised the options when the stock is worth $100. As a result, you owe AMT on the difference between the exercise price and the grant price—or $25.

Now let's assume that after you exercised the options, the stock's price plummeted to $50. Because the share price went down, you may not be able to sell shares to raise enough money to pay the tax owed under the AMT.

That's why consulting a tax planner before you exercise stock options is so important. There may be ways to avoid the AMT liability by using one strategy over another.

■ *Receiving income from certain muni bonds and funds.* Certain types of muni bonds are taxable under the AMT's rules. Such bonds are those offered by states and cities for private activities such as industrial development and low-income housing.

If it looks as if you'll be subject to the AMT, call your broker to be sure you don't hold such bonds in your portfolio or in a bond fund. You also should call the company holding your bond funds to be sure that they don't hold munis in their bond portfolios that can trigger the AMT.

If they do own such bonds, consider selling them before year-end and investing the assets in other types of muni bonds or muni bond funds.

- *Itemizing employee business expenses.* If you're an employee, watch out. You may be subject to the AMT if you deduct itemized business expenses. Talk to your tax planner about ways to minimize the impact and steer clear of the AMT by having your employer reimburse these expenses instead.
- *Claim the AMT credit.* If you are eligible to take the AMT credit because you paid taxes under the AMT in earlier years, take the credit in a year when you face the regular tax. Remember, you create an AMT credit only on items that were the result of a deferral of tax, such as exercising incentive stock options or taking accelerated depreciation.

Q&A

Q. What are the big AMT triggers?

A. Events that can trigger the ATM include:

- Paying large amounts of state and local taxes and taking the deduction
- Exercising incentive stock options
- Deducting interest payments on a home-equity loan used to consolidate credit-card debt
- Taking a deduction for unreimbursed medical expenses
- Taking a deduction for unreimbursed business expenses
- Deducting a large amount of investment expenses
- Other miscellaneous itemized deductions
- Having lots of kids

Q. Can't I simply avoid claiming deductions to avoid the AMT?

A. You can avoid itemizing your deductions and take the standard deduction instead. Or you can itemize only some of your deductions. But then these deductions will be wasted. The whole purpose of a deduction is to reduce your regular tax bill. If you don't take them just to avoid falling into the AMT, you will not be any better off. In fact, you may be worse off because you may push your regular tax above the AMT and thus exceed the 28% rate you would have paid under the AMT rules.

Q. What tax credits can trigger the AMT if I take them?

A. Some nonrefundable tax credits do not lower your AMT. These nonrefundable credits include:
- Child and dependent-care credit
- Credit for the elderly or disabled
- Lifetime Learning and Hope scholarship credits

Q. Can I skip taking the education credits to avoid the AMT?

A. You cannot avoid taking the Hope or Lifetime Learning credit. Either you are eligible for those credits or you are not. If they push you into the AMT, that's the way it goes. Your only move is to factor them into your plans as you attempt to avoid the AMT next year.

Q. Does it pay to correct a mistake on an old return?

A. Many taxpayers find a mistake in an old tax return and rush to correct it, thinking it will mean cash back in their pockets. But before you complete and send in IRS Form 1040X—which is required to amend an earlier return—have your tax planner run the numbers. You want to be sure that the credit or deduction you're claiming won't suddenly jolt your old return into AMT territory.

Q. What are nonqualified stock options?

A. In general, there are two types of stocks options—incentive stock options and nonqualified stock options.

With nonqualified stock options, you can buy shares from your employer at a price fixed at the date of grant. When you exercise them the spread is taxable as ordinary compensation income.

Here are the benefits of nonqualified stock options:
- As the value of the stock increases, you get to share in that appreciation without having to make any upfront investment.
- Gains accruing after exercise are taxed at the maximum 20% long-term rate starting 12 months and a day after you exercise the options.

If you own both types of stock options, ask your tax planner how to time the exercise of your nonqualified stock options so they offset the AMT adjustment from the exercise of your incentive stock options and minimize the risk of triggering the AMT. For much more information, go to *www.mystockoptions.com*.

Q. How can I exercise options?
A. There are four different ways to exercise your stock options:
- *Pay cash.* If you're at a volatile company, paying cash means trading money for a potentially rocky investment—so make sure you're not investing money you can't afford to lose.
- *Borrow money to exercise.* Many employers offer loans at relatively low interest rates. Just keep in mind that you'll have to pay the loan back, with interest—usually whether or not the stock you got from the options you exercised is worth anything.
- *Use a "swap exercise."* This strategy works best for employees who own stock that has soared in value. A swap exercise uses the market value of some of your shares to pay for the exercise price of the options.

  > **Example:** Let's assume you own 100 stock options with an exercise price of $1 per share. Let's also assume that the stock has a market value of $10 per share. Rather than paying $100 to exercise all your options, you would trade 10 of your shares—with a market value of $100— for the 100, which have a total value of $1,000.

- *Use a "cashless exercise."* Take the last example. Instead of paying the exercise price, your employer gives you 90 shares in exchange for the option. The value of the 90 shares— $900—represents the value of the spread in the 100 options.

4

Married Couples

THE BIG NEWS

- Married couples filing jointly can take a higher standard deduction starting in 2005.
- The 15% income bracket for married couples filing jointly widens starting in 2005.
- Married and single taxpayers in the 15% tax bracket are eligible for a larger earned income credit starting in 2002.

THE FIRST CHANGE

Married couples filing jointly can take a higher standard deduction starting in 2005.

Do You Qualify for This?

Yes. If you are married and file a joint tax return in 2005 and beyond.

BACKGROUND

Married couples have been screaming about the "marriage penalty" for years. While the new tax law doesn't completely eliminate the different ways that married individuals and single individuals are taxed, the new law has eased the burden.

Under the tax law, married couples are taxed on their combined taxable income rather than as two individuals. That may sound fair and logical—until you learn that the rates used to tax married couples correspond to income brackets that are higher than those used for single taxpayers.

What this means

Let's say three individuals earn the exact same amount of annual income. And let's say that the amount they each earn is $100,000. Two of the individuals are married to each other. Because they are married, their $100,000 amounts are taxed more heavily than the $100,000 earned by the single individual.

Sure, married couples can file separate returns, but it doesn't pay. The tax rates and provisions are structured in such a way that married couples who file separately will owe a higher tax than if they had filed a joint return.

Ironically, the inequity puts the government in the position of encouraging couples to live together unmarried in order to qualify for a lower combined tax rate. That's why this part of the tax law is know as the "marriage penalty." The government seems to be penalizing couples for marrying by providing them with a big financial incentive to stay single.

The so-called marriage penalty was born in 1969, when Congress changed the tax law to ease the tax burden on single taxpayers. Up until that year, a single taxpayer actually paid more tax on his income than two individuals who earned the same amount of income but happened to be married.

Back in 1913, when the income tax was introduced, the tax law treated everyone as individuals, regardless of marital status. But by the 1930s, how much you were taxed as a married couple varied, depending on the state in which you lived.

Some states had "community property" laws, which said that all property in a marriage belonged to both husband and wife, no matter who earned it. Most other states had "common-law rules," which said that property belonged to the individual who legally owned it. As a result, married couples in common law states paid higher income taxes than those in community property states.

In 1941, Congress tried to standardize all of the states under the common-law rules. The plan would allow the federal government to charge married couples a set of rates that was different than that for single taxpayers.

But the attempt by Congress failed, and a new problem emerged. With the community property laws still in place, married couples began to take advantage of a huge tax loophole. They were able to reduce their total tax bill by shifting ownership of investment income to the lower-earning spouse. So, common-law states began converting to the more favorable community property law to ease the federal tax burden on married residents.

In 1948, however, Congress put a halt to the law-swapping trend. It established a "joint-return provision" and allowed married couples to combine income and deductions on a joint return. Married couples would pay twice the tax that an individual earning half their income would pay. Married couples would be treated as a "household" rather than two individuals living under the same roof.

While the law standardized the tax bite for all married couples, two single people with the same income as a married couple paid higher taxes. This inequity was addressed in the tax law of 1969, which shifted a greater tax burden to married couples.

Some relief for married couples arrived in 1981 with the Economic Recovery Act. It eased the marriage penalty through the adoption of a 10% second-earner tax deduction. In 1986, the Tax Reform Act repealed this deduction but trimmed the marriage penalty by cutting the number of tax brackets for everyone and lowering the tax rates.

In 1993, Congress increased the number of tax brackets. But the highest tax rate hit couples in the top bracket with an additional marriage penalty of as much as $15,000 a year.

In 1995, Congress tried again to reduce the marriage penalty by doubling the standard deduction married couples were allowed to take on joint returns. But the bill was vetoed by President Bill Clinton, who also rejected another Congressional attempt to cut the marriage penalty in 1999.

The new tax law attempts to even the playing field, if only just slightly.

THE NEW LAW

Higher standard deduction

Married couples who file a joint return will be able to take a higher standard deduction starting in 2005 (see Table 4.1).

Table 4.1   Higher Standard Deduction

In the year:	Married couples filing a joint return will be allowed to take a standard deduction that's the following percentage of the deduction allowed for single returns:
2005	174%
2006	184%
2007	187%
2008	190%
2009+	200%

WHAT YOU NEED TO KNOW

Know when to take the standard deduction

A "standard deduction" is the amount the IRS gives you if you do not itemize your deductions.

Deductions play a major role in calculating your taxable income. To determine your taxable income, you first reduce your total gross income by the adjustments the IRS allows. The result is your adjusted gross income (AGI).

Then the IRS gives you two choices:

- You either itemize your tax-deductible expenses, or
- You choose the standard deduction, which the government created to even the playing field. The standard deduction is adjusted annually to match the rate of inflation.

It's worth itemizing your deductions only if they exceed the standard deduction.

While debating the new tax law in early 2001, the House wanted to give married couples who file jointly a standard deduction that was double the one for single taxpayers. The House wanted that bigger standard to start in 2002. The Senate had no problem with the increase but wanted to phase in the increase over a longer period of time. Congress ultimately went along with the Senate's extended timetable.

While the new law does not roll back the clock to 1969, when there was no marriage penalty, it boosts the standard deduction for married couples beginning in 2005.

The law brings relief to married taxpayers who have few or no itemized deductions.

Don't itemize until you've checked your state's rules first

Some states require that you itemize deductions on your state form if you do so on your federal return. What's wrong with that? State income taxes are not deductible on most state returns.

Hence, itemizing deductions on your state form may produce a number that's lower in value than your state's standard deduction. In this case, you may have been better off taking the standard deduction on your federal return.

Know what deductions can be itemized

Here are the big deductions that you can itemize on your regular tax return:

- Certain employee business expenses
- Qualified mortgage interest
- Unreimbursed medical and dental expenses in excess of 7.5% of your AGI
- Property taxes
- Charitable contributions
- Casualty and theft losses in excess of set thresholds
- State income taxes
- Investment interest

Create year-end deductions to lower your tax bite

Make the following moves before year-end and include them as part of your itemized deductions:

- Donate old clothes, appliances, and stereo equipment to a church or charity.
- Buy equipment or software that helps you invest.
- Prepay your property taxes.
- Accelerate the payment of state income-tax liability.
- Contribute securities that have appreciated in value to a qualified charity.

Know how to calculate your federal itemized deductions

If the total of your itemized deductions exceeds the standard deduction, you must complete and attach Schedule A, Itemized Deductions, to your Form 1040.

Q&A

Q. Is there a fast way to estimate whether it pays to itemize or take the standard deduction?

A. There is no fast way except to sit down and work through an estimate.

Q. When must I itemize my deductions, regardless of whether the standard deduction is higher?

A. You have to itemize your deductions if you are:
- Married but filing separately and your spouse itemizes
- You are a nonresident alien
- You file a short-period return because of a change in your accounting period

Q. What is commonly overlooked when itemizing deductions?

A. Make sure you claim any payroll deductions that qualify as an itemized deduction. Such payroll deductions include contributions to the United Way and any state unemployment or disability taxes that are required to be withheld.

THE SECOND CHANGE

The 15% income bracket for married couples filing jointly will expand starting in 2005.

Do You Qualify for This?

Yes. *Everyone qualifies, including higher-income taxpayers because part of their taxable income is taxed at the 15% rate.*

BACKGROUND

The 15% tax bracket was the result of the 1986 Tax Reform Act, which established just two income-tax rates—15% and 28%. The Act's objective was to put in place a 15% income tax bracket for all low- and middle-income wage earners and a 28% bracket for wealthier people. Just a year earlier, the lowest rate was 11% on taxable income up to $3,000.

The rates took effect in 1988. Married couples filing jointly qualified for the 15% rate if their taxable income did not exceed $29,750. The top tax bracket of 28% was nice while it lasted—but it didn't last long. The top rate jumped in 1991 to 31% and again to 39.6% in 1993.

But the 15% rate remained in place and is still in effect—although it's no longer the lowest rate. The new 10% rate took effect in 2001.

Under the old law, single taxpayers paid only about 60% of the rate that married couples who filed jointly did. The new law does not create immediate relief for married taxpayers filing jointly but it does widen the 15% bracket.

Both the House and Senate wanted to raise the income bracket needed to qualify for the 15% rate for married couples filing jointly. But the House wanted to phase in the increase over six years, starting in 2004. The Senate wanted the increase phased in over five years starting in 2005.

In the end, Congress decided to expand the 15% income bracket to twice that of a single taxpayer. The phase in of this rate bracket expansion begins in 2005 and is complete in 2008.

THE NEW LAW

Higher 15% bracket. The top end of the 15% tax bracket will rise for married couples filing jointly starting in 2005. The bracket's ceiling will continue to rise incrementally until 2008, when it will be twice the level that affects single taxpayers.

Table 4.2 shows how the 15% tax bracket will expand for married couples.

Table 4.2 Higher 15% Tax Bracket

In the year:	The top end of the 15% bracket for married couples filing a joint return will be the following percentage of the rate bracket amount for single taxpayers:
2005	180%
2006	187%
2007	193%
2008+	200% (double)

WHAT YOU NEED TO KNOW

Remain below the rising maximum level

The best way for married couples to do this in 2004 is to defer earned income until 2005, when the 15% bracket rises.

For example, if you are in this tax bracket and are an independent consultant, ask to be paid in January 2005 so that more of your earned income in 2004 falls into the 15% rate and is absorbed by the higher bracket in 2005.

Q&A

Q. What will the 15% bracket's ranges be in 2005?

A. By raising the income level for married couples filing jointly starting in 2005, more dual-income households will qualify for the 15% rate.

But it's impossible to know now what the income bracket will be because all income tax brackets are adjusted annually for inflation. We won't be able to estimate its new range until late 2004.

Q. How can a recent college grad reduce income?

A. Even though most recent college graduates are single and won't qualify for the higher 15% bracket for married couples filing jointly, there are ways they can continue to qualify for the 15% bracket when they're nearing the borderline:

- Deduct student loan interest
- Contribute to retirement plans such as a 401(k) or deductible IRA (A Roth IRA will not provide a current tax break)

Q. How can a retired married couple reduce income?

A. The goal clearly is to remain in the 15% bracket if you're married and qualify for the expanded range in 2005. If you're retired and your income puts you on the borderline, it may pay to limit your retirement-plan withdrawals until the following year. By doing so, you'll stay below the threshold for the 15% bracket. This assumes, of course, that you already have other assets for support.

Assuming you've met your plan's annual minimum distribution requirement and you have sufficient income, deferring withdrawals from tax deferred retirement plans would reduce current income and provide tax-deferred growth of the funds.

Another option would be for you to withdraw assets from a Roth IRA. Withdrawals from a Roth IRA are not taxable if certain requirements are met.

Q. Does it pay to borrow money rather than take income if I'll be bumped into a higher tax bracket?

A. The answer depends on the savings you will achieve by deferring the tax until the next year and the interest you will pay on the borrowed funds.

Generally credit cards charge high interest rates. So it will be very important to calculate your benefit before borrowing money on your credit card.

As an alternative to borrowing money on your credit cards, consider alternatives such as opening a line of credit with your bank, which may provide you access to the funds at a lower cost of borrowing. An equity loan might even give you a tax deduction for any interest you pay.

THE THIRD CHANGE

Married and single taxpayers in the 15% tax bracket are eligible for a larger earned income credit starting in 2002.

Do You Qualify for This?

Yes. If you are married and filing a joint return or are a single taxpayer, and you are in the 10% or 15% tax bracket.

BACKGROUND

To ease the financial strain on low-income taxpayers, the government allows married couples and single taxpayers in the 15% tax bracket to claim an "earned income credit."

This credit is refundable, which means the government sends you a check if you qualify.

The earned income credit was introduced in 1975 to help ease the burden that low-income working parents faced when social security taxes were removed from their paychecks. It also was viewed as a way to encourage low-income parents to work.

The amount a married couple receives varies depending on their income and the number of children in their care.

In 2001, you qualify for the full earned income credit if your wages, salaries, tips, and other employee compensation, plus net earnings from self-employment, do not exceed these "earned income" amounts:

- $10,020 (caring for two or more children)
- $7,140 (caring for one child)
- $4,760 (not caring for any children)

To qualify, the children in your care must be yours or descendants of your children. This means you qualify if you are caring for a grandchild. In addition, the children in your care must have lived at your address for more than six months of the tax year. And under the new law, beginning in 2002, the person can be a brother, sister, step-brother, step-sister, or descendants of such relatives.

Because the purpose of the earned income credit is to help low-income taxpayers, the credit declines as your earned income rises above a specific level or drops below the levels mentioned above. It is not available at all if your disqualified income (interest, dividends, rent, capital gains, etc.) is more than $2,450 in 2001.

In 2001, your earned income credit starts to shrink if your earned income:

- Exceeds $13,090, or falls below $10,020 (if you care for two or more children), or falls below $7,140 (if you care for one child).
- Exceeds $5,950, or falls below $4,760 (if you have no children).

In 2001, you do not qualify for the credit if your earned income:

- Exceeds $32,121 and you take care of two or more children.
- Exceeds $28,281 and you take care of one child.
- Exceeds $10,710 and you don't take care of any children.

Under the new law, the income range used to start the phase out and end the credit entirely will rise starting in 2002. This will make it easier for low-income taxpayers to claim a larger credit, slightly easing the marriage penalty.

How is the earned income tax credit calculated?

Your earned income credit is determined by taking the rate that applies in your child-care category and multiplying it by your joint earned income amount.

Example: If you and your spouse have $10,000 in earned income in 2001 and you care for one child, you'd multiply your earned income amount ($7,140) by 34% (the established rate for someone in your category) or $2,428.

You'll receive a credit for only $2,428. That's the maximum allowable credit in this income and child-care category. There would be no reduction since your income is below the threshold phase out amount of $13,090.

THE NEW LAW

Higher cutoff point for the full credit

Under the new law, the cutoff point for the full earned income credit will increase by:

- $1,000 in 2002, 2003, and 2004
- $2,000 in 2005, 2006, and 2007
- $3,000 after 2007

Starting in 2009, the cutoff point will be adjusted annually for inflation.

This means that in 2002–2004, the size of your credit will start to decline if your earned income:

- Exceeds $14,090 or falls below $10,020 if you care for two or more children, or falls below $7,140 if you care for one child.
- Exceeds $6,950, or falls below $4,760 if you have no children.

WHAT YOU NEED TO KNOW

Get a piece of the credit early—and in cash

Instead of waiting until April of the following year to file for the earned income credit, you can receive it in advance.

Ask the payroll department at your company whether you qualify. You'll be asked to fill out a W-5 form. Then you'll receive a piece of the earned income credit owed in your check each pay period.

You must properly identify your children and their social security numbers to receive the benefits. Otherwise the IRS will disallow the earned income credit.

Q&A

Q. What can I do if it looks like my earned income is going to reduce my credit?

A. To receive the full credit, your earned income cannot exceed a set level based on the number of children in your care. If your income is about to rise above that level, see if you can defer any income until the following tax year.

5

Tax Credits for Children

THE BIG NEWS

- The tax credit for children rises in 2001.
- Adoption tax breaks start to rise in 2002.
- Dependent-care tax credit starts to rise in 2003.

THE FIRST CHANGE

The tax credit for children rises in 2001.

Do You Qualify for This?

Yes. If you care for one or more children under age 17 and your adjusted gross income does not exceed certain thresholds.

BACKGROUND

The child tax credit was established as part of the Taxpayer Relief Act of 1997, which included many features that benefited families. These features were the government's way of rewarding taxpayers who were raising children.

The child credit should not be confused with the personal exemption, which allows you to reduce your adjusted gross income (AGI) based on the number of people in your household. Think of the child credit as a second tax break for families with kids.

The credit was nonrefundable for most taxpayers—meaning you didn't get a check from the government. Instead, you are allowed to reduce your tax liability by a specific amount for each child.

But the amount you can take as a credit gets tricky if you're in a higher tax bracket. If your AGI exceeds certain levels, depending on your marital status, the government no longer feels you need the tax break and starts to reduce the size of the credit it offers you.

There are two major factors that determine the size of the credit and whether you qualify for it:

- *The first factor* is the size of the credit itself. Under the old law, taxpayers whose income met the standard for a full credit could claim $500 for each child under age 17 in their care. Under the new law, taxpayers who qualify for the full amount can claim $600 per child in 2001 and higher amounts in the years that follow.
- *The second factor* is your AGI and marital status. To qualify for the full child credit, your AGI cannot exceed the level established for your marital status.

Under the old and new law, the full credit starts to shrink when your AGI rises above these thresholds:

- $110,000 for married couples filing jointly
- $75,000 for single head of households
- $55,000 for married couples filing separately

Once your AGI exceeds a certain point, yor child credit disappears entirely and you are no longer qualified to claim one.

How does the child credit phase out? Your credit is reduced by $50 for every $1,000 of AGI above your threshold. Clearly, how much of the full credit you receive depends on the number of children in your care as well as your AGI.

> **Example:** You would not qualify for a child credit if you are married filing jointly, have one child and an AGI of $123,000. But if you have two children and the same AGI, you would qualify for $550.

Under the old law, you had to have three or more children to qualify for a refundable credit. There also were two ways to calculate the amount, both of which were tricky and complex.

The government's heart may have been in the right place when it originally created the law's child credits, but it missed the big picture. Instead of making life easier for low- and middle-income taxpayers by providing tax credits for children, the law actually made it so difficult for these taxpayers to determine what they were owed that most missed claiming the benefit entirely.

Under the new law, Congress made changes to the old law to make the child tax credit more understandable. However, it will still be difficult for lower-income taxpayers to comprehend the rules.

THE NEW LAW

■ *The child tax credit rises to $600 in 2001 and increases over the years to $1,000 by 2010 (see Table 5.1).*

Table 5.1   The Full Credit for Each Child under Age 17

$600 in 2001–2004
$700 in 2005–2008
$800 in 2009
$1,000 in 2010+

You are no longer eligible for the full amount once your adjusted gross income (AGI) hits:
— $110,000 for married couples filing jointly
— $75,000 for single head of households
— $55,000 for married couples filing separately

As your AGI rises above the threshold, the amount you can claim for each child starts to decline. Your credit is reduced by $50 for every $1,000, or part thereof, of AGI that's above the threshold. Eventually, your AGI could hit a level that causes you to lose the credit entirely.

Here is the range of AGI when your child credit starts to shrink and when you are no longer eligible for it at all in 2001:
— Married filing jointly with one child: $110,000–$121,000
— Married filing jointly with two children: $110,000–$133,000
— Single head of household with one child: $75,000–$86,000
— Single head of household with two children: $75,000–$98,000
— Married couples filing separately with one child: $55,000–$66,000
— Married couples filing separately with two children: $55,000–$78,000

Example: Table 5.2 shows the size of the child credit under the new tax law if you're married filing jointly and you and your spouse have one child.

■ *Part of the child credit is now refundable for all taxpayers.* In tax-talk, "refundable" means you can request the credit in the form of a check rather than a tax break on your return.
   — *In 2001–2004,* the child credit is refundable to the extent of 10% of the amount that your earned income exceeds $10,000. Obviously the amount that's refundable cannot exceed the $600 credit per child—if you qualify for the full amount.
   — *In 2005 and beyond,* the child credit is refundable to the extent of 15% of the amount that your earned income exceeds

Table 5.2   How the Child Credit Phases Out for Married Couples Filing Jointly with One Child

Income up to:	2001–2004	2005–2008	2009	2010+
$110,000	$600	$700	$800	$1,000
111,000	550	650	750	950
112,000	500	600	700	900
113,000	450	550	650	850
114,000	400	500	600	800
115,000	350	450	550	750
116,000	300	400	500	700
117,000	250	350	450	650
118,000	200	300	400	600
119,000	150	250	350	550
120,000	100	200	300	500
121,000	50	150	250	450
122,000	0	100	200	400
123,000		50	150	350
124,000		0	100	300
125,000			50	250
126,000			0	200
127,000				150
128,000				100
129,000				50
130,000				0

the $10,000 threshold. The $10,000 threshold is indexed for inflation after 2001.
— Families with three or more children get a refundable credit for the amount their social security taxes exceed their earned income credit, if that's more than the amount calculated on the formula above.

WHAT YOU NEED TO KNOW

Calculate carefully if you qualify for the child credit

The credit can significantly reduce your tax liability.

Example: A married couple who files jointly has an adjusted gross income of $100,000 at the end of 2001. After calculating their taxes, the couple determines that their taxes owed before taking any credits is $10,000.

The couple has two children under age 17 living at home. So they take the child credit for the two children, which is $1,200 ($600 for each child). Their net tax liability now is just $8,800.

But wait. They also have a federal withholding of $9,500. After they apply the withholding against their tax liability, their refund is $700.

Defer income to the following year if necessary

Ideally, you want to do this in years when you expect your AGI to rise to a level where you won't be eligible for the highest allowable credit.

Don't goof when applying for financial aid

Don't include the nonrefundable portion of the credit as income when filling out forms for a government grant or financial aid. Federal programs and federally sponsored programs do not count the credit as part of your income.

Change your W-4 and put cash in your paycheck

If you anticipate that you'll be eligible for a child credit refund next year, change your W-4 form now. Then you'll get the refund in your check rather than waiting until you file your income tax return.

The payroll department at your job will give you a W-4 form and instructions to revise your federal withholding. Ask for the full W-4 form, which has the worksheets, so you can make the proper computations.

In a divorce, the credit depends on income and care

In cases of divorce the couple needs to plan who will claim the child credit. Obviously, both parents can't claim it if they are filing separate returns.

Under the new law, the credit becomes more valuable to the parent who qualifies to claim the full amount.

But in some situations, income restrictions may mean that only one spouse is eligible to claim it—provided that the eligible spouse also is the parent caring for the child.

Example: A family with one child is divorcing. Larry is a sculptor and has taxable income of $5,000 in 2001 and tax liability of $0. So Larry would not be eligible for the nonrefundable credit because of the tax liability limitation. He also would not be eligible for the refundable portion because his income is not over $10,000.

However, his former spouse, Leticia, has income of $75,000 in 2001 and a tax liability of $12,000. She also is caring for their child. Hence, her refundable credit would be $600. Leticia has a tax liability before the credit of $12,000, so she first would use the $600 credit to reduce her final tax liability. But if Leticia did not fully use the full $600 credit against her tax liability, she would be entitled to an actual refund of the credit.

What is the law's definition of a child?

You qualify for the child credit if the child . . .

- Is related to you
- Is a dependent, meaning you support the child financially
- Has not turned 17 during the tax year for which you're claiming the credit
- Is a citizen or resident of the United States.

THE SECOND CHANGE

Adoption tax breaks increase in 2002.

Do You Qualify for This?

Yes. If you are married filing jointly or single, adopting an American or foreign child, and your adjusted gross income does not exceed $190,000 in 2002 and beyond.

BACKGROUND

Thanks to the Tax Payer Relief Act of 1997, couples today who adopt receive two significant tax breaks. These tax breaks occur in the year your adoption is finalized:

■ *A tax credit.* In 2001 you can claim an adoption credit of $5,000 on the amount you spent during the adoption process. Under the new law, the amount doubles.

■ *Employer-paid expenses are not considered earned income.* The government does not consider the adoption benefits of up to $5,000 that you receive from an employer as earned income.

You're allowed to claim both of these tax breaks for the same adoption—but not for the same specific expense. So, you can claim the tax credit for the amount paid to the adoption service and exclude from your tax return the payment received from your employer for the child's medical exam.

Like most other tax credits and exclusions, both of these have AGI thresholds. The benefits start to decline once your AGI rises above a set threshold and disappear entirely when your AGI hits a maximum level.

THE NEW LAW

■ *Higher adoption tax credit.* The top amount you can claim as a credit in 2002 rises to $10,000.

■ *Higher employer-benefit exclusion.* In 2002, the top amount you can exclude from your earned income rises to $10,000 per adopted child.

Your credit and income exclusion in 2002 and thereafter will start to decline once your AGI reaches $150,000 and will disappear completely when your AGI hits $190,000. That's for married couples filing jointly and single taxpayers.

Cost of living adjustments will be made to the income threshold and the $10,000 limitation each year.

If you're married filing separately, there are special rules that will apply in order to qualify. Ask your tax planner about these rules.

WHAT YOU NEED TO KNOW

Adoptions of special-needs children are treated as any other adoption

The adoption of special-needs children no longer receives a higher credit. They are treated like any other adoption—and all receive the same higher new benefits under the new law. However, after 2002, a $10,000 credit will be allowed for special-needs adoptions regardless of whether you actually have adoption expenses.

Money spent in earlier years is eligible for the credit

Expenses and benefits that are paid or incurred prior to the tax year in which your adoption is finalized still qualify for the credit.

All employer expenses count

The $10,000 limit for qualified expenses includes all employer expenses or benefits during the time period needed to complete the adoption.

Q&A

Q. How can I reduce the financial stress of adoption?

A. The average private adoption today costs anywhere from $4,000 to $30,000. Here are strategies that can help you get started on the road to adoption and limit the stress.

    1. Know your adoption options. There are three major ways to adopt. Each has different pros and cons to consider:

- *Agency adoption.* Your name goes on a waiting list until an appropriate child is selected for you—or you are selected by a birth parent. You're likely to receive an extensive medical history of the birth parents and child.

- *Private/independent adoption.* You or your attorney locates a pregnant birth mother by placing an ad or by using other outreach methods. Your attorney handles the legal and practical aspects of the adoption plan.
- *International/overseas.* You hire a U.S. agency, which contacts an overseas agency to select a child. You need Immigration and Naturalization Service approval for the child's visa. You'll also have to travel to the child's country for a one- to four-week stay to complete the necessary legalities.

   2. Protect yourself against high prices. Get all agency fees and attorney fees in writing first. And make sure your attorney is a member of the American Academy of Adoption Attorneys or your state's association of adoption lawyers. He or she should have several years experience and should have done at least 100 successful adoptions.

   3. Anticipate paying for a "home study." Whether you use an agency or a lawyer, you are required to present a state court with a written evaluation of you and your family. This evaluation is called a "home study."

> **How it works:** A state-licensed social worker visits your home to discuss your health and social background, your finances, parenting styles, and feelings about adoption. The visit costs $750 to $1,200 and often is included in an agency's fee.

   4. See if your health benefits cover child exams. Check your health insurance policy for your prospective child's coverage. If you are adopting overseas, visit the child in person if possible. What constitutes a healthy or stable child in a Third World country may be very different from U.S. standards. Obtain as much medical information as possible as well as a video of the child. Also, have a skilled physician review the information.

   5. Purchase adoption insurance. Coverage cushions your financial loss if the adoption falls through. Such insurance is important if the birth mother has no medical coverage. Coverage is also key if your expenses for the mother's care will exceed $5,000.

6. **Consider an adoption loan.** Inquire about adoption loans at larger banks.

7. **Claim the credit on your federal income tax return.** Starting in 2002, you can claim up to $10,000 in travel, legal, or agency expenses associated with each adopted child in the year the adoption is finalized. In 2001, the limit is $5,000.

8. **Ask your company about its benefits.** Many companies now offer pre-adoption counseling, resources, and reimbursement for expenses. Under the new law, the top amount you can exclude from your earned income in 2002 is $10,000 per adopted child.

THE THIRD CHANGE

The dependent-care tax credit rises in 2003.

Do You Qualify for This?

Yes. If you pay someone to care for a child under age 13 or to care for an incapacitated adult dependent.

BACKGROUND

If you pay someone to take care of your child, you are eligible to take a credit for the cost—assuming the expenses are qualified, your dependent is qualified, and you have earned income. The credit is nonrefundable, meaning it comes in the form of a tax break, not a government check. The credit is usually only available if the care is necessary for you to be able to work.

How the credit is calculated

The annual expenses you pay the care-provider is multiplied by the percentage allowed by law. The current top amount you can claim is capped at $2,400 if the person you hired cares for one dependent, and is capped at $4,800 if that person cares for two or more dependents.

Under the old law, if your adjusted gross income (AGI) was $10,000 or less, the care-provider credit equaled 30% of employment-related expenses. If your AGI was higher than $10,000, the 30% credit rate dropped by one percentage point for each $2,000 in AGI over $10,000. The lowest the percentage could drop was 20%.

The new law raises the levels across the board.

THE NEW LAW

Higher percentage of expenses. Starting in 2003, the maximum percentage of employment-related expenses that can be claimed as a credit rises to 35%.

Higher level of expenses. The top amount of eligible employment-related expenses jumps to $3,000 for one child and $6,000 if there are two or more children in the person's care. As a result, the maximum credit is $1,050 for one child and $2,100 for two or more children.

Higher AGI threshold. You're eligible for the full credit if your adjusted gross income (AGI) does not exceed $15,000.

Once your AGI exceeds $15,000, the 35% rate starts to drop by one percentage point for each $2,000 in AGI over the threshold.

If your AGI exceeds $43,000, you qualify for the credit but the credit percentage used for the calculation is capped at 20%. That means you'll only receive part of the credit.

WHAT YOU NEED TO KNOW

You only get a credit if the IRS gets a W-2

To claim the credit, you have to give the person you're paying to care for dependents a copy of Form W-2 to report their wages.

If you are married, there's a catch

If you're married, both you and your spouse need to have earned income in order to qualify for the credit. The AGI restriction applies to the spouse with the lowest income. So employment-related expenses claimed for this purpose cannot exceed the earned income of the spouse who earned less.

Q&A

Q. I'm divorced but we share the cost of a care provider. Who gets the credit?

A. In the case of divorce, the credit is given to the parent who has custody for a greater portion of the calendar year, regardless of financial support.

Q. Does a day-care center qualify as a care-provider?

A. Yes, expenses incurred for daycare would qualify for the credit, assuming the other requirements of the dependent-care credit are met.

6

IRAs

THE BIG NEWS

- Higher annual IRA contributions start in 2002.
- Special catch-up rules for taxpayers age 50 or older start in 2002.
- New tax credit for IRA contributions starts in 2002.

THE FIRST CHANGE

Higher annual IRA contributions start in 2002.

Do You Qualify for This?

Yes. Anyone who has earned income qualifies for an IRA and the new, higher annual contribution levels.

BACKGROUND

The Individual Retirement Account (IRA) may be the single largest asset you own. If it isn't the largest one now, it probably will be soon.

If you're like most people, you've been making annual contributions for more than 20 years. You also probably transferred 401(k) and pension assets from former employers into a Rollover IRA. And in the coming years, the new tax law will allow you to make higher annual contributions. Assuming the stock market cooperates, the value of your IRA assets will likely rise considerably over time.

That's why you need to be absolutely sure you understand the basic rules that govern IRAs, how the new tax law affects those rules, and how to make the most of them.

How IRAs work:

There are two types of individual retirement accounts for retirement savings—the Traditional IRA and the Roth IRA.

You open a Traditional IRA and Roth IRA at a qualified financial institution, such as a bank, brokerage, insurance company, etc. Once you've made a deposit in an IRA account, you generally can invest in stocks, bonds, and virtually any other security offered through your IRA's custodian. You decide how to allocate your money.

You also can trade securities in your IRA as often as you wish without having to pay taxes on the gains. The only rule is that the assets must remain in the IRA or be transferred to another IRA to avoid capital gains taxes.

In addition you can hold several IRA accounts at different financial institutions and contribute as little as you wish monthly—although some institutions may require you to invest a higher initial amount.

About 60% of taxpayers who own an IRA contribute the maximum the law allows each year, and the percentage of employees who are covered by any retirement plan is about the same as it was in the mid-1970s. As a result, the IRA plays a critical role in helping individuals save for retirement. Its assets over time will likely grow to make up a large slice of your overall investment pie.

Prior to the new tax law, the maximum annual contribution allowed was $2,000. Starting next year, the maximum contribution levels will rise.

THE TWO TYPES

Now that you know how the IRA works, let's look more closely at the details of two types of IRAs for retirement savings—the Traditional IRA and the Roth IRA.

The Traditional IRA. In the early 1980s, everyone could take a tax deduction for contributing to an IRA. But five years later, the Tax Reform Act of 1986 set limitations on who could take a tax deduction for making a contribution.

The deduction rule today: If you participate in a company retirement plan, such as a 401(k), you cannot deduct your IRA contribution on your 2001 tax return if your adjusted gross income (AGI) exceeds $63,000 (married filing jointly) or $43,000 (single).

The full IRA deduction starts to shrink once your AGI exceeds $53,000 (married) or $33,000 (single).

But if your company does not offer a retirement plan or you choose not to participate in it for whatever reason, the IRS considers your IRA your retirement plan. As a result, it lets you deduct the maximum annual contribution.

You generally cannot start withdrawing contributions from a Traditional IRA until you turn age 59½ without paying a 10% penalty. Starting at age 59½, withdrawals are taxed as regular income.

Then, beginning at age 70½, you no longer can make contributions to your Traditional IRA. You also must begin withdrawing from your Traditional IRA no later than April 1 of the year following the one in which you turn 70½.

All of the assets in your Traditional IRA are allowed to compound tax-free. That's a powerful feature.

Example: John and Jane each have $2,000 to save for retirement. John invests his money in a taxable account. Jane invests the same amount in the exact same investment and at the exact same time as John. But she invests through a Traditional IRA.

After 25 years, assuming the investment returned 10% a year, taxes were 25% on the annual returns, and both John and Jane left their investments alone and never added another dime, John would have $12,200 in his taxable account while Jane would have $21,700—or $9,500 more in her tax deferred account than John.

When you start to withdraw assets from your Traditional IRA, they will be taxed as income. But the tax bite will likely be lower than it would have been when you were working. That's because when you retire, you'll likely be in a lower tax bracket than you were when you were holding down a job and making contributions.

The Roth IRA was created by the Taxpayer Relief Act of 1997. There are several big differences between a Roth IRA and a Traditional IRA. Unlike the Traditional IRA:

- There are no taxes when you withdraw assets at age 59½. Roth IRA assets can be withdrawn tax-free starting at age 59½—if you've held the account for at least five years.
- You can withdraw assets sooner for special reasons. You can withdraw assets tax-free at an earlier age if you are disabled or are buying a first-time home and need the money. The maximum amount you can withdraw tax-free in the case of a home is $10,000 over the course of your lifetime.
- You can leave the assets in there until you die. You don't have to withdraw assets from a Roth IRA after you turn 70½. You can leave the assets in the account to compound tax-free until you die.
- But—there is no tax deduction for making Roth IRA contributions. There is a tax deduction for Traditional IRA contributions, if you qualify.

Who is eligible to make the full Roth IRA contribution?

- Only married taxpayers filing jointly whose adjusted gross income (AGI) does not exceed $150,000 and single taxpayers whose AGI does not exceed $95,000.
- As your AGI rises above those levels, the amount you can contribute starts to decline.
- You cannot contribute to a Roth IRA at all if you're married filing jointly and your AGI exceeds $160,000 or if you're single and your AGI exceeds $110,000. If you're married filing separately, you're out of luck. You can't contribute to a Roth IRA at all.

Anyone who qualifies can own a Traditional IRA and a Roth IRA. But your total IRA contribution for the year cannot exceed the maximum annual contribution level.

Example: In 2001, the maximum annual contribution to an IRA is $2,000. If you own a Traditional IRA and a Roth IRA, you can contribute $800 to the Traditional IRA and $1,200 to the Roth IRA.

THE NEW LAW

Higher contributions. Starting in 2002, the maximum annual contribution to a Traditional IRA and Roth IRA will rise to $3,000 from the current $2,000 level. This level will rise again in 2005 and in 2008, after which it will be adjusted annually for inflation (see Table 6.1).

Table 6.1   Maximum Annual Contribution to an IRA

2001	2002	2003	2004	2005	2006	2007	2008+
$2,000	$3,000	$3,000	$3,000	$4,000	$4,000	$4,000	$5,000

Higher deduction threshold. The Traditional IRA deduction threshold also will rise in future years. As your adjusted gross income (AGI) increases, your eligibility for the full deduction declines—until you hit a point where you are not longer qualified to take any deduction.

Table 6.2 shows the AGI levels at which your deduction starts to drop and the point at which you are no longer eligible for it.

WHAT YOU NEED TO KNOW

Invest $5,000 in January 2002

If you neglect to make the $2,000 maximum IRA contribution in 2001, you have until April 15, 2002, to do so. While you're at it, write out another check in January 2002 for $3,000—the maximum IRA contribution allowed in that year. As a result, your $5,000 investment will start compounding tax-free much sooner.

Don't think you'll have the money?

Try setting aside $38 a day between December 1 and April 11, 2002. There are 132 days between these dates (132 × $38 = $5,016). On Friday, April 12, make the contributions in two separate payments ($2,000 for 2001 and $3,000 for 2002). If you qualify to take the de-

Table 6.2 AGI Levels When the Deduction Starts to Phase Out and No Longer Exists

	2001	2002	2003	2004	2005	2006	2007+
Married filing jointly	$53,000–$63,000	$54,000–$64,000	$60,000–$70,000	$65,000–$75,000	$70,000–$80,000	$75,000–$85,000	$80,000–$100,000
Single taxpayer	$33,000–$43,000	$34,000–$44,000	$40,000–$50,000	$45,000–$55,000	$50,000–$60,000	$50,000–$60,000	$50,000–$60,000

duction, be sure to factor that into your taxes in advance rather than waiting until April 12. Tax returns are due Monday, April 15, 2002.

If you can't save $38 a day, how about $15.16 a day?

That will produce $2,000 by April 11, enough for your 2001 contribution—and a tax deduction if you qualify.

Shift old 401(k) assets into a Rollover IRA

Whenever you leave a job, you are no longer allowed to make contributions to the company's 401(k) plan. Your assets can still grow tax-deferred, but you can't add to them.

So, no matter how good the old 401(k) plan is, it almost always pays to transfer your assets into a Rollover IRA. That's because a 401(k) is limited by its investment choices. In a Rollover IRA, your investment choices are unlimited.

> *Word to the wise:* Be sure the assets you're transferring into a Rollover IRA are placed in that account. If the custodian of your Rollover IRA makes a clerical error and accidentally puts the assets into a taxable account, you will owe taxes and a 10% penalty if the mistake isn't corrected within 60 days.

Under the new law, if your employer allows it, you can roll over your Traditional IRA into your employer's 401(k) plan. Why would someone do that? If the 401(k) plan offers an asset mix that has produced desirable returns for you over the long-term, you may want to roll over Traditional IRA assets.

Max out your 401(k)—and your IRA

Many people who own a 401(k) don't bother investing in an IRA. They assume that their annual 401(k) investment is sufficient. They also insist that they don't have the extra money to make an IRA contribution.

Here's how to make the maximum contribution to both accounts: Calculate how much you'll need to contribute to your 401(k) each month to max out in September 2002. The maximum 401(k) contribution level is $11,000 in 2002, up from $10,500 in 2001.

Once you've maxed out your 401(k), continue to have the same amount withdrawn and automatically deposited into an IRA account. You'll max out your IRA by December. The top contribution level for an IRA in 2002 is $3,000 ($3,500 if you're age 50 or older, but more about that later).

By using this strategy, you'll never miss the money coming out of your paycheck because you will have already adjusted to your net income by then.

> **Example:** Olivia's annual gross income is $150,000. Her gross pay is $12,500 a month. If she contributes 7.33% of her annual salary—or $916.25 a month—to her 401(k) in 2002, she will max out by the end of the year.
>
> But if she contributes a little more each month—$1,222 (or 9.78% of her gross pay)—she will reach the $11,000 limit in September. Then she can have roughly the same amount—$1,000—automatically deposited each month into her nondeductible IRA for the remaining three months of the year. The result? Olivia maxed out her 401(k) and her IRA in 2002 without feeling a cash crunch.

And Olivia will be glad she used that strategy thanks to the IRA's tax-shelter feature. Look at the comparison between someone who contributes to an IRA and someone who saves the same amount in a taxable account (see Table 6.3). This example assumes that $3,000 was contributed each year for 20 years, a 35% marginal tax rate and a pre-tax ordinary return of 8%.

It also assumes that the entire IRA is paid out in a single amount in the last year. If distributions from the IRA are deferred it would be even more valuable.

Table 6.3   IRA Growth v. Taxable Account

Post-tax balance after	IRA	Taxable account
20 years	$117,375	$106,589
30 years	229,066	176,958
40 years	470,198	293,784

How to take early IRA withdrawals—penalty-free

There is a way to avoid the 10% penalty for withdrawing IRA assets before age 59½. You simply ask to take an annuity in "substantially equal payments." The annual payments are computed based on the life expectancy of someone your current age.

The IRS lets you make withdrawals this way because it views them as annuity payments—your money returned to you little by little. You still have to pay income tax on the annual withdrawal. But there's no penalty. The money that remains in your IRA continues to enjoy tax-deferred status. And you can continue to make the maximum allowable IRA contribution—although you'd probably make the contribution to a different IRA.

> *Warning:* Keep in mind that it's unwise to withdraw assets early from your IRA for frivolous reasons. The amount you remove will no longer grow tax-free. Such an annuity withdrawal plan makes sense only if you retire early and need the assets to bridge the gap between your retirement date and the date that you are able to receive social security or other retirement benefits.

If you still want to withdraw assets this way, here are the rules:
- You can take an annuity only from a Traditional IRA.
- You can take an annuity from just one Traditional IRA and leave your other IRAs untouched.
- You must complete a form supplied by your IRA custodian.
- Your annual withdrawal will be based on three different methods:
  — *Life expectancy method.* The account balance is divided by your life expectancy, based on IRS tables.
  — *Amortization.* It uses life expectancy, the account balance, and interest rates established by the IRS.
  — *Annuity factor.* It uses a formula similar to an annuity to determine your payout.
- The withdrawn assets will be taxed as income on that year's tax return. So before you go forward, have your tax planner be sure such a withdrawal won't trigger the alternative minimum tax, a separate set of tax rules that offer far fewer deductions and exemptions than the regular tax rules.

(continued)

- You must take the withdrawal payments from your IRA based on the schedule until you turn 59½ or for five years, whichever period is longer.
- An IRA annuity is not reversible. You must take the payments for five years or until age 59½. Otherwise you face a penalty. Of course, what you decide to do with the assets is up to you.
- If you withdraw more than the required annual amount, you will owe a penalty on all of your withdrawals up to that date.

Before you agree to an IRA annuity payment plan, have your tax planner review the forms and the statement that accompanies the first payment. A mistake made by your IRA custodian is your responsibility. Mistakes can be costly in terms of taxes and penalties if they are not reversed immediately and explained to the IRS. In addition, be aware that withdrawing assets under the annuity plan will erode one of your most valuable retirement savings opportunities.

Name your spouse as the beneficiary of your IRA

Your IRA will pass to your spouse when you die, thus avoiding estate tax. And under the new estate tax rules, the amount you can pass to heirs estate-tax-free rises each year starting in 2002. So the IRA assets may escape estate tax entirely in the future when the assets pass to heirs.

Another option for your IRA assets is a Qualified Terminable Interest Property (QTIP) trust. This trust can handle the lifetime financial needs of your spouse and pass the amount your spouse didn't use on to your heirs when your spouse dies. This trust comes in handy when you've remarried and you want to ensure that your IRA passes to the children of your first marriage.

Choose the right mandatory payout method

When you turn age 70½, you must begin withdrawing assets from a Traditional IRA. How do you determine the minimum amount you must withdraw?

You have two choices. The first choice is based on the life expectancy of you and your spouse if your spouse is more than 10 years younger than you. The second is based on your life expectancy and hypothetical beneficiary. Ask your tax planner or the custodian of your Traditional IRA for details.

In most other cases, it's best to use the "joint life expectancy" method, which requires the lowest withdrawals each year.

Q&A

Q. Which type of IRA should I invest in?

A. If you qualify for a Roth IRA, go for it. You will have more years of tax-free compounding, since you don't have to withdraw the money—ever. You also will be able to make contributions after age 70½ if you wish. And all of your withdrawals after age 59½ will be tax-free. You also can pass along a Roth IRA income-tax-free to your heirs. The same can't be said for a Traditional IRA. The rules are a bit more complicated.

Q. Can I convert my Traditional IRA to a Roth IRA?

A. Yes, if your adjusted gross income (AGI) does not exceed $100,000 (married or single taxpayers). Simply call the custodian of your Traditional IRA and ask what papers you need to complete to have the assets moved into a Roth IRA. You can even reverse the conversion without penalty up until October 15 of the year after the year in which the conversion took place.

Why would you want to undo the conversion? Because you may have been near the $100,000 cut-off point when you made the conversion but exceeded it once you computed your taxes at the end of the year. Or the market value of your Roth IRA may have decreased dramatically.

Q. Are there any tax drawbacks related to converting?

A. Yes. The market value of the assets you move from a Traditional IRA to a Roth IRA (minus your nondeductible contributions) are considered taxable income. In addition, the value of the assets you convert may fall rapidly in value soon afterward.

What can you do in both situations? You can ask the Roth IRA custodian to undo the conversion, returning your Roth IRA to its original Traditional IRA status.

Q. What if my AGI rises after the conversion?

A. Remember, if you make the conversion and your AGI rises above the $100,000 limit that same year, you'll be charged an early withdrawal penalty of 10% and a 6% excess contribution penalty for the time your ineligible assets sat in the Roth IRA, in addition to the income tax.

The following are rules of thumb that apply:

- If you plan to convert, ask your tax planner to run the numbers to see how the move will affect your tax bill. Make sure he or she takes into consideration surprise year-end mutual fund distributions, which can bump up your AGI.
- If you have already converted, ask your planner in January to see if any tax problems were created and whether it pays to undo the conversion before filing your federal return.

Q. Are there strategies for minimizing a conversion's tax hit?

A. Yes. When you convert a Traditional IRA to a Roth IRA, you will owe income tax on the market value of the assets. If your Traditional IRA assets are invested in stocks at the time of conversion and your portfolio has declined with the stock market, you will owe less tax. That's because the value of your portfolio is lower.

When the stock market bounces back and the value of your newly converted assets increase in the Roth IRA, you won't owe a dime in income tax—nor will you owe tax when you withdraw the amount under the Roth IRA rules starting at age 59½.

> *Example:* Let's say your adjusted gross income in 2001 is $80,000. So you qualify to convert a Traditional IRA to a Roth IRA. And let's say that your Traditional IRA is invested in stocks and the portfolio is now worth $250,000.
>
> If you are in the 40% cumulative tax bracket—meaning federal, state, and local taxes combined—you will owe $100,000 in additional tax this year if you converted immediately. But you decided to wait, and the stock market

declined again. By December 2001, the value of your Traditional IRA portfolio slipped to $185,000. If you converted in December, you would owe $74,000 after a conversion instead of $100,000 had you converted earlier.

Q. What if my company offers a 401(k) but I don't participate?
A. You can deduct your Traditional IRA contribution for the year if you didn't participate in a 401(k). But not participating in a 401(k) that's available to you is almost always a bad move. Your 401(k)contributions are made on a pre-tax basis. That means they are removed before they are counted as part of your gross income, thereby lowering your possible tax liability.

But that's not all. The maximum contribution levels for a 401(k) are higher in future years and higher than IRA levels, allowing more of your money to compound tax-deferred over time.

The only situation in which you should consider investing outside of a 401(k) is when the investment options in the plan are so bad that your money would be at risk. But even in such a situation, complaining about the plan to your company's benefits department might cause a review and action.

Q. What types of investments are ideal for an IRA?
A. The IRS ignores investment gains in an IRA. That makes a Traditional IRA and Roth IRA ideal for investments you plan to sell once they reach target prices or if you rebalance your portfolio. However, a Roth IRA is more ideal for growth investments, since they can remain tax-sheltered forever. Remember, withdrawals from a Traditional IRA are taxed as regular income. Withdrawals from a Roth IRA are not taxed at all, and you can keep the assets in there for as long as you wish.

Q. Can I open an IRA for my child?
A. Yes, if your child has earned income for the year. You even can give your child a gift up to the amount of his or her earned income, not to exceed $2,000 this year, for the specific purpose of opening an IRA. Or you can contribute to your child's existing IRA. In 2002, under the new law, you can give up to $3,000.

Q. Which type is best for a child?
A. Ideally, your children should open a Roth IRA. Their AGI is probably low enough to qualify. As your children age and their AGI

rises and prohibits them from contributing to a Roth IRA, they'll still have their old Roth IRAs and all of the benefits that go with them.

Q. How is a Traditional IRA deduction handled?

A. The deduction for a Traditional IRA contribution is subtracted from your gross income. The deduction is considered part of the adjustment that takes place to arrive at your AGI.

> *Strategy in action:* Bob and Mary are married and file a joint tax return. Each contributed $2,000 to a Traditional IRA in 2001. Their adjusted gross income in 2001 is $60,000 before taking the full Traditional IRA contribution deduction and neither participates in their employer's plan. As a result, the couple can subtract $4,000 from their $60,000 AGI.
>
> Here's the cute part: After taking the deduction for tax year 2001, they can convert the Traditional IRA to a Roth IRA, since they qualify for the conversion. However, they won't be able to deduct the amount they contribute next year, since Roth IRA deductions are not available. They also will pay tax on the $4,000 plus any increase in value.

Q. Can I deduct my Traditional IRA contribution if my spouse is covered by an employer plan?

A. Yes, but the deduction is phased out between $150,000 and $160,000 of AGI.

Q. Is there a difference between the two IRAs for estate planning?

A. Yes. Assets in a Roth IRA can be passed on to a spouse and heirs without income tax liability. Even though the Roth IRA is subject to the minimum distribution rules upon the owner's death, the distribution will not result in income taxes.

By contrast, assets in a Traditional IRA that are inherited by anyone but a spouse face income taxes and possibly estate taxes. With the estate tax starting to decline and the estate tax exemption starting to rise, it makes sense to check with your estate planner to determine the tax consequences.

And even though a spouse won't be subject to estate taxes, income taxes will still apply.

Q. How can I preserve a Traditional IRA's value for my heirs?
A. When heirs other than a spouse inherit a Traditional IRA, the assets in the IRA can be withdrawn in a lump sum. Generally, that means a large tax bill. Or the assets can be paid out little by little each year based on your life expectancy.

> **Strategy:** The best way to keep most of the assets compounding and minimize your heirs' tax liability is to use this simple strategy:
> Take a minimum distribution from your IRA starting after age 70½. Upon your death, leave your IRA to your spouse, who can roll over the assets into his or her IRA.
> Then he or she should name new beneficiaries for the IRA (since you're no longer around) and begin to take a minimum distribution based on his or her life expectancy.
> After your spouse dies, your heirs should elect to take a minimum distribution over their life expectancies, which can be 40 years or more. As a result, most of your Traditional IRA will remain intact and left to compound and grow over time.

Q. How can I ensure that my IRA gets into the right heirs' hands?
A. Estate planning when a Traditional IRA is involved can be tricky.

> **Example:** Leaving an IRA to your three children may seem equitable and fair. But if one of the children dies before you do, and you neglect to update the paperwork, the IRA will pass to the other two, leaving nothing for your deceased child's children—your grandchildren.

In the example above, the smarter solution would be to set up three different IRAs—each one naming a different child as the beneficiary. Then when you die, each IRA will pass directly to your designated heir.

> **Example:** You may want to set up three IRAs, each holding 33% of your total IRA assets. To be equitable, be sure that each IRA holds the same mix of assets. Then name each of your three children as the beneficiary of each IRA,

adding the other children's names as co-beneficiaries. This strategy will ensure that each of your children will inherit an equal part of your IRA assets. Should any of your children die, the other two would inherit 50% each.

If your spouse is still living, it makes the most sense to leave your IRA to him or her so that the assets escape taxation. Your spouse, in turn, should leave his or her IRA to you. The first spouse to die would then set up the IRA beneficiaries according to the example above.

Again, IRAs and estate planning can require complex solutions. That's why it's best to talk to an estate planner.

Q. What do I have to tell my IRA custodian?

A. If there isn't room on the IRA form to express your exact beneficiary wishes, attach a letter with clear instructions. Store a copy of the beneficiary designations with your will. If your IRA custodian misplaces it over the years, you and your estate planner will have a copy of it.

While you're at it, find out now whether the custodian of your Traditional IRA will let your spouse and children take minimum withdrawals upon your death. Some custodians won't and insist that a lump sum payout be made at the time of death. If that is the case with your current custodian, you or your spouse and heirs should move the IRA to a financial institution that will allow for the staggered payout.

Speeding up your IRA decisions

- *Roth or Traditional?* If your adjusted gross income (AGI) exceeds $160,000 (married) or $110,000 (single), you can't contribute to a Roth IRA.
- *Convert or not?* If your AGI is not higher than $100,000, you can convert your Traditional IRA to a Roth IRA. Just be aware that you will owe income tax on the market value of the Traditional IRA at the time of conversion.
- *Don't qualify for a Roth IRA?* Consider contributing to a Traditional IRA. It still allows your money to grow tax-deferred.

- *What's the top IRA contribution?* $2,000 in 2001, $3,000 in 2002–2004, $4,000 in 2005–2007, and $5,000 in 2008. The level will be adjusted annually for inflation in years after 2008.
- *Can I take the Traditional IRA deduction?* If your AGI does not exceed $63,000 (married) or $43,000 (single) in 2001. The ceilings rise in future years.
- *Hate taxes?* Open a Roth IRA, if you qualify. There's no tax liability when you withdraw Roth IRA assets starting at age 59½.
- *Don't want to withdraw at age 70½?* Open a Roth IRA, if you qualify. There's no age when you must start withdrawing assets.

Q. Can I borrow from an IRA?
A. Technically you cannot borrow from an IRA. But you can withdraw money from an IRA before age 59½ without paying taxes or early-withdrawal penalties, provided you return the money within 60 days. You can only do this once every 12 months.

THE SECOND CHANGE

Special catch-up rules for taxpayers age 50 or older starts in 2002.

Do You Qualify for This?

Yes. If you are age 50 or older in 2002, you can make a higher annual maximum contribution to a Traditional IRA or Roth IRA.

BACKGROUND

Under current law, all taxpayers with earned income may open an IRA and make the maximum annual contribution. Taxpayers are free to invest their contributions any way they wish and can own several IRAs at different financial institutions.

The best part is that the assets grow without being taxed. When you turn age 59½, assets can be removed from a Traditional IRA without penalty and are taxed as income depending on the bracket you're in at the time. Assets can be withdrawn from a Roth IRA starting at age 59½ but they aren't taxed at all. You also do not ever have to withdraw from a Roth IRA.

Because of its favorable tax-shelter feature, either type of IRA is considered one of the best ways to save for retirement—although a Roth IRA is more favorable if you qualify for it.

Many stay-at-home moms were able to take advantage of either IRA based on their husbnand's income. But these women were not earning income in many cases and couldn't afford to contribute to an IRA. They were able to resume making annual contributions only after they returned to the workplace.

Most older women who returned to work after raising children faced a stark IRA savings gap of 18 years or more, depending on the number of children they stayed home to raise.

Over the past five years, sentiment in Congress and on the state level has been growing to correct this inequity. Legislators know that allowing women to "catch up" with their retirement savings isn't just about women but families as well. Not only do families suffer financially when mom stops earning an income but they also suffer in the future as a result of a drop in her tax-deferred savings.

Adult children risk facing a greater financial burden in the future should mom run short of retirement savings. They also may be burdened should mom and dad have to rely on only dad's savings. Such burdens become even more painful in cases where women who stayed home to raise children wind up divorcing and have little income on which to retire as a result of not being able to contribute to an IRA over the years.

While the new law doesn't provide mom with compensation for her lost years of savings, it does allow her to catch up. The new law is aimed at women age 50 or older who presumably make up the largest number of people who were out of the workplace for the longest period of time and unable to afford to make annual IRA contributions.

But because it would be unfair (and probably unconstitutional) for the new law to discriminate between women and men—or women who stayed home and women who didn't—the new catch-up contribution rule applies to everyone age 50 or older. After all, in many cases, dad may have stayed home all those years to care for the kids while mom worked, depriving him of making annual IRA contributions.

In either case, all taxpayers age 50 or older caught a break with the new law and should take advantage of it.

THE NEW LAW

Higher catch-up contribution

Starting in 2002, all taxpayers age 50 or older can contribute a higher maximum amount each year to their IRA than other taxpayers (see Table 6.4). You're considered to be 50 for the entire year if you're 50 by the end of that year.

Table 6.4   Top Annual IRA Contribution for All Taxpayers

	2002	2003	2004	2005	2006	2007	2008+
Under age 50	$3,000	$3,000	$3,000	$4,000	$4,000	$4,000	$5,000
Age 50 and over	$3,500	$3,500	$3,500	$4,500	$5,000	$5,000	$6,000

WHAT YOU NEED TO KNOW

Don't underestimate the new law

Glancing at the comparative chart above, you may notice the slim difference between the two groups and wonder what all the "catch-up" fuss is about. While the difference may not seem like a big increase for people age 50 and over, it's a huge benefit when you compare the new rates to the old ones and then run the numbers.

By the fifth year of investing, a person who is age 50 or older can wind up with more than twice as much under the new law than the person could under the old one.

> **Example:** A woman who earns $75,000 a year makes the maximum contribution each year starting in 2002. If you assume that the investments in her IRA earn an average of 10% a year, here's how her returns would look under the new law versus how they would look if the new law didn't exist (see Table 6.5).

Get the benefit of a deduction and a Roth IRA contribution

Taxpayers age 50 or older who qualify for a Roth IRA as well as a deduction for making a contribution to their Traditional IRA have some thinking to do. The Traditional IRA deduction will lower their tax

Table 6.5   The Power of Compounding, Assuming a 10% Average Annual Return

	2002	2003	2004	2005	2006	2007	2008+
Under the old law	$2,000	$2,000	$2,000	$2,000	$2,000	$2,000	$2,000
Investment total	2,000	4,200	6,620	9,280	12,210	15,430	18,970
Under the new law	3,500	3,500	3,500	4,500	5,000	5,000	6,000
Investment total	3,500	7,350	11,590	17,240	23,970	31,360	40,500

liability but a Roth IRA allows for tax-free withdrawals starting at age 59½. The solution may be to do both, given the higher contribution level under the new law.

For instance, you can contribute $2,000 to your Traditional IRA and take the deduction. Then you contribute the remaining $1,500 to your Roth IRA for tax-free withdrawals in the future. Ask your tax planner which move makes the most sense for someone in your situation.

Convert to a Roth IRA if you are eligible

Taxpayers age 50 or older are nearing the traditional age of retirement. But fewer and fewer taxpayers want to retire at that age anymore. Many work full time or part time into their 70s or even 80s. As a result, a Roth IRA makes more sense at this point in your life if you qualify for one. It may even pay to convert your Traditional IRA to a Roth IRA if your adjusted gross income is no higher than $100,000.

There are three big reasons why. In a Roth IRA, your assets will continue to be tax-free as long as they are held there. You can withdraw Roth IRA assets starting at age 59½ without paying income tax. And you don't have to start withdrawing assets starting at age 70½ if you don't need the money because you are still working.

Q&A

Q. **If I turn age 50 in January 2003, should I wait until then to make my 2002 contribution?**

A. The government is way ahead of you. If you are planning to wait until January 2003 to make your 2002 contribution to claim the higher $3,500 maximum, you will be disappointed. Even though you will be 50 years old in January and can make 2002 contributions up until April 15, 2003, the IRS views these contributions as a 2002 tax event. Because you will be 49 in 2002, the most you can contribute is $3,000, not the $3,500 max people age 50 can contribute in that year. However, you can make your 2003 contribution at that time as well, which will indeed qualify for the higher maximum.

Q. **Will putting contributions to work early in the year help?**
A. Big time. Just look at Table 6.6, which shows the performance of a January and December contribution over time, assuming it earns on average 10% a year.

Table 6.6 Growth of January v. December IRA Contributions

	2002	2003	2004	2005	2006	2007	2008+
Contributed Jan. 1st	$3,500	$3,500	$ 3,500	$ 4,500	$ 5,000	$ 5,000	$ 6,000
Year-end total	3,500	7,350	11,590	17,240	23,970	31,360	40,500
Contributed Dec. 31st	3,500	3,500	3,500	4,500	5,000	5,000	6,000
Year-end total	0	3,500	7,350	11,590	17,240	23,970	31,360

Q. **What if I turn age 50 in June 2002 but contribute in January 2002?**
A. You will still qualify for the higher maximum annual contribution ($3,500) for people age 50 or older. When it comes to the higher IRA contributions for people in this age group, the IRS considers you to be 50 years old in the tax year you turn 50.

THE THIRD CHANGE

New tax credit for IRA contributions starts in 2002.

Do You Qualify for This?

Yes. If your AGI does not exceed $50,000 (married filing jointly), $37,500 (head of household), and $25,000 (single or married filing separately).

BACKGROUND

Low- and middle-income taxpayers usually don't have much left after they pay their bills to save for retirement.

Recognizing that these taxpayers need an extra incentive to save, Congress included in the new law a tax break for low- and middle-income taxpayers who make contributions to retirement plans.

THE NEW LAW

Specific plans qualify for new credit. Contributions to these retirement plans qualify for the new credit under the new law:

- Traditional IRA
- Roth IRA
- 401(k)
- 403(b) (nonprofit organizations)
- 457 (government agencies)
- SIMPLE (salary reduction plan offered by small employers)
- SEP (employer and employee contribute to IRA)
- Qualified plan

The new credit is nonrefundable—meaning it's a tax break rather than a cash refund. The credit is designed to be a reward in the form of lower taxes for making a contribution to a retirement plan.

To determine your credit, a little math is required. Here's how to calculate your credit:

First find your AGI in the chart below (see Table 6.7) under the marital status that applies to you.

Then take the percentage next to your bracket below and multiply it by your annual retirement savings contribution. Your credit cannot exceed $1,000.

Table 6.7 Calculating the IRA Contribution Credit

Percentage to use in calculation of credit	When your adjusted gross income (AGI) is					
	Married filing jointly		Head of household		Single or married filing separately	
	Over	But not over	Over	But not over	Over	But not over
50%	0	$30,000	0	$22,500	0	$15,000
20%	$30,000	$32,500	$22,500	$24,375	$15,000	$16,250
10%	$32,500	$50,000	$24,375	$37,500	$16,250	$25,000
0	$50,000		$37,500		$25,000	

Example: In 2002, Bruce and Judy's adjusted gross income is $31,000. They contributed $1,000 each to their IRAs in 2002 and $5,000 each to their 401(k) plans at work. Because they qualify for the retirement plan contribution credit, they scan the chart above for their percentage. It's 20%. So they multiply 0.20 times $12,000—the total joint contribution they made in 2002 to their retirement plans. The result is $2,400. However, the credit they can take on their return is $2,000 ($1,000 for each of them), because that's the max the law allows.

A few more rules under the new law:

- *Phase-out rules.* You are not eligible for the credit when your AGI exceeds $50,000 (married filing jointly), $37,500 (single head of household), and $25,000 (single and married filing separately).
- *Other requirements.* You are not eligible for the credit if you're under 18, are a dependent or are a full time student.
- *Distribution trap.* You must reduce the retirement-plan contribution that you use to calculate the credit by any distributions you received from retirement plans during that year, the two preceding years and up to the due date of your return.
- *AMT rule.* The credit can be claimed when calculating your tax liability under the regular tax rules as well as the alternative minimum tax rules.
- *The credit isn't forever.* The credit is considered "temporary" and won't be available after tax year 2006.

Tip: The credit should not be confused with the exclusion or deduction from gross income you receive when you make certain retirement-plan contributions. If you qualify for all of them, you can claim all of them.

WHAT YOU NEED TO KNOW

Recent college grads may qualify for the credit

If your children recently graduated from college and aren't earning executive salaries yet, they qualify for the credit if their AGI is under $25,000, assuming they are single.

Retirees may qualify for the credit

Retirees with a low AGI who make contributions to a Roth IRA or Traditional IRA qualify for the credit. Does it make sense for retirees with a low AGI to contribute to their retirement plans? Absolutely. Many retirees have tax-exempt incomes, which would be excluded from their AGI. So retirees can be comfortable, have a low level of AGI, make a retirement plan contribution, and claim the credit!

Watch out for the low- and middle-income taxpayer trap

The retirement savings credit is available only *after* you apply the child tax credit and childcare credit. These two credits are common for people in lower income tax brackets. As a result, it's wise to take steps so that you can maximize your retirement plan credit.

The retirement-plan credit is nonrefundable—meaning it's a tax break, not a check. So you want to do everything possible not to reduce the size of the credit if you can help it.

Hence, see if your employer's benefits department offers any dependent-care accounts that will help you defray childcare expenses. By reducing these costs, you will avoid claiming the childcare credit and maximize the one for retirement savings.

Q&A

Q. If my AGI is about to rise over the limit, what can I do?

A. You can defer income to the following year if the income would otherwise put you over the limit. But you have to be sure deferring income as a low-income earner makes financial sense just to qualify for the retirement savings credit.

Q. Will distributions from a plan that I roll over to an IRA reduce my retirement plan contribution amount?

A. No. A distribution from a plan only reduces your contribution amount if it's taxable. A rollover makes it nontaxable.

7

401(k) and Other Company Retirement Plans

THE BIG NEWS

- Annual contribution levels rise starting in 2002.
- Special catch-up for taxpayers age 50 or older starts in 2002.
- New hardship-withdrawal rules start in 2002.
- Hardship waiver for 60-day rollover starts in 2002.
- New Roth plan may be offered by employers in 2006

THE FIRST CHANGE

Annual plan contribution levels rise starting in 2002.

Do You Qualify for This?

Yes. If you participate in a 401(k), 403(b), SEP, SIMPLE, or 457 retirement savings plan.

BACKGROUND

If you work, there's a tax-friendly retirement plan out there for you. Starting in 2002, the most you can contribute each year to these plans will go up, making these plans even more attractive and essential than they were before.

Many taxpayers have become so used to hearing about these plans that they may have forgotten how new most of them are. Retirement savings plans didn't exist when most baby boomers' parents were in their prime working years. Or their parents didn't qualify for them.

These plans include:

- 401(k)
- 403(b)—public sector and nonprofits only
- SIMPLE—small companies with under 100 employees or less
- SEP—self-employed and other companies
- 457—government employees and nonprofits only

Times were different before these plans were introduced. People were expected to work until they reached retirement age. Then they lived on whatever savings they socked away and on their social security checks.

Social security was meant to assist those who didn't have enough money to support themselves in retirement. It was a lifesaver for those who had nothing left after years of work. But for the majority of people of that generation, it was supplemental income in addition to assets saved in taxable accounts.

And before social security there were no government-subsidy plans to help individuals support themselves when they were too old to work. Back then, you saved some money in a mattress and hoped your children would help support you. If your kids couldn't kick in, you and your spouse were at the mercy of local charities and churches.

In fact, before social security, there was no such thing as retirement. You worked until you dropped or were no longer able to get out of bed. The image of leaving the workplace at age 65 with enough money to put up your feet and reel in fish is a relatively modern dream.

Today, about 70 million people—or half the country's workforce—do not have a retirement plan. When a plan is offered, only about two-thirds participate in it. Which is why it's especially important not to take company-sponsored retirement plans for granted. If you start saving early enough and properly diversify your assets, you will likely have plenty to live on when you no longer want to work full time or no longer can.

The new tax law affects most employer-sponsored retirement plans, which allow you to contribute part of your income to accounts where they grow tax-deferred.

It's wise to know a little about the five big plans. You never know when you're going to switch from the private sector to a nonprofit corporation or become self-employed.

THE 401(k) PLAN

The 401(k) is probably the best-known retirement savings plan because of the sheer number of employees who participate in one.

Like many great inventions, the 401(k) was an accident. In the late 1970s, Ted Benna, a benefits consultant, was designing a benefits plan for a client when he noticed a loophole in the 1978 Tax Reform Act. Benna had long been concerned that rank-and-file employees did not have an adequate way to save for retirement, while top executives had compensation packages that left them little to worry about.

Ted Benna also knew there was little financial incentive for employees to sock enough away to make a difference in their later years. Taxes would nibble away at the gains, which wouldn't be able to keep pace with annual inflation. As a result, savings that went into an account would likely emerge with less purchasing power over time.

Benna's discovery back in 1978 changed the rules. He found a loophole in Section 401(k) deep inside Section 401, which outlines the rules that companies must follow when offering a retirement savings plan and who in the company qualifies to participate in one. Section 401(k) focuses on how companies could fund such plans— specifically stating that companies can use their own cash or they can defer part of an employee's income to do so.

Here's where Benna found the opportunity: The law did not state whether the income had to come out of the employee's check before taxes were taken out of gross salary or afterward. Clearly, allowing for contributions on a pre-tax basis was far more attractive for employees than after-tax income.

Employees would be able to put more of their hard-earned money to work in their accounts. And because the contributions were made on a pre-tax basis, they would not be considered part of income and therefore would likely lower their income taxes.

Benna also noticed that Section 401(k) did not prevent companies from matching their employees' contributions to help them save for retirement and getting a corporate tax break in the process. Everyone would emerge a winner.

As Benna began setting up plans based on his interpretation of Section 401(k), many benefits lawyers thought the move might be a stretch and would attract federal lawsuits. But the IRS didn't seem to have a problem with it. If employees could save enough for retirement, the odds that the government would have to create new federal support programs when millions of baby boomers started retiring in the future would be reduced.

By allowing for pre-tax contribution, the government agreed to give up collecting revenue on the front end for taxing the assets as income when withdrawals were allowed starting when the employee turned age 59½.

Once it became clear that the IRS wasn't going to make trouble for Benna's Section 401(k) interpretation, attitudes in the benefits-consulting world changed almost overnight. By 1981, the IRS officially approved Benna's use of the law, and a year later companies began offering the first 401(k) plan.

How the 401(k) plan works

The 401(k) plan is offered by a company for the benefit of its full time employees. You decide how much of your pre-tax income you want to contribute each pay period up to a set maximum. Your company handles the paperwork and a financial institution provides the investment mix available to you in the 401(k) plan. You are responsible for deciding how to invest your money and when to buy or sell investments.

Once invested in the 401(k) plan, your money grows on a "tax-deferred basis." That means your investments aren't taxed on the profits they earn for you nor do you face income taxes until the assets are withdrawn. This lets you keep more of your money and lets the investment generate larger returns and hopefully outpace inflation over time. Why? Because of something called "compounding."

Compounding isn't complicated to understand. First you need to recognize that a large sum will grow faster than a small sum if both earn the same amount of interest. To illustrate this point, 5% of $100 is $5. But 5% of $1,000 is $50.

Once you understand that simple concept, compounding is a breeze. When money sits in your wallet, it doesn't grow. When your money is invested, it earns a rate of return because the institution that borrowed it pays you something for the privilege. If the money is left alone for a year, it earns an annual rate of return. In the second year, a larger amount earns interest—the amount you initially invested plus the interest you were paid for loaning it out the year before. As you can see, compounding means your money grows larger simply by sitting still.

> **Example:** Let's say you put $1,000 into an investment that earns 5% interest a year. You will have $1,050 in the account at the end of the first year. If that larger amount again earns 5% in the second year, you will have $1,102.50—or the result of 5% × $1,050 ($52.50) added to last year's $1,050. After the third year, you will have $1,157.63. After 30 years, if your investment continues to earn on average 5% a year, your initial investment will grow to $4,322.

So, you will have earned interest on the money you put into the account (also known as your "principal") and on the interest that the sum generated during that period. Remember, this example does not include any additional sums you may invest nor does it take into consideration that your sum might earn a higher rate of interest over the investment period.

A 401(k) plan offers many advantages that help your money grow over time:

- Your contribution comes from pre-tax income.
- Your company may provide matching contributions.
- You decide how to invest your money within the plan choices.
- Your assets grow without facing taxes until withdrawal.
- You can take your assets with you when you leave your job.
- You can borrow from the account in some cases.

The secret of compounding

Think of compounding as a forest left undisturbed. You plant a tree. It grows. It flowers. Seeds fall onto the ground. More trees and other foliage grow. Soon, your forest is huge.

Compounding works the same way. The money you invest grows. It earns interest. There are dividends. Soon the investment grows as increasingly larger sums earn interest.

The IRS in this analogy would be a chainsaw or bulldozer. If part of the forest is taxed, its total size will grow but at a much slower rate.

So, the longer your money sits undisturbed in a well-diversified tax-deferred account, the faster it will grow.

The 401(k)'s Rules

The 401(k) plan has many benefits to help you save for retirement. But there are a number of rules the companies and employees must follow:

Your annual contribution is capped. There's a cap on the amount you can contribute each year to your 401(k) plan. The tax law sets that ceiling. Under the new tax law, the amount you can contribute will rise starting in 2002.

You can contribute as little or as much of the maximum annual amount. Just tell your company the total you want to contribute for the year and what percentage of your income each pay period you want diverted on a pre-tax basis into the plan.

You also tell your company how you want your contributions invested among the securities in the plan. Your company handles the rest. You can sell the securities in your plan and invest the assets in other securities at any time by calling the financial institution that manages your plan.

Your contribution is limited if you're a big exec. To keep the 401(k) from becoming an exclusive plan for highly compensated employees who can afford to make regular contributions, the IRS included a rule to encourage all employees to contribute.

If a low percentage of the company's lower earners are participating in the plan, the employer must limit highly compensated employees to a lower contribution level. Your benefits department can tell you whether you are considered one of the company's highly compensated employees as well as your maximum annual level.

However, companies are allowed to offer high-level executives a nonqualified deferred compensation plan, which allows them to contribute up to 100% of their compensation. This type of plan does not fall under Section 401(k)'s qualifications and therefore escapes its stringent rules. It also does not get the same benefits as a 401(k) plan.

Your company's contribution is capped. If you work for a generous employer or your employer wants to encourage employees to participate in the plan, it can make matching contributions. Some companies contribute 50 cents for every $1 you contribute. Other companies match employees' contributions dollar for dollar while many others match a multiple of your contributions.

There are two other rules you need to know about here:

1. The amount your company contributes usually does not compromise your ability to contribute your maximum annual contribution allowed under the law. In other words, you can make your full contribution. Your company's contributions are added to that amount, provided the total is below certain caps.

   > ***Example:*** Let's say you earn $120,000 in salary and you contribute the full $11,000 allowed under the new tax law in 2002 for someone under age 50. And let's say your company matches your contribution dollar for dollar—up to 6% of your salary. Hence, your company could contribute $7,200, and your total combined contribution for the year would be $18,200.

2. Your company must stop contributing to your plan in a year when your contributions and your employer's contributions combined hit a set level outlined in the new tax law ($35,000 in 2001 and $40,000 in 2002) or it reaches 25% of your salary (100% after 2001), whichever is less.

Your company must deposit the assets fast. Your employer must transfer your contribution and its matching contribution into your plan no later than 15 days after the end of the month when your money was diverted from your pay. If your company fails to do this, let the benefits coordinator at your company know.

You can borrow from your plan. The IRS allows you to borrow from your plan only if your company allows it. The law sets a period during which the loan must be paid back—five years, though first-time homebuyer loans can be longer.

You must repay it on a regular basis with cash or payroll deductions and you have to pay interest on the loan. The interest payments, however, are not tax-deductible.

Need to know I: When you borrow from your 401(k) plan, you're being taxed twice on the loan. First, you will be making your loan repayments with after-tax dollars. Second, the money you repay to your plan will be taxed as income when it's withdrawn later in life.

Need to know II: If you leave your company before you've repaid the 401(k) loan and you are unable to repay it, the loan is treated as a distribution. As a result, it will be taxed as income and you may face a penalty as well.

You must wait to begin withdrawing your assets. You may begin withdrawing money from your 401(k) plan when you turn 59½. These amounts will be taxed as income. You can't withdraw money from the plan before then if you're still employed with the plan sponsor. If you withdraw assets before that age, the amount will be taxed as income and be hit with a 10% penalty. At age 70½, you must begin withdrawing a set amount each year from your 401(k) based on your life expectancy, which is determined by special IRS tables, unless you're still working—in which case you can wait until retirement.

You can withdraw your assets when you leave your job. When you leave your company—whether you leave on your own, you are fired, or you retire—the amount you contributed to the plan over the years is yours.

You can leave your assets in the plan and take advantage of the investments available to you in the plan, you can have the sum transferred to a Rollover IRA or qualified plan, or you can spend it.

The last option isn't advisable. The taxes and penalties on such a move are costly, and spending the savings will seriously compromise the long-term potential of your retirement portfolio.

Because not all companies provide employees with a 401(k) plan or do not let them participate in it right away, the IRS allows departing employees to transfer 401(k) assets to a Rollover IRA. In some cases, you may have to liquidate the investments in your 401(k) if the custodian of your Rollover IRA will not accept the securities.

Example: Let's say your 401(k) plan assets are invested in the mutual funds of one company. When you leave your job, you want to open a Rollover IRA at another mutual fund company. The second company may require you to sell your shares first and move in cash so you can invest in its selection of funds.

There is a way around this, of course. If you like the securities in which your money is invested, open a Rollover IRA at the same financial institution where your 401(k) was held. In either case, there are no taxes to pay when you sell securities in your 401(k) and then transfer the assets to a Rollover IRA.

Once transferred, assets in a Rollover IRA can be invested any way you wish. You eventually may want to move the assets into a new employer's 401(k) plan. Again, in such a situation, you may be required to convert investments to cash before transferring money from a Rollover IRA to a new employer's 401(k).

It's also important to remember that many people don't bother transferring assets from a Rollover IRA into a new 401(k). That's because your investment choices in a Rollover IRA are virtually unlimited compared to the fixed number offered by a 401(k) plan.

Your company's contributions may not be available to you. When you enroll in a company's 401(k) plan—or any defined contribution plan for that matter—the company can choose to match your contribution.

But pay careful attention to your company's vesting period. "Vesting" is a fancy word for the time period that must elapse before you can consider the company's contributions your own and take it with you when you leave your job.

To receive tax-exempt treatment, a qualified plan must adhere to the rules that outline when an employee is eligible to leave the company with the employer's contributions. Under the old law, an employer's plan could choose one of two methods of calculating how much the employee could take.

The first formula said that the employee could remove 100% of the employer's contributions if he or she worked there for five years or longer. The other formula said that the employee could leave with 20% of the employer's total contributions after three years of service—with an additional 20% for each subsequent year.

The new law changed this vesting schedule, making it more attractive for employees.

Retiring from the company has its own set of rules. When you retire from the company, you can transfer your 401(k) plan assets to a Traditional IRA or to a Roth IRA if you qualify.

If you're 55 or older when you leave your company, you can withdraw all of the money as a lump sum without paying a 10% penalty. The lump sum will be taxed as income unless rolled over into a Traditional IRA.

What should you do with the lump sum? You have two choices:
1. You can deposit the lump sum in a taxable account. Then, depending on your age, you can withdraw a set amount each month.
2. Or you can have the lump sum transferred into a Traditional IRA, where it will continue to grow tax-deferred. You'll have to withdraw the money starting at age 70½ based on the IRS's life-expectancy tables.

If you continue to work at the same company after age 70½, you don't have to start withdrawing from the 401(k) held there and you can continue to make contributions, if you wish, until you retire.

THE 403(b) PLAN

The 403(b) plan is really the father of the 401(k) and most other modern tax-deferred exempt retirement plans. The 403(b) dates back to 1958, when Congress created a tax-exempt savings program for employees of nonprofit organizations. Educational institutions were able to offer the 403(b) plan starting in 1961. Starting in 1974, all organizations offering this plan could offer a wider range of investments, including mutual funds.

By the 1980s, employees who were invested in 403(b) plans were allowed to borrow from them and roll assets into IRAs when they left their jobs.

How the 403(b) Works

The 403(b) isn't that much different from the 401(k). The key difference is who can participate in it. Only schools and tax-exempt organizations such as charities and churches can offer a 403(b). If you look at Section 501(c)(3) of the tax code, you'll find that to be qualified, the tax-exempt organizations must be "organized and operated exclusively for religious, charitable, scientific, public-safety testing, literary or educational purposes."

The other big difference is that a 403(b) plan cannot offer individual stocks. Many don't even offer mutual funds. Participants are often forced to invest solely in annuities sponsored by insurance companies. While many 401(k) plans do not offer individual stocks as part of their investment mix, they are not prohibited from doing so. In fact, as taxpayers have become more sophisticated, more 401(k) plans have offered the ability to invest in individual stocks.

The 403(b)'s Rules

Investors in a 403(b) plan face many of the same rules that govern a 401(k):

- Regular pre-tax contributions come out of your salary.
- You decide how to invest your money among the plan's choices.
- Investment gains within the plan are not taxed.
- Withdrawals before age 59½ face a 10% penalty.
- Withdrawals after age 59½ are taxed as income.
- Withdrawals must begin starting at age 70½.
- When you leave your job, you can transfer assets to a Rollover IRA.
- You can borrow from the account in some cases.

But there also are key differences:

Asset transfers are permitted if you hate annuities. The problem with annuities is that they often aren't aggressive enough for investors with many years to go until retirement. Ideally, you want a portion of your long-term assets in stocks if you have 10 years or more until retirement.

If you participate in a 403(b) and stock mutual funds are not part of your plan's investment mix, try to convince your benefits coordinator to look into adding them. If you are unsuccessful in getting your employer to include them, you can perform an "asset transfer." This means moving the assets in your annuity to a financial institution that you prefer.

However, there usually is a surrender penalty and fees for transferring assets out of an annuity. The penalty usually starts out at a high level when you buy the annuity and then phases out over a period of years after you own it. The penalty exists to discourage you from buying and selling retirement assets sooner than is prudent.

SIMPLE Plan

The Savings Incentive Match Plan for Employees (SIMPLE) was created by the Small Business Protection Act of 1996 to help people who work at small companies save for retirement in a tax-deferred account. There are two types of SIMPLE plans—a SIMPLE IRA and a SIMPLE 401(k).

Many small companies offer a SIMPLE plan because they cannot afford the high administrative costs to manage a regular defined contribution plan. Less is involved to operate a SIMPLE IRA, so a small company that offers one has fewer costs and headaches.

How the SIMPLE works

The SIMPLE's purpose is similar to that of other defined contribution retirement plans. A company can offer a SIMPLE plan if it has 100 employees or less, counting employees who earned at least $5,000 each in salary in the past year. The company cannot offer a SIMPLE plan if it already provides employees with another employer-sponsored retirement plan.

Employees who own either type of SIMPLE plan make pre-tax contributions. With a SIMPLE IRA and a SIMPLE 401(k), you can contribute up to $6,500 this year and $7,000 next year. That amount goes up by $1,000 each year from 2003–2005, when it will be $10,000.

A company that offers a SIMPLE plan must match its employees' contributions. If your company offers a SIMPLE IRA, it must match your contribution dollar for dollar—up to 3% of your annual salary, or make a non-elective 2% contribution to all employees. If your company offers a SIMPLE 401(k), it can use the 3% formula outlined above or it can make matching contributions using a lower percentage, depending on how many employees participate in the plan, the rate of employee turnover, and other factors.

If the company offers a SIMPLE 401(k) and uses the lower formula, it has to do so for all employees. In addition, the company cannot use the lower formula in more than two years out of the last five years. And it does not have to contribute at all to your plan if you do not make an annual contribution.

The SIMPLE's rules

Investors in a SIMPLE plan enjoy many of the same benefits of other defined contribution plans:

- Regular pre-tax contributions come out of your salary.
- You decide how to invest your money among the plan's choices.
- Investment gains within the plan are not taxed.
- Withdrawals before age 59½ face a 10% penalty.
- Withdrawals after age 59½ are taxed as income.
- Withdrawals must begin starting at age 70½.
- When you leave your job, you can transfer assets to a Rollover IRA.
- You can borrow from the account in some cases.

But there is a key difference:
- You face a 25% penalty if you withdraw money from the plan before you reach age 59½ and during the first two years you're enrolled in the plan. (In most other plans, you face only a 10% penalty for early withdrawal.)

SEP Plan

The Simplified Employee Pension (SEP) plan was created by the Tax Reform Act of 1986. A SEP can be set up by self-employed individuals, independent contractors, or any small business with 25 employees or less. In fact, you don't even have to be incorporated to qualify for a SEP.

How the SEP works

The SEP is considered an IRA, so it enjoys all of the benefits, flexibility, and restrictions of a Traditional IRA.

The most that you or your employer can contribute to your SEP plan in 2001 is 15% of your annual salary, up to the maximum dollar amount set by the new law. Starting in 2002 the range extends to 25%.

Your employer can vary the amount it contributes to your plan each year, provided it's done in writing and the change affects all employees.

In the past, a Keogh was the only plan available to you if you were self-employed. But a Keogh is a qualified plan that requires you to file paperwork with the IRS. The SEP doesn't have that problem.

While you can't convert an existing Keogh into a SEP, you can roll the Keogh into a Rollover IRA and open a new SEP as your business retirement plan for future contributions.

The SEP's rules

Owners of a SEP must follow many of the rules faced by participants in other defined contribution plans:

- You decide how to invest your money among the plan's choices.
- Investment gains within the plan are not taxed.
- Withdrawals before age $59\frac{1}{2}$ face a 10% penalty.
- Withdrawals after age $59\frac{1}{2}$ are taxed as income.
- Withdrawals must begin starting at age $70\frac{1}{2}$.
- You can borrow from the account in some cases.
  But there are key differences:
- There is no vesting period with a SEP, so you are immediately eligible to transfer out all of the assets contributed by your employer when you leave your job.
- In addition to your employer contributing to a SEP, you can contribute the maximum annual amount to a Traditional IRA or Roth IRA, assuming you meet the eligibility rules for these plans.
- Contributions to a SEP-IRA may disqualify you from claiming a deduction for your Traditional IRA contribution depending on your income.
- You can no longer make employee contributions to most SEPs.

457 PLAN

The 457 plan is named for the section of the tax code that allows state and local governments as well as tax-exempt organizations to offer employees a nonqualified plan.

Many of the 457 plan's features are similar to those of other types of defined contribution plans. But there are big differences as well.

How the 457 Plan works

Participants in a 457 plan can contribute 25% of their annual income up to $8,500 in pre-tax income in 2001. Next year the amount rises to $11,000.

The 457 Plan's rules

Some of the 457 Plan's rules are similar to those of other defined contribution plans:

- Regular pre-tax contributions come out of your salary.
- You decide how to invest your money among the plan's choices.
- Investment gains within the plan are not taxed.
- Withdrawals are taxed as income.
- Withdrawals must begin starting at age 70½.

THE NEW LAW

You can contribute more to your company-sponsored retirement plan starting in 2002

Tables 7.1 to 7.3 show the maximum annual contribution levels for participants who are *younger* than age 50.

Table 7.1   Top Amount You Can Contribute to a 401(k), 403(b), or SEP plan

2001	$10,500
2002	$11,000
2003	$12,000
2004	$13,000
2005	$14,000
2006	$15,000*

*After 2006, the top annual contribution will rise based on inflation in increments of $500.

Table 7.2   Top Amount You Can Contribute to a SIMPLE Plan

2001	$6,500
2002	$7,000
2003	$8,000
2004	$9,000
2005	$10,000*

*After 2005, the top annual contribution will rise based on inflation in increments of $500.

Table 7.3   Top Amount You Can Contribute to a 457 Plan Is 33% of Annual Pay or the Amount Below, Whichever Is Less

2001	$8,500
2002	$11,000
2003	$12,000
2004	$13,000
2005	$14,000
2006+	$15,000

*After 2006, the top annual contribution will rise based on inflation in increments of $500.

Under the old law, there was a special catch-up rule in a 457 plan that allowed participants who were three years away from retirement to contribute up to $15,000 over that three-year period.

Under the new law. The higher amount is more favorable. Participants who are three years from retirement can contribute up to two times the top annual amount allowed under the new law.

Example: In 2002, if you are three years from retirement, you can contribute up to $22,000 in that year.

Your contribution plus your employer's match will rise

Under the old law, the total contribution—yours and that of your employer combined—could not exceed 25% of your salary, or more than $35,000, whichever figure was lower.

Under the new law. The total annual amount contributed to your plan now can be 100% of your salary or the amount below, whichever is less (see Table 7.4):

Table 7.4   Top Total Amount You and Your Employer Can Contribute to Your Defined Contribution Plan

2001	$35,000
2002	$40,000
2003	$41,000*
2004	$42,000*
2005	$43,000*
2006	$44,000*

*Depending on inflation.

Example I: Let's say you're under age 50 and earn an annual salary of $120,000 in 2002. And let's say you contribute $11,000 to your 401(k)—the max allowed in 2002. Your company contributes 50 cents for every dollar you contribute—but only up to 5% of your salary. As a result, your company can contribute $3,000 if you contribute the $11,000 max ($120,000 × 5% × 50% = $3,000).

The $14,000 total is under the $40,000 combined max allowed under the new law in 2002—and much lower than 100% of your $120,000 annual salary Your employer could actually contribute another $26,000 to your account.

You can leave a job sooner with more of your company's matching contributions

Companies that offer a qualified retirement plan and make contributions to it must decide how much time must elapse before employees can leave the company and take company contributions with them. This is called the vesting period.

Under the old law, a company had two choices: It could elect to have employees work five years before keeping 100% of its matching contributions. Or it could elect a graduated method, allowing employees to keep 20% of its matching contributions after three years, another 20% after four years, and so on until you worked there seven years, when you could take it all with you.

Under the new law. The amount of time you are required to work at a company before you become vested—or eligible to take all or part of its matching contributions—has been reduced.

Starting in 2002, companies that selected the all-at-once vesting schedule must let employees leave with 100% of matching contributions after working there for three years.

As for companies that originally selected the little-by-little vesting schedule, they too must reduce the time period employees are partially vested (see Table 7.5).

Table 7.5   Starting in 2002, Employees Can Leave a Company and Take Part of Their Employer's Matching Contributions

After	You can leave with
2 years	20%
3 years	40%
4 years	60%
5 years	80%
6 years	100%

Example: Let's say you went to work for a company in January 1999. The company offered you a matching contribution that had a five-year, 100% vesting period. That means if you left prior to January 2004, you would not be able to take a dime of your employer's matching contributions.

But under the new law, that five-year waiting period has been reduced to three years. Hence, you can leave your job after two years and keep 20% of your employer's matching contributions.

Highly compensated employees catch a break

The percentage of income that an employee can contribute to a plan and how much a company can match that contribution depends on the employee's level of compensation. In 2001, if an employee earned annual compensation of $170,000 or more, there are limitations.

Under the new law, the threshold rises to $200,000 in 2002—and rises in $5,000 increments afterwards, based on inflation. This new threshold will allow more compensation to be taken into consideration when determining the limits that affect highly paid participants.

You can roll 401(k) assets into a 403(b) or 457 plan

Under the new law, if you leave your job in the private sector to take a job in your state or local government or at a nonprofit corporation or public school, you can transfer your 401(k) assets into your new 403(b) plan or 457 plan.

In the past, you could only roll 401(k) assets into another qualified plan or into a Rollover IRA.

You can take a tax credit for your contribution—if you qualify

In 2002, you can take a nonrefundable tax credit if your adjusted gross income (AGI) is less than $30,000 (married filing jointly), or less than $15,000 (single), and you contributed to one or more of the following retirement plans:

- 401(k)
- 403(b) (nonprofit organizations)
- 457 (government agencies)
- SIMPLE (salary reduction plan offered by small employers)
- SEP (employer and employee contribute to IRA)
- Traditional IRA
- Roth IRA

To determine the size of your tax credit, a little math is required:
- Find your AGI in Table 7.6 under the marital status that applies to you.
- Take the percentage next to your bracket and multiply it by your annual retirement savings contribution. Your credit cannot exceed $1,000.

Table 7.6

| Percentage to use in calculation of credit | When your adjusted gross income (AGI) is | | | | | |
| | Married filing jointly | | Single head of household | | Single or married filing separately | |
	Over	But not over	Over	But not over	Over	But not over
50%	0	$30,000	0	$22,500	0	$15,000
20%	$30,000	$32,500	$22,500	$24,375	$15,000	$16,250
10%	$32,500	$50,000	$24,375	$37,500	$16,250	$25,000
0	$50,000		$37,500		$25,000	

What You Need to Know

Contribute the max—and use the leftovers for your IRA

Before the end of 2001, figure out how much you're going to contribute to your plan next year.

Be sure to calculate your contribution level and your company's matching contributions carefully. The key is to contribute to your plan at the right pace so you can maximize your company's matching contribution.

> **Example I:** Let's say you earn $120,000 in 2002 and you're under age 50. Your maximum contribution will be $11,000. And let's assume your company contributes 50 cents for every dollar you contribute—up to 5% of your salary.
>
> Let's also say you're an aggressive saver and want to max out over nine months instead of 12 months.
>
> Watch out. If you do the math, you're going to miss out on your company's maximum contribution.
>
> Why? Using the numbers above, your monthly contribution would be $1,222 ($11,000 divided by 9). But nine months of salary in your case would be $90,000, the base which your company would use to calculate its contribution. Hence, your company would contribute only $2,250. That's $750 less than it would have contributed had you contributed over the entire 12 months of the year.

If it turns out after doing the math that you can max out your 401(k) sooner than December without compromising your company's matching contribution, then do it. When you no longer can make contributions to your company retirement plan, have the monthly amounts that would have been contributed diverted to your Traditional IRA or Roth IRA.

Max out for sure if you'll drop to a lower tax bracket

Contributions to a 401(k) plan come out of your pre-tax earnings. If you contribute the $11,000 maximum allowed next year for someone under age 50, your gross income will be reduced by $11,000.

That's great because your taxable income will be lower, especially if removing that $11,000 drops you into a lower tax bracket.

Remember, you receive several big benefits by contributing to your company's defined contribution plan:

- Your contributions are in pre-tax dollars, so your gross income will be lower. That may result in your paying a lower amount of regular income taxes.
- If your company matches your contributions, you'll be receiving free money.
- The money in your plan will grow free of taxes.
- Next year's higher top contribution level will allow more of your money to compound.
- If you qualify, you can claim a tax credit for your contribution.

But watch out for the AMT

By putting money into a defined contribution plan, you're lowering your gross income and your AGI as well. Great news—unless you find yourself subject to paying taxes under the alternative minimum tax (AMT) rules instead of the regular tax rules. Lowering your income won't cause a problem, unless your income drops while your level of exemptions and credits soars. Such an imbalance could trigger the AMT.

Before you max out your contribution, have your tax planner run the numbers. Do your taxes both ways—under the AMT rules and the regular tax rules.

Even if it looks like you might be subject to the AMT, you still should contribute the maximum to your company-sponsored retirement plan. But you may want to discuss with your tax planner whether it makes sense to generate income by exercising options or selling stocks at a gain.

Note your plan's new vesting schedule

Next year, the period a company-sponsored plan requires before it will let you leave with all or part of your company's matching contribution will shrink. Plans either can let you leave with 100% of your employer's matching contributions after three years or 20% or more after just two years.

As a result, it may pay to stay at your current job a bit longer to be eligible for a larger amount of your company's contributions.

Example: You work at a company whose retirement plan uses a partial vesting schedule. That means starting in 2002, if you work for the company for two years, you can leave with 20% of its matching contributions, if you work there for three years you can leave with 40%, and so on.

Let's assume you started working there January 8, 1999. If you get a job offer in December of 2001 and leave, you'd only walk away with 20% of the contributions the company put into your account. Remain at the job until your anniversary in January 2002, and you'll leave with 40% of those contributions.

Or you may be able to leave your job sooner than you thought. If you were waiting until you became completely vested under the old law, the period of time may be much shorter now, making you instantly vested in 2002.

Your company's benefits coordinator will know the number of years your plan requires for full or partial vesting and the date when you become partially or fully vested.

Participate in a 401(k) and a SEP

Many people have a full-time job but also earn income from a weekend job or sideline business. If you're in this category, you can contribute to your company's 401(k), 403(b), or 457 plan *plus* open a SEP, which is a retirement savings IRA available to self-employed taxpayers. You can even continue to contribute to your Traditional IRA or Roth IRA. To open a SEP, you must have self-employed income.

Laid off? Open a SEP or Keogh

Many people over the past year were laid off as companies reorganized in the wake of the economic slowdown. Unfortunately, these people can no longer contribute to their former employer's 401(k) should they begin to earn income consulting or freelancing.

But because they are self-employed, they can open a SEP or Keogh, even if they aren't incorporated.

Call your favorite financial institution, such as a brokerage or mutual fund company, for more information about how to open a tax-deferred SEP or Keogh account.

Negotiating an employment contract?

Have your attorney try to negotiate a clause that says that if you are terminated within two months of your anniversary, you will remain on the payroll at least through that date. This not only will let you collect extra income but also qualify you for more of your employer's matching contributions.

> **Example:** Let's assume that in December of 2001, you're hired as an executive at a major company. Your attorney was able to include a clause in your contract that says you will remain on the payroll until your anniversary if you are terminated within two months of that date.
>
> You sign up for your company's 401(k) plan. It uses the partial formula to determine employee vesting. In 2002, you contribute $11,000—the maximum allowed for someone under age 50. Your company matches your contribution, dollar for dollar. So you have $22,000 invested that year.
>
> In 2003, you can contribute $12,000 to your plan. By September, you've contributed $10,000 and your employer's dollar-for-dollar matching contribution brings your total that year to $20,000.
>
> But in October, your company reorganizes and you are let go.
>
> Under the terms of your contract, you will remain on the company's payroll at least until December 1, allowing you to leave with 20% of your company's contribution—or $4,600. Without the clause, you would have left with none of your company's contributions.

Don't let old 401(k) money sit

If you've left your job, transfer your 401(k) assets to a Rollover IRA. No matter how good your former employer's 401(k) seemed, a Rollover IRA offers the same investments plus as many choices as you'll find in a taxable account, including individual stocks.

When your old 401(k) is a better bet . . .

There is one exception to the rule about always moving your assets out of a former employer's 401(k) and into a Rollover IRA: When the 401(k) offers exceptional investment advice or a cohesive allocation that worked well for you.

The fact is that you may find you are more comfortable with your asset mix in that 401(k) than in a Rollover IRA. Don't forget, it's not uncommon for people to make the wrong investment decisions when they have the kind of unlimited choices found in a Rollover IRA. You also run the risk of doing nothing in a Rollover IRA as the large number of complex choices keeps you from making any decision.

Recent college grads may be able to take the credit

While the new tax credit for retirement contributions was created for low-income taxpayers, a recent college grad may qualify if his or her adjusted gross income does not exceed $25,000, assuming he or she is single.

Encourage your company to offer a matching contribution

If you're a highly compensated employee, then you know that your annual retirement-plan contribution may be limited because not enough of the rank-and-file employees at the company are participating. One of the most powerful ways your company has to encourage workers to sign up for the plan—and improve your maximum contribution—is by offering the matching contribution. It's free money, and compounded over time your savings will grow much larger than if only your contributions were invested.

Don't count your contributions when calculating growth

Many people look at their plan statement, see that it has grown and assume they're doing well. What they forget, however, is that the increases in the account could be due only to monthly contributions. To find out how well the fund has performed, call the financial institution that manages your plan and ask for the investment's rate of return since January and over a period of five years. Then compare both rates with the index the investment uses for comparison.

Q&A

Q. Can company plans change their vesting schedules before 2002?

A. No. Company plans are locked into the schedule they originally chose—either 100% vesting after a set number of years or partial vesting over shorter periods. Otherwise a company could change its vesting schedule with the passage of the new law just to avoid the shorter fixed period and to discouraging employee turnover.

> **Example:** Let's assume you're about to reach your fifth year of employment and your company's plan originally chose the fixed 100% vesting schedule. Under the old law, you would have been fully vested after five years and could have left with 100% of your employer's contributions.
>
> Under the new law, though, the five-year period has been reduced to three years, which means you can leave your job now and take all of your employer's contributions with you.
>
> But under the new law, the partial vesting schedule allows employees to leave with 100% of their employer contributions after six years. If the company's plan were able to switch schedules, you'd be forced to work an extra year before you could leave with all of your employer's contributions.
>
> That's why company plans are prohibited from switching schedules.

Q. If my company goes out of business before I'm vested, can I keep the company's matching contributions?

A. If the company's plan is terminated you will be fully vested in all contributions in your account.

Q. Can I own a 401(k) and a SEP for my consulting work?

A. Yes, provided you meet the qualification for each plan.

Tips for investing in your retirement plan

Knowing how to invest in your company-sponsored retirement plan can be tricky, especially as the number of choices in your plan expands.

Here are a few basic guidelines to help you as your contribution levels rise under the new law:

- *Choose your asset allocation carefully.* How your contributions are divided among your investment choices is important. Handled correctly you will spread your risk among several different types of investments. Ideally, the investments you chose will behave differently when the markets rise and fall. Call the financial institution that manages your plan to find out where to turn for help allocating your assets.
- *Stocks are key to any retirement savings plan.* Historically, stocks have tended to outperform bonds over long periods of time. How much you should have invested in stocks and what types of stocks depends on your tolerance for risk and when you will need your retirement savings.
- *Don't equate risk with recklessness.* The more time you have until you'll need your money, the more risk you can afford to take. However, this does not mean you should put most of your money in investments that might not be around in a few years. As we saw in 2000 and 2001, some sector stock funds can collapse in value and may not recover for years.
- *If your company offers its own common stock* as part of your investment mix, allocate no more than 5% of your assets to its shares.
- *Rebalance your portfolio periodically.* Let's assume the right allocation for you is 70% stocks and 30% bonds. Major shifts in the stock market or economy could alter that allocation. After 12 months, you could wind up with 60% of your money invested in stocks and 40% in bonds.

  To return your portfolio to the 70%/30% mix, you can have more of your new contributions invested in stocks. Or you can sell 10% of your bonds and invest the assets in stocks. Remember, gains on securities you sell in a retirement savings plan are not currently taxed.
- *At retirement, avoid taking a lump-sum distribution.* The lump sum will no longer be able to grow tax deferred and the withdrawal will be taxed as income. Instead, leave the assets in the 401(k) or transfer them to a Traditional IRA.
- *In retirement, withdraw money from your taxable accounts first.* Why? Because your retirement savings will continue to compound tax-deferred if you leave them in there.

THE SECOND CHANGE

Special catch-up rules for taxpayers age 50 or older starts in 2002.

Do You Qualify for This?

Yes. *If you are age 50 or older by the end of 2002 and your employer offers a qualified retirement plan.*

BACKGROUND

Under the new tax law, your maximum contribution to a company-sponsored retirement plan and to an IRA are higher than other taxpayers if you are age 50 or older in 2002. The intent of Congress was to help women age 50 or older who stayed home to raise children "catch up" to everyone else's savings levels.

The thinking behind the law is that millions of women who left the workplace to raise children and did not earn income were not eligible to contribute to workplace retirement plans or receive matching contributions from employers.

Because they weren't working, these women couldn't afford to invest in an IRA and, more important, they couldn't contribute to a company-sponsored plan, such as a 401(k). Congress viewed this situation as unfair. Unless something was done, millions of baby boomer women would be retiring over the next 15 years with very little saved because they had stayed home to raise a family.

Congress also recognized that this problem could be compounded by the high divorce rate. If a woman who wasn't able to work for the past 20 years while raising children became divorced, she would have far less savings than a married woman who had been working and saving all those years.

But because company-sponsored retirement plans have very strict rules governing nondiscriminatory practices, Congress could not very well approve legislation that allowed only women over age 50 who stayed home with kids to benefit more than others.

There also would be bureaucratic and qualification nightmares for companies and the IRS. How would you structure the law so that a woman who raised two children and was home for 15 years could contribute more than a woman who raised one child and returned to work sooner? And what about families in which a man quit work for a period of years to raise the children while his wife returned to a job that was more lucrative?

Ultimately, Congress decided to write this part of the law so that if affected all taxpayers who are age 50 or older in 2002.

> *Example:* Beth and her neighbors, Judy and Frank, all turn 50 years old in 2002. They all work for companies that provide employees with a 401(k) plan. Beth has worked all her life. But Judy stayed home for the past 20 years to raise three children and didn't work during that period. Her husband Frank worked during those years. Under the new law, all three can contribute the same higher amount—$12,000—in 2002.
>
> But even though the law favors all three equally, Beth will still do much better over the years than she would have had this part of the law not been included. This is especially true when you factor in company matching contributions and compounding.

THE NEW LAW

If you are 50 years old or older in 2002, you can contribute more to your company retirement plan than other taxpayers

Tables 7.7 to 7.9 show the maximum annual contribution levels for plan participants age 50 and older:

Table 7.7 If You Are Age 50+, the Top Amount You Can Contribute to a 401(k) or 403(b) Plan

2001	$10,500
2002	$12,000
2003	$14,000
2004	$16,000
2005	$18,000
2006+	$20,000

Table 7.8   If You Are Age 50+, the Top Amount You Can Contribute to a SIMPLE Plan

2001	$6,500
2002	$7,500
2003	$9,000
2004	$10,500
2005	$12,000
2006+	$12,500

Table 7.9   If You Are Age 50+, the Top Amount You Can Contribute to a 457 Plan is the Amount Below or 33% of Compensation, Whichever is Less

2001	$8,500
2002	$12,000
2003	$14,000
2004	$16,000
2005	$18,000
2006+	$20,000

Special 457 rule: Under the old law, there was a special rule that allowed plan participants who were three years away from retirement to contribute a higher maximum.

Under the new law, the amount is more favorable. Participants who are three years from retirement now can contribute up to two times the top amount allowed each year under the new law for up to three years.

The maximum amount you and your employer can contribute is not the same as other taxpayers

The new law created higher maximum contribution levels for taxpayers who are age 50 or older. The combined amount you and your employer can contribute has been increased by that amount. For example, in 2002 the maximum amount that you and your employer can contribute is $41,000, not 40,000.

What You Need to Know

Do the math if your company makes contributions

If you are 50 years old or older, every dollar you and your company can contribute to your workplace retirement plan is critical. But you don't want to be in a situation where you max out too soon. Remember, your company's contributions may be based on your income during the period in which you are making contributions.

If you max out too soon, you could lose valuable contributions from your employer. Call your employer's benefits coordinator now to find out how much you would have to contribute each pay period next year to qualify for all of your employer's contributions.

Be sure to name plan beneficiaries

The older you get, the more important it is that your financial accounts are in order. By law, your spouse is your plan's primary beneficiary. He or she will inherit your 401(k) assets estate tax-free. Your other heirs could face estate and income taxes.

But if your spouse dies before you do and you failed to list other beneficiaries on your 401(k) and how much you want each of them to inherit, your heirs might not receive the assets immediately or at all.

Once a year, review your list of 401(k) beneficiaries and the percentage of assets you want each one to receive.

Leave time for transfers when you retire or leave a job

It can take four to six weeks to have assets in a 401(k) transferred over to another company's 401(k) or qualifying IRA.

Unlike an IRA, which is an account you own, a 401(k) functions as a trust held by your company for your benefit. As a result, there is more paperwork to fill out, documents to be notarized, and regulations to follow with a rollover.

Ideally, you want to initiate the transfer of assets as early as possible. In some cases, plan administrators handle such transfers only once a quarter. If you miss the date, you'll have to wait until the next quarter before the four-to-six-week transfer period begins.

Q&A

Q. What if I don't turn 50 until December 2002?

A. You still qualify to make the higher contribution starting January 1, 2002. Under the new law, you are 50 years old in 2002 if you turn that age at any time next year.

Q. I don't expect to have enough to make higher contributions to both my 401(k) and IRA. Which one is best?

A. The answer depends on your company's generosity, your tax bracket, and your investment choices in each account.

> *Option 1:* If your employer makes matching contributions, you're better off making the higher contribution to your company-sponsored plan.
>
> Your contributions to your company-sponsored plan come out of your income on a pre-tax basis. As a result, your higher contribution will reduce your gross income, which could put you in a lower tax bracket. Again, contributing to your company-sponsored plan makes the most sense in this case.

> *Option 2:* If the investment choices in your company-sponsored plan are terrible and your company does not seem ready to improve them, making the higher contribution to your IRA may be more beneficial, especially if it's a Roth IRA, where assets grow tax-deferred and can be withdrawn after age 59½ tax-free.

THE THIRD CHANGE

New hardship-withdrawal rules start in 2002.

Do You Qualify for This?

Yes. *If you must withdraw assets from a 401(k) plan before you leave your job and prior to age 59½ for hardship reasons.*

BACKGROUND

You know you can borrow from a 401(k) plan without paying income taxes or a penalty—provided you repay the loan. If you withdraw assets from a 401(k) plan before you reach age 59½, you will face income taxes and a 10% penalty. If you still work for your employer, the 401(k) plan is prohibited from making a distribution to you until you're 59½.

An exception to the early withdrawal prohibition on a 401(k) plan is when you face a financial hardship and other financial resources are not available to you. At that point, your company can authorize a withdrawal that will be subjected to regular income tax and, perhaps, to the 10% penalty, depending on your age and what you do with the money. Under the old law, the catch was that you couldn't resume making contributions to your 401(k) plan for 12 months after a hardship withdrawal.

The old law was written this way for two reasons:

1. If you need to take an emergency withdrawal from a tax-deferred retirement plan, you shouldn't make contributions to your plan immediately but should wait until your hardship is under control and finances are in order.
2. Without a blackout period, you could request a hardship withdrawal and take advantage of the tax-deferred 401(k) by continuing to make contributions.

THE NEW LAW

■ Starting in 2002, you only have to wait six months after receiving a hardship withdrawal instead of 12 months before you can make contributions to a 401(k).

> **Example:** Molly takes a hardship withdrawal from her employer's 401(k) plan on March 5, 2002. She decides to have $4,000 removed from her check in 12 monthly installments.

Under the new rules, she will be able to resume making 401(k) contributions September 6, 2002.

She also will be able to raise the amount she originally chose to contribute to the plan to catch up—if she can afford to.

Congress decided that the 12-month ban under the old law placed a different type of hardship on the very people it was trying to help. By preventing people who needed a 401(k) hardship withdrawal from making new contributions for so long, the law was depriving them of the best way to save for retirement.

■ The new law's hardship rule is somewhat retroactive. So, if you request a hardship withdrawal in the second half of 2001 instead of 2002, you will only have to wait six months before you can resume making pre-tax contributions.

Example: Molly takes a hardship withdrawal from her employer's 401(k) plan on December 3, 2001. She will have to wait only until June 4, 2002, to resume making contributions.

Q&A

Q. What exactly is considered a hardship?

A. An immediate and heavy financial need is considered a hardship. Money needed for college or to buy a house is viewed as a hardship even though the payments should have been anticipated, as long as resources are not available from elsewhere. Money needed to repair a house severely damaged by a storm or flood would be a hardship. It's up to the plan administrator to decide whether to grant you the withdrawal.

Q. What do I have to show to prove it's a hardship?

A. You have to show immediate and heavy financial need in the following areas:
■ Medical care
■ Home purchase
■ Education
■ Eviction
■ Others such as funerals, disasters etc.

In addition, the distribution must satisfy your pressing need. As a result, you have to show that you used up all other means within reason.

Q. Is there any appeal or is my employer the last word?
A. Your plan administrator is the last word based on the hardship rules outlined in the company-sponsored plan.

Q. Does my employer's matching contribution stop as well?
A. Yes, your employer cannot match if you are not contributing.

Q. When exactly does the six-month blackout period begin?
A. The blackout period begins as soon as the check is issued.

THE FOURTH CHANGE

Hardship waiver for 60-day rollover starts in 2002.

Do You Qualify for This?

Yes. If you transfer assets from one plan to another but the assets fail to arrive in the new plan within 60 days due to circumstances outside of your control.

BACKGROUND

When you leave your job at a company, you can roll your 401(k), 403(b), or 457 retirement plan assets over to a similar retirement plan or a Rollover IRA.

The easiest way to do this is by having the assets transferred between accounts, so you never have to touch the money. The electronic transfer between trustees lets you avoid having to pay income taxes and a penalty on the withdrawn assets, and no withholding tax is taken out.

You also can avoid taxation and a penalty if you have the plan send you the check but made out to the new financial institution that will be managing your Rollover IRA. Then you send the check to your Rollover IRA's custodian.

However, many people still choose to have the check made out and sent to them. They do this either because they want to be sure the money gets to where it's supposed to go or they haven't decided whether to put it in a Rollover IRA or spend it. Whatever the reason, these people have 60 days to put the check into a Rollover IRA. Otherwise, the amount is considered a distribution and faces income taxes and possibly a penalty if you're younger than 59½. In addition, the plan will usually withhold 20% of the distribution for taxes. To avoid tax, you have to roll over that amount also.

Under the old law, the only way you could get off the hook with the IRS if you didn't roll it over in time is if you lived in an area that the President declared a disaster or you were in the military and were suddenly shipped off to war.

In all other cases, the IRS did not have the authority to waive this 60-day deadline.

THE NEW LAW

The IRS now has the power to waive the 60-day rollover period in cases that include casualty, disaster, or other events it feels were beyond the reasonable control of the individual. These events now can include screw-ups by financial services institutions. For example, you authorize assets to be transferred, but the person responsible for wiring the assets or receiving them drops the ball and the assets never arrive in the account or they are put into the wrong account.

Don't laugh. It turns out that the No. 1 reason why people had to pay taxes and a penalty on a distribution was because of a clerical error. And in such cases under the old law, the IRS's hands were tied. You had to pay the tax and the penalty.

The new law not only gives the IRS a heart but also widens the scope of situations in which a hardship can occur. After all, the number of people who can't complete a 60-day rollover because their town is flooded or they were sent off to war is relatively small. Now, however, many other more common situations that are out of the taxpayer's control can receive an IRS break.

> **Example:** Under the new law, the IRS can grant an extension if it wishes when a house burns down with the rollover check inside.

What You Need to Know

You still need to be careful

While the new law allows the IRS to use its discretion when granting a 60-day extension, it did not outline exactly what situations qualify. The new law asks the IRS to provide rulings and regulations to clarify exactly who qualifies for an extension and who does not.

If you read the new law, you'll see that Congress "authorizes" the IRS to extend the 60-day period in hardship cases but it does not "require" it to do so. As a result, the new law merely grants the IRS permission to do what it thinks is best in each situation.

The law's limits will likely be framed by decisions in future situations as people come forward seeking relief for hardships.

Always have your assets transferred electronically

The best way to reduce mistakes is to have your former plan transfer the assets to your new plan electronically. In today's highly technological world, there's really no need to have the check sent to you and risk it being lost or accidentally destroyed.

Make sure assets arrive in a timely manner

Even if you have the assets transferred electronically, don't assume that the financial institutions involved are perfect. Find out how long it will take for the assets to arrive in your Rollover IRA. If they don't arrive by the time the benefits coordinator at your former employer said they would, call him or her up to see if the location of the assets can be verified.

The Fifth Change

A new Roth plan may be offered by employers in 2006.

Do You Qualify for This?

Yes. If your company decides to offer one. There will be no income restrictions to prevent you from making contributions.

BACKGROUND

The new type of Roth retirement savings plan created by the new tax law and due to begin appearing in 2006 is something of a royal wedding. The new plan will continue features of the two most popular and favorable retirement plans. To understand what's coming, you need to know how the Roth IRA and the 401(k) and 403(b) work.

Roth IRA. In the 1990s, Senator William Roth of Delaware led the charge for a new type of IRA. The old IRA was a great way for people to save using a tax-deferred account, but there were serious limitations for low- and middle-income taxpayers. Withdrawals from IRAs made during retirement faced income tax, you had to start withdrawing at age 70½, and your heirs had to pay income taxes on the inherited assets.

So when Senator Roth's alternative IRA was approved as part of the Taxpayer Relief Act of 1997, it came to be known as the Roth IRA. It allowed taxpayers who qualified to save for retirement in a tax-sheltered account and then withdraw assets tax-free starting at age 59½. And you didn't have to start withdrawing your money starting at age 70½. In fact, you never had to withdraw the assets if you didn't want to, making it far more attractive from an inheritance viewpoint. The tradeoff was that you couldn't claim a deduction by making a contribution as you could with a Traditional IRA.

So it's no wonder that when the full Roth IRA was first introduced in 1998, it was immediately embraced by taxpayers who qualified. Today, the only qualification to open a Roth IRA is that your adjusted gross income (AGI) must be below $150,000 (married filing jointly) and $95,000 (others). The amount you can contribute to a Roth IRA is phased out between $150,000 and $160,000 of AGI (married filing jointly) or between $95,000 and 110,000 (others).

If you qualify, you can contribute the same top annual amount of after-tax income that you can to a Traditional IRA. In fact, you can own both if you want to. You can convert your Traditional IRA into a Roth IRA and even undo the conversion if it turns out that your AGI is higher for the year than the qualification threshold.

But the maximum annual contribution is relatively low and doesn't allow taxpayers to save enough—and the contribution was limited for upper income taxpayers.

401(k). By contrast, the 401(k) let taxpayers save more than twice as much each year. It was created in 1980 after Ted Benna, a pension consultant, discovered a loophole in Section 401(k) of 1978 Tax Reform Act. As Benna interpreted the law—and the IRS eventually allowed everyone to interpret it—full-time employees for companies in the private sector could fund retirement savings accounts with pretax dollars and employer matching contributions.

The 401(k) lets your assets grow tax-deferred until you can start withdrawing them at age 59½. The amounts you withdraw are taxed as income, and you must usually start to withdraw your plan's assets regularly starting at age 70½.

The big benefit of the 401(k) is the size of your annual contribution. Not only is the amount you can contribute significantly higher than in a Traditional IRA or Roth IRA, but your employer could kick in a sizable amount as well.

403(b). The 403(b) works pretty much the same way as a 401(k) except it is offered to employees of public schools and certain non-profit organizations. Also, its investment mix usually is more limited than a 401(k)'s.

But there are drawbacks to the 401(k) and 403(b) plans—as good as they are. The big one is that contributions are taxed as income when you withdraw them starting at age 59½ and you have to withdraw assets at 70½, whether you need the money or not.

The Roth IRA and the 401(k) and 403(b) are very different types of plans that were for a merger. Under the new tax law, companies will be able to offer just such a hybrid plan.

THE NEW LAW

The new Roth starts in 2006. Starting in 2006, employers that offer a 401(k) or 403(b) plan can also sponsor a Roth savings plan if they choose to do so.

All employees will qualify.   because there are no adjusted gross income restrictions like those found with a Roth IRA.

How contributions will be made.   Employees can divert part or all of their 401(k) or 403(b) contribution into a company-sponsored Roth plan. That means that when the plan is first offered in 2006, you can contribute all or part of the $15,000 you're allowed to contribute to a company-sponsored retirement plan maximum if you're under age 50. Or you can contribute all or part of the $20,000 you're allowed to contribute if you're age 50 or older.

Tax-free status.   The company-sponsored Roth plan will allow your contributions to grow without taxation. Withdrawals can be made tax-free starting at age 59½. And the assets in the plan probably do not have to be withdrawn starting at age 70½.

>   *Drawback I:* Your contributions to a company-sponsored Roth plan must be with after-tax dollars rather that the pre-tax dollars used for regular 401(k) or 403(b) contributions.

>   *Drawback II:* Your employer cannot make matching contributions to your company-sponsored Roth plan. Only your after-tax dollars can be contributed.

Unlike the Roth IRA, which is an account you open, your employer must administer the company-sponsored Roth plan.

And like with any other tax-favored retirement plan, your assets will be subject to penalty for excess contributions, early distributions, flawed rollovers, etc.

WHAT YOU NEED TO KNOW

Don't expect companies to jump at the chance to offer them

There will likely be a delay in acceptance of the new Roth plan as companies view their 401(k) plans as sufficient for employee retirement savings when balanced against the complexity of managing a company-sponsored plan. However, look for employees to lobby hard for their employers to sponsor one.

You can spread your contributions over both types of plans

If you are offered both a 401(k) or 403(b) and a company-sponsored Roth plan, you can contribute your entire annual amount to a Roth. Or you can split the maximum annual contribution any way you wish.

> **Example:** In 2006, you're under age 50 and can contribute $15,000 to your company-sponsored retirement plans. So you may decide to contribute $11,000 to your 401(k) and $4,000 to your company's new Roth plan.

Weighing the pros and cons will be tricky

Employees will have a hard time determining how much of their after-tax income, if any, should be diverted to the new company-sponsored Roth plan.

Before you determine what percentage of your contribution should be used in a company-sponsored Roth plan, you'll have to ask yourself these questions:

- *Is it worth giving up pre-tax contributions?* After all, one of the big benefits of contributing pre-tax dollars to a 401(k) or 403(b) plan is that they reduce your gross income and likely your tax bracket.
- *How will assets perform in a company-sponsored Roth IRA vs. a 401(k) or 403(b) plan?* If your employer makes matching contributions to your 401(k) or 403(b), you may not want to give them up. Over time, the extra money is likely to grow faster than the amount in your company-sponsored Roth IRA, which will hold only your contributions. Your decision here will depend mainly on whether or not your company matches your contributions and up to what amount.
- *When will you need to withdraw retirement plan assets?* The sooner you'll need the money, the more attractive a company-sponsored Roth IRA will become. Withdrawals from a Roth plan are tax-free vs. withdrawals from a 401(k) or 403(b) plan—or a Rollover IRA for that matter—which are taxed as income.

    However, it's important to remember that it's better to withdraw assets from a taxable account first before you dip into your retirement savings. Assets in a company-sponsored retirement plan or a Rollover IRA continue to grow tax-deferred until withdrawn.

- *What will your income tax rate be when you need to withdraw 401(k) or 403(b) assets?* If you do not plan to withdraw assets from a 401(k) or 403(b) plan until you turn 70½, your tax bracket will likely be much lower than it is while you're working. That means you'll pay less in income tax on the withdrawals. If you expect to be in a higher bracket because you're still working or receiving income, then the Roth plan is more advantageous.

Heirs will prefer that you use the Roth plan

Assets from a 401(k) are taxed as income when inherited by heirs. But inheriting a company-sponsored Roth plan is painless. Like a Roth IRA, the assets withdrawn after death under the minimum distribution rules escape income tax. In addition, the assets can continue to grow tax free if they are left in the inherited plan.

People over age 50 at the time may find it most beneficial

While younger people may prefer to stick with their pre-tax contributions to 401(k) and 403(b) plans to reduce their tax hit, older taxpayers are likely to be more interested in the tax-free withdrawal feature of the company-sponsored Roth plan, especially as these people near retirement and their maximum annual contribution rises. However, some younger people may favor the Roth over the 401(k) because of its tax-free withdrawal benefit starting at age 59½.

Nevertheless, when these company-sponsored Roth contribution programs are offered starting in 2006, they will lead to a frenzy similar to the excitement that occurred in 1998 when the Roth IRA was first introduced.

Q&A

Q. **Will I have to hold assets in a Roth plan for at least five years before distributions are tax-free?**

A. Yes, similar to the Roth IRA rules, the plan distributions will only qualify for tax-free treatment if the account has been in existence for at least five years.

Q. When I leave my job, where will be the best place to transfer my Roth plan assets?

A. In order to continue the tax-free buildup of the plan's assets, the assets should be rolled over into a Roth IRA if you qualify or a Traditional IRA if you don't qualify.

Q. I'll be 61 years old in 2006 and plan to retire at 65. Does it pay at that age to open a Roth plan at work?

A. Probably not. Remember, if you open a Roth plan with your employer, the employer is not allowed to match your contributions to the Roth plan (although it could make the match on a pre-tax basis).

This match may provide a significant economic benefit that offsets the tax-free withdrawal benefit of your Roth plan. Roth plans will be better suited for younger employees who have a significant time horizon to accumulate tax-free assets within a Roth plan.

Q. Is there a way to max out my 401(k) using my employer's matching contributions and still have money left over for the Roth plan?

A. This is unclear at this time. However, what is clear is that if your adjusted gross income is low enough that you qualify for a Roth IRA, you could max out your employer's 401(k) plan along with the employer's match—and still contribute the maximum after-tax dollars to a Roth IRA.

8

Education

THE BIG NEWS

Starting in 2002:

- "529" tuition-plan withdrawals are tax-free.
- Education IRA contribution limit rises and can cover non-college costs.
- The student-loan interest deduction rises.
- Deduction for college expenses increases.
- More liberal Hope and Lifetime Learning credit rules.

THE FIRST CHANGE

Most "529" tuition-plan withdrawals are tax free starting in 2002.

Do You Qualify for This?

Yes. If you are invested in a "529" college savings plan or intend to invest in one. Anyone can contribute to a 529 plan.

BACKGROUND

Nothing grows faster than the cost of a college education. Despite the relatively low 2.9% rate of annual inflation, college costs shot up 4.5% to 5% in the 2000–2001 academic year.

The price of a four-year college education at a state school—tuition plus room and board—now stands at about $34,000 while four years at a private school will run you about $90,000. That means you have to come up with between $8,500 and $22,500 a year, depending on where your child attends college. And this assumes you have only one child who is college bound.

But those tabs are today's college costs. If your child is 10 years old now, you need to calculate how those figures are going to rise based on the 5% average annual rate of college-costs inflation.

The estimated totals give you a sense of how aggressively parents have to save for their children's college education. The savings challenge is made even more daunting by parents' need to save regularly for retirement as well.

The government is well aware of how expensive it is to educate your kids. To help offset these costs, the tax code allowed states to offer Qualified State Tuition Programs starting in 1986.

Under the rules of these plans, states let you buy tuition credits in advance or contribute to a savings account specifically set up to help you save for a child's or other beneficiary's college tuition and certain costs.

To qualify, a state plan has to meet requirements under Section 529 of the IRS code, which is why such programs are known as "529" plans.

There are two types of 529 plans:

1. **Prepaid plan.** You transfer assets to an account with the state. The account is limited to the growth rate of public-college tuition increases in your state. If your plan is a tuition contract, you agree to prepay a lump sum or a set amount in monthly payments.

    Other plans sell credits. Each credit is worth a percentage of your future college costs, which you buy on a schedule or whenever you wish. Under the new law, colleges will be able to offer these plans along with states starting in 2002.

    These plans were popular when the inflation rate for college costs were about 9% a year. With the rate of inflation for college costs much lower now, the college savings plans outlined below offer a better chance to achieve the former rate of growth.

2. **College savings plan.** Under the old law, your assets were deposited in one or more state-run investment funds that are professionally managed. When your child reaches college age, the assets must be used to pay part of the education costs.

There are several big advantages to a 529 plan:

- *Everyone qualifies to participate.* There are no restrictions based on your income or the age of the person you want to put through college. That person could even be you.

  Some state plans allow you to contribute as much as $250,000 at once or over the life of the investment. You also are allowed to contribute up to $50,000 at once without incurring a gift tax.

- *Tax breaks on the federal and state level.* Your deposits in a 529 college-savings plan grow tax-deferred. Under the old law, the gains on your investments were taxed at the student's low tax bracket when withdrawn to meet college costs. The new law eliminates that tax, and makes withdrawals for college expenses tax-free.

  On the state level, your state may offer a tax deduction or exemption for investing in its plan. You are usually not required to use your assets in the plan to pay for a state school. Your assets can be used to cover costs at any accredited university in the country.

- *Your assets are allocated for you.* One of the trickiest parts of saving for college is knowing when to shift your assets out of stocks and into safer investments as your child nears college age.

  Many people learned this lesson the hard way in 2000 and 2001. They assumed that the run-up in stock prices in 1999 would continue, so they remained fully invested in stocks with a year or two to go until they needed the money. When the market began its crash in March 2000, many people watched their assets decline by 30% or more.

  The point here is that you don't want to be too heavily invested in stocks when your child is within five years of becoming a freshman.

  A 529 college savings plan takes care of the asset shifting for you. You only have to decide which funds in the plan are ideal based on your risk-tolerance. Then the fund you chose will shift your assets into safer investments over the years based on the age of your child when you started investing.

  Keep in mind, however, that although the asset-shifting process is done for you, you still must carefully select which plan to invest in and how much of your assets you'd like invested in each fund that the plan offers. Once invested, you cannot move the assets out of one investment and into another. You can invest new money in the different fund choices. Or, under the new law, you can transfer all of the assets to another plan once every 12 months.

New investments can be made regularly by automatic deposit or periodically by check.

■ *You control when to withdraw the money.* The money you save in the plan can only be used for your child's college costs. But just because the money is for your child doesn't mean your child can withdraw the money to buy a new set of drums. Your child also cannot control where the money will be invested. You make those decisions.

If you withdraw your 529-plan assets for purposes other than college, you will likely face two different taxes. The gains your principal investment earned would face regular income tax and you'd face a 10% withdrawal penalty.

If your child chooses not to attend college, you can leave the money in the account and hope it's just a phase. You won't be taxed unless you withdraw the money for purposes other than college for the person named as the beneficiary.

If it becomes apparent that your child won't attend college at all, you can avoid taxes by crossing your child's name off the plan and adding a new beneficiary who intends to attend college. That person could be another one of your children, your spouse, you, or a brother or sister's child.

Again, the only way to withdraw the assets tax-free is if the money is used to pay for the college expenses of the beneficiary named on the plan.

■ *Oh, yeah, and this, too.* If you withdraw the money for purposes other than college costs, any state deductions you took over the years would be reversed when you reported the nonqualified withdrawal. Which is why it's important that college is definitely in the cards for your child when you begin saving in one of these plans.

How exactly is your money invested by the funds? Each state offers a different selection. You need to review them carefully and their long-term and short-term performance before you invest. You also want to see if there is an enrollment fee and an annual management fee. Then you want to invest in a plan that offers the best-performing funds with the lowest fees. A comparison of the various 529 plans can be located at *www.savingforcollege.com*.

Will your child's chances for financial aid be compromised by your investment in a 529 plan? It depends on your withdrawals, which are considered a dollar-for-dollar offset in eligibility for financial aid.

Example: if you withdrew $20,000 for college costs this year, your need for financial aid will be considered to be $20,000 less.

The 529 plan offers many advantages including potentially tax-free savings, much higher annual deposits, and handling your asset allocation for you. But you still must be sure you're investing in a plan with a good track record and a fund that suits your risk tolerance.

THE NEW LAW

1. *New tax-free status.* Starting in 2002, plan withdrawals are tax-free when they're used for college costs. This is a huge break. Under the old law, your account's earnings were taxed at your child's tax bracket when they were withdrawn for college costs.

   Although a child's bracket is usually the lowest one—10% under the new law—taxes are still taxes. Now you have more money to pay for college.

   Example: You have $100,000 saved in your 529 plan. Your child will be attending college in the fall of 2002. The bill will be $20,000. Under the old law, you would have owed $2,000 in taxes—if your child were in the 10% bracket. Now, the entire amount you withdrew can be used to pay for college, tax-free. This tax-free status applies to school-sponsored 529 plans after 2003.

2. *New definition of "room and board."* If your child lives off campus and not at home, be aware that the definition of "room and board" for students has changed. Beginning in 2002, there is no longer a $2,500 per-year cap on college-related expense. That amount has been expanded to "a reasonable allowance."

3. *Private colleges can get into the act.* In the past, only state governments could offer 529 college savings plans. Under the new

law, private colleges are now allowed to set up prepaid educational accounts and sell credits for payment in the future starting in 2002.

   Again, the savings do not have to be used at the college that offers the plan. They can be used to pay costs at any college.
4. ***Plan-to-plan rollovers are OK.*** This is a big change. In the past, once you invested in a state plan's fund, you were stuck with it. Now, if you're unhappy with the performance of your 529 plan or you find a better 529 plan alternative, you can roll all of your assets into that plan. The catch is that you can do this only once every 12 months without it being viewed as a taxable event.

> ***Example:*** You saved a nice sum—$150,000—in a 529 plan for the benefit of your son. But it turns out that you son is so brilliant (just as you expected, right?) that his college of choice gave him a full scholarship.
>
> What should you do with the assets you saved for him? You can remove his name as beneficiary and name his little brother, who is 13 years old. But wait. When you set up the plan, it was for your son who is about to begin college. As a result, the 529 plan has shifted the assets into the most conservative allocation, expecting that you needed the money now.
>
> In this case, it may pay to move the assets to another plan where you'll find a slightly more aggressive investment for your younger son. Remember, you are five years away from that child's first college bill and eight years away from his final bill (senior year).

   To find out how exactly to name a new beneficiary to your existing 529 plan and when you need to move the assets to another plan next year, contact your current 529 plan custodian.

WHAT YOU NEED TO KNOW

Put off withdrawing 529 plan assets in 2001 if possible

Remember, the new rules don't take effect until 2002. If you already withdrew assets in 2001 to pay for the fall 2001 semester, you're out of luck. You will have to pay taxes on your withdrawal's gains. The good news is that the gains will be taxed at your child's rate, which could be as low as 10% in 2001.

If you haven't paid your 2001 bill yet, determine the implications of delaying your college tuition payments until January 2002. While you won't be taxed on the assets withdrawn in 2002 if they're used for college costs, you may owe the college a late-payment fee. Compare which will hurt more—the tax or the penalty. The other factor to keep in mind is that assets left in the account until January will be able to compound tax-free a little longer.

Higher-income parents take note

All taxpayers, regardless of their income or the age of the person due to attend college, can invest in this plan. Also, your savings can be used to pay tuition at any college, including Harvard. This makes a 529 plan especially beneficial for parents whose level of income is high enough that their children won't likely receive much financial aid from their college of choice.

Take advantage of the gift-tax loophole

You typically face a gift tax (or at least use up your unified credit) when you give more than $10,000 in a single year to a child. A contribution to a 529 plan is still considered a gift. However, the IRS waives the annual $10,000 limitation in this situation.

When you contribute up to $50,000 (or $100,000 for a married couple) to a 529 plan, the gift is treated as if you had given the amount over a five-year period instead of over one year. That's $10,000 a year, which keeps you out of gift-tax trouble.

> *Example:* Your child's grandparents are loaded and want to contribute to their granddaughter's college education fund. Her grandmother and grandfather can contribute $100,000 to the 529 plan ($50,000 each) without facing a gift tax. Not only are they doing a good thing by putting their granddaughter through college but the move will also reduce the size of their estate and limit their estate tax liability.

The example above makes sense when a child has many years to go until college. However, if the child in our example is 18 years old and about to attend college, her grandparents would be better off writing a check for tuition and sending it directly to her university. There are no gift taxes when the checks are made out to the school and paid directly. In fact, anyone can pay her tuition directly and avoid the gift tax.

If the child is within a few years of college and her grandparents— or rich uncle and aunt, for that matter—want to send her money and reduce the size of their estates now, they can contribute up to $50,000 each to her 529 plan and avoid the gift tax. You then can allocate the cash to the plan's money market account to preserve its value and avoid investment risk altogether.

Before you invest, shop around

About 40 states offer a 529 plan. Soon, colleges will begin marketing them as well. How can you tell which plans are better than others? There are three key factors:

1. *You want a plan with low fees.* The average annual fee is around 1%. Just be sure the fund's beneficiary can be changed easily if your child decides not to use the money and you want to name another child.

2. *You want a plan with funds that held up in tough times.* While the funds in a 529 plan are professionally managed, there's no guarantee of strong performance. You need to take a careful look at the plans you're considering and the funds they offer. Some funds in 2000 were down as much as 30%.

   Remember, the initial amount you invest in a savings plan (your principal) is not guaranteed. Just because you're investing in a state or college plan and both want you to earn as much money as possible to offset college costs, there's no guarantee that your fund will produce your desired amount by your child's freshman year. In some cases, an inferior state plan may *underperform* investments held in another plan or even a taxable account.

3. *You want a plan that didn't do too badly in the past few years.* Your 529 plan's fund manager allocates your assets among stocks, bonds, and cash depending on the age of your child. The manager allocates more assets to stocks than bonds and cash when your child is young, shifts to a less aggressive mix when your child nears college, and adopts a conservative mix when your child is nearly college age.

   Ideally, you want to find a 529 plan with funds that didn't do too badly over the past two years for beneficiaries who were about to go to college. Over the past two years, the stock market has performed poorly. Looking at how the fund performed in its most conservative phase will give you a sense of how the fund tends to perform in tough times. The performance rate will tell you how badly the fund can perform in a worst-case situation and let you plan accordingly.

These three factors make a very strong argument for shopping carefully when comparing 529 plans and why it's important now to put all of your college investment assets in a 529 plan. One of the best sites for reviewing state-sponsored 529 plans is *www.savingfor-college.com*.

Be careful not to invest more than you need

If you still have money in a 529 plan when the college dean is handing your child his or her diploma, you saved too much. The only way to escape taxation on withdrawal of the excess is to change the name on the plan from your graduating child to another child who is in college or plans to go. Or, the money could be used for graduate school. A 529 plan is exclusively for college costs. Using the assets for any other purpose results in taxation and a penalty.

Think twice if your child won't be a freshman by 2010

One of the biggest oddities of the new tax law is its "sunset" provision. In short, if the new tax law isn't amended to extend many of its provisions, the new law will expire at the end of 2010 and revert to the old tax law.

As you know, most qualified withdrawals from a 529 plan are tax-free from 2002 through 2010. But in 2011, if this part of the law remains unchanged, you will owe tax on the gains at your child's tax bracket again when you withdraw the money. While the 529 plan is still a beneficial way to save for college, it's impossible to know whether the gains you withdraw after 2010 will be taxed or not. What you do know is that once your savings are earmarked for college costs, they must remain there or face taxation and a penalty.

By all means, use a 529 plan to save for college. It's the best deal for the most number of taxpayers. But talk to your tax planner whenever the law changes to determine how much more you should put away and whether there are steps you should take if the law looks as if it's going to remain unchanged.

Consider investing in your state's plan

Your state may offer a tax deduction on your state return for investing in its 529 plan. Ask your tax planner whether such a deduction is available and whether it's valuable to someone in your tax bracket. Or visit your state's tax Web site for more details on its deductions.

Q&A

Q. What if I planned for my child to go to college in 2007 but she doesn't go until 2009?

A. As long as the assets are used ultimately for the costs of the person named on the plan, the assets won't be taxed.

As you know, the 529 plan's fund automatically shifts assets into less risky investments so that they are in a safe place when your child is scheduled to begin college. In the case of your daughter who put off college for two years, the assets will sit in the most conservative mix during the period, because the fund was originally set up under the assumption that your child was going to college in 2007.

Q. Can I change the plan's beneficiary to my brother's child?

A. Yes. If you originally set up a 529 plan to save for your child's college education but your child decides not to go or doesn't need the money, you must change the plan's beneficiary or pay the tax and penalty on the withdrawn assets.

But let's say you have only one child. Rather than pay the tax and penalty, you could name your brother's child the beneficiary of the plan and pay his or her college tab as a gift when the child is ready to attend. Or you could ask your brother for the current market value of the amount in the account with a promise that you will withdraw the assets for his child when the child is ready for college.

If your brother's child is many years away from college, it's probably best to transfer the assets to another plan, where you can invest them in a fund that will allocate the assets more aggressively. The problem with keeping them in the fund you set up for your child is that the asset allocation will be conservative by that point. Your brother's child likely needs a more aggressive mix, given how many years that child has left until the child needs the money.

Q. **What happens if the beneficiary can't go to college due to hardship?**

A. There is no hardship clause in the law. Either the beneficiary uses the money for college, you name a new beneficiary who is expected to use the money for college, or you withdraw the assets and pay the tax and penalty.

Q. **What if the value of my 529 plan is down? Do I have to use the assets now?**

A. No. If your portfolio is down—and many 529 plans were down in 2000 and 2001—you don't have to use the assets immediately. You can use them when your child is a sophomore, junior, or senior. The only rules are that the assets must be used for the child's college or other higher education costs and that they have to be exhausted by the time your child is graduating. Otherwise you have to name a new beneficiary for the remaining assets in the plan. Again, the alternative is taxes and a penalty on the withdrawal.

Q. **Can I transfer assets from a Rollover IRA?**

A. Sure, but your Rollover IRA assets will be taxed and hit with an early-withdrawal penalty if you're younger than age 59½. Although both the 529 plan and the Rollover IRA are tax-deferred accounts, they cannot be merged, tax-free. If you withdraw Rollover IRA assets to pay college expenses directly, you'll be subject to income tax but not the early-withdrawal penalty.

Paying for college when stocks are down

Many parents use a 529 plan for part of their college costs. Others prefer to use a taxable account because they can control the investments.

In a 529 plan, the manager controls the asset mix depending on how soon you need the money. In a taxable account, you have to shift your assets yourself.

(continued)

But what if you forgot to shift the assets to a more conservative mix or, you got greedy and left them in stocks too long? Here are some tuition strategies that will help you buy your stock portfolio some time:

■ *Sell only what you need.* Identify stocks that have fallen way below what you paid for them. Then find the ones that have risen dramatically in value. Then sell them both.

By selling stocks that have lost money and stocks that have made money, you can use the losses to offset the gains and reduce your taxes owed next year on the sales. Talk to your tax planner first to be sure you're executing this strategy properly.

■ *Ask grandma to pay for part of the first year.* While annual gifts are limited to $10,000 each before the donor is taxed, the child's grandparents can foot the tuition bill, even if it exceeds $10,000 as long as the check is sent directly to the college.

In fact, anyone, whether it's a grandparent, relative, neighbor, or friend can make this payment directly to the college for tuition and not be subject to the gift tax.

■ *Borrow against your portfolio.* If you don't want to sell any of the stocks in your taxable account, consider borrowing against the value of your investments. The interest payments are not tax-deductible, but you'll raise the money without having to sell your assets.

Talk to your financial planner first, however. You don't want to expose too much of your portfolio to this kind of risk should the value of your investments drop before you can pay back the money you borrowed. Otherwise, you could lose your securities as your broker sells them to raise cash to cover the loan.

■ *Use a home-equity line of credit.* Instead of borrowing against your investments, you borrow against the equity in your home. The interest payments on home-equity lines of credit used for college costs are tax-deductible on loans up to $100,000 for regular income tax purposes but not for the AMT. Again, talk to a financial planner to assess the risks and how comfortable you are with them. Fail to make your loan payments and you could wind up losing your home.

■ *See if the college has a "level payment" plan.* Most colleges offer "level payment plans," which allow you to make monthly payments rather than sending in a lump sum.

THE SECOND CHANGE

Education IRA contribution limit rises and can be used to cover non-college costs.

Do You Qualify for This?

Yes. *If your AGI does not exceed $220,000 (married) and $110,000 (single).*

BACKGROUND

The Education IRA (officially known as the Coverdell Education Savings Account) was created by the Taxpayer Relief Act of 1997 to allow taxpayers to save money each year for a child's education, tax-free. The assets in the account grow without being taxed and they can be withdrawn for college costs without being taxed either.

But there are two big restrictions:

1. You can contribute the full annual amount only if your adjusted gross income (AGI) does not exceed a specific level.

    In 2001, you can make the full $500 maximum annual contribution to an Education IRA if your AGI is below $150,000 (married filing jointly) and $95,000 (single). Above those levels the maximum amount you can contribute starts to shrink. You become ineligible to make any Education IRA contribution when your AGI reaches $160,000 (married) and $110,000 (single). The new law raises all of these levels.

2. Contributions can be made by you or anyone else provided the beneficiary of the Education IRA is under age 18.

    You can open as many Education IRAs as you wish, provided your annual contributions when added up do not exceed the maximum allowed based on your AGI. An Education IRA is opened in your child's name, but you control how the assets are invested and when to sell them.

    Withdrawals must be used to pay for tuition and room and board and are tax-free. If they're not used for this purpose, you must pay income tax and a 10% penalty.

    If the assets aren't used for college costs by the time your child turns 30 years old, the Education IRA account must be closed and you must pay taxes and a penalty on the assets withdrawn. The only way around this is to name a new, younger beneficiary who plans to attend college.

You can use the assets for children attending school as long as the students attend half-time.

There is no deduction for making deposits to an Education IRA.

Important: Tax-free withdrawals from an Education IRA to cover college costs disqualify you from claiming the Hope and Lifetime Learning tax credits for that year.

The Hope credit is $1,500 and can be taken only in your child's first or second year of college. The Lifetime Learning credit gives you a tax credit of up to $1,000 per year if you qualify and cannot be taken in the same year as the Hope credit for the same student.

THE NEW LAW

1. *Higher contribution level.* Starting in 2002, the annual contribution to an Education IRA rises to $2,000—up from $500.
2. *Higher AGI levels.* The level of adjusted gross income (AGI) that you can have and still make a contribution has gone up. You can contribute the full amount to an Education IRA if your AGI does not exceed $190,000 (married filing jointly) and $95,000 (single). When your AGI exceeds those levels, your credit starts to shrink.

   You are ineligible to make any Education IRA contribution when your AGI exceeds $220,000 (married) and $110,000 (single).
3. *More educational uses.* You can make tax-free withdrawals for virtually all levels of education—from elementary, secondary, public, private, or religious school tuition and expenses to college costs. Expenses include tuition, tutoring, room and board, some computer technology, uniforms, transportation, and extended-day programs. This is a big change, considering that under the old law, Education IRA assets could be used only for college costs.
4. *Companies can contribute.* Companies now can contribute to your child's Education IRA, provided your AGI is low enough that you qualify for your employer's deposit.
5. *Special-needs children.* There are special rules for children with special needs. You can continue to make contributions to an

Education IRA after the child turns 18 years old. Special needs include a physical, mental, or emotional condition or a learning disability that requires additional time to finish his or her education.

Also, the funds in the Education IRA do not have to be removed once the child with special needs turns age 30. The assets do, however, have to be used for the child's educational purposes eventually or face taxation and a penalty.

6. *Later contribution deadline.* You can make annual contributions up until April 15 of the following year, as is the case with a Traditional IRA or Roth IRA.

7. *Switch names on the IRA.* You can change the name of the beneficiary on the Education IRA if your child can't use the assets—or no longer needs them. The only catch is that the new beneficiary must be a family member. Then the assets will remain in place and continue to enjoy tax-free status.

8. *No excise tax* for contributing to both a 529 and an Education IRA in the same year.

WHAT YOU NEED TO KNOW

Open an Education IRA when your child is young

The math works out in your favor if you start saving early.

> *Example:* If you qualify to make contributions and you deposit $2,000 in January 2002, when your child is born, you will have a nice sum saved by the time your child is ready for college in 2020. If you assume a 6% rate of return, your child will have $73,571. Under the old law, assuming your contributed the $500 max each year, you would have saved just $18,393. Keep in mind that a 6% average annual rate of return is conservative and could be higher.

Education IRAs offer you a much larger investment selection

Like a Traditional IRA or Roth IRA, an Education IRA offers you an unlimited range of investments, from individual stocks to mutual funds. Ideally, you need to establish two things before you invest:

1. *A smart asset allocation,* so the money is well-diversified and won't decline in value too much when the market falls.
2. *An asset-shift plan,* so that you know when to move out of aggressive investments. You want to be invested in more moderate investments when your child becomes a teen and a more conservative mix when your child is five years away from needing the assets to cover college or other educational costs.

Your financial planner should be able to help you with both points.

Use your Education IRA assets to fund a 529 plan

Under the new law, funding a 529 plan is considered an education expense. In fact, under the new law, you can use the assets in an Education IRA to pay for virtually any type of educational expense, not just college.

Hence, consider using Education IRA assets to fund a 529 plan. Why would you want to do this? Here are a few scenarios:

- If you want to open a 529 plan so that your parents can contribute a sizable amount but you don't have other assets available to do so.
- If you like the state or university 529 plan that is available to you.
- If you no longer want the responsibility of deciding how your assets are invested or allocated. The 529 plan takes care of that automatically for you.
- If you don't want to be tempted to use the Education IRA assets to pay for any other education expense except college

If you don't qualify, have a relative contribute

Under the new law, the AGI levels have risen to allow more taxpayers to qualify to contribute to an Education IRA. If you don't qualify, you can't contribute.

But there is a way around this. Have a relative who meets the AGI standards consider opening an Education IRA and naming your child as the beneficiary.

Defer 2001 income until 2002

If your AGI will rise into the range that starts to limit your contribution or prohibits you from making one, determine whether you are able to defer any taxable income coming your way until January.

By holding down your AGI, you may be able to make the full $500 contribution this year under the old AGI rules and next year under the higher levels.

Deposit $500 this year and $2,000 in January

Just be sure to monitor your AGI late next year to be sure you're not over the limit for your Education IRA contribution. If you are, try to defer income until 2003 so that you can take the full contribution.

Q&A

Q. What if I contribute $2,000 in January but my AGI for the year is too high for such a contribution?

A. You have a problem. You'll have to notify the plan's custodian and withdraw the amount prior to April 15 of the following year. Any income you earned on the $2,000 investment while it was invested would be taxable.

Q. Which one is better, a 529 plan or an Education IRA?

A. It depends. If you qualify for the Education IRA, you can control the investments in your account. You can't control the investments in a 529 plan.

The downside of an Education IRA is that you may be tempted to take too many risks to achieve your goals. By contrast, a 529 plan will gradually shift your money into lower-risk investments as your child nears freshman year. If the 529 plan isn't to your satisfaction, you can always switch to a different state or college plan. The other big plus of a 529 plan is that this plan allows for much higher contributions. They're capped at $2,000 max with an Education IRA.

Q. Does it still make sense to invest in an Education IRA if my child is 10 years old?

A. Yes. When the maximum contribution was $500, you had to start investing when your child was born for the amount to be meaningful after 17 years. But now that the annual max will be $2,000 in 2002, you can start saving as late as when your child is age 10 (if you qualify) and still wind up with a sizable sum.

Example: If you put $2,000 in an Education IRA when your child is 10 years old and your portfolio earned an average annual 6% over that seven-year period, you'd wind up with $19,794.

Q. What if my child doesn't use the full amount saved?

A. Whatever is left can be rolled over into a second child's Education IRA. You would not have to meet the $2,000 annual maximum contribution rule nor would you have to qualify for the AGI standards at the time of the rollover.

In other words, if you have $25,000 left in the first child's Education IRA, you could roll it all over into your second child's Education IRA—without regard to the $2,000 annual maximum deposit.

Why? Because all of the assets in the first child's plan are assumed to have been qualified when they were originally deposited. According to the IRS, you're just moving around old money.

Q. What if I make my 2001 contribution in 2002?

A. It's not clear whether the new April 15 deadline applies to contributions for 2001 made in 2002.

Q. Can I save in an Education IRA for private school and in a 529 plan for college?

A. Yes, assets in an Education IRA can now be used to pay for costs at virtually every level of education. Assets in a 529 plan, however, must be used only for college.

Q. Can I own an Education IRA and a Traditional IRA or Roth IRA?

A. Yes, and you can max out an Education IRA with $2,000 if you qualify in 2002 and max out a Traditional IRA or Roth IRA (if you qualify) with $3,000. They're considered two different savings vehicles.

Q. If my AGI is too high, can a grandparent open an Education IRA and contribute?

A. Yes, provided the Education IRA is in your child's name. If the grandparent dies, the trustee of his or her estate would then be in charge of controlling the assets.

Q. I'm confused—under the new law, which plan does what?

A. Many people want to know which makes more sense under the new law—the 529 college-savings plan or the Education IRA.

Take a look at the comparisons in Table 8.1. All answers are based on the new law, which takes effect in 2002.

Q. Is there an easy way to know which plan is better for me?

A. Yes, the information in Table 8.2 can help.

Table 8.1 Education IRA v. 529 Plan

Your Questions	Education IRA	529 Plan
Am I eligible to contribute in 2002?	Only if your AGI is under $220,000 (married) and under $110,000 (single)	Yes
How much a year?	$2,000	Up to maximum allowed by the plan.
How can I use the savings?	To cover virtually any educational cost	College and graduate school only
What are my investment choices?	Unlimited	Limited to choices in the plan
Do assets grow tax-deferred?	Yes	Yes
Are assets taxed when withdrawn for school?	No	No
Can I buy/sell investments of my choosing?	Yes	No
What if I don't like my investment?	You can sell it.	You can transfer all plan assets to another plan, once every 12 months.
Are my returns guaranteed?	No	No
Can I invest in both at once?	Yes, if you qualify	Yes
What's the biggest drawback?	If you qualify, you can only invest up to $2,000 a year.	The plan decides how to allocate your assets based on the age of your child.

Table 8.2   Which Education Plan is for You?

Situation	Education IRA	529 Plan
Your income is high.	**Forget about it.** Your AGI must be less than $220,000 (married) or $110,000 (single).	**Consider it.** There is no income limit.
You qualify for both.	**Consider it.** But remember that the annual max is low—$2,000—and you must make the investment decisions.	**Consider it.** Deposits are limited to the maximum allowed by the plan. But the plan decides the investment mix based on the age of your child.
You may need money to pay for private school.	**Consider it.** You can use assets for virtually any educational cost.	**Forget about it.** Assets are for higher education only.
You want to control your investments.	**Consider it.** You decide where to invest and when to sell.	**Forget about it.** The plan controls the investment.
You don't know much about investing.	**Think twice.** You must decide where to invest and how to allocate assets as your child nears college age.	**Consider it.** Assets are shifted to lower-risk investments as your child nears college age.
You're not sure if your child will go to college.	**Consider it.**. Assets can be used to pay nearly any educational cost.	**Consider it.** Assets must be used for college but can be withdrawn for other reasons, subject to income tax and penalty.
Your child is almost a teen.	**Consider it.** If you qualify, you can invest up to $2,000 a year and offset part of your child's education expenses.	**Consider it.** The plan will invest your assets for you by taking your child's age into consideration.

How to save for college—and retirement

Both goals are important but there's only so much money to go around, right? Yet it is possible to accomplish both goals if you plan carefully:

Attach numbers to both goals. Start by setting financial targets for each goal.

- *College.* For a public college in your state, you'll need about $40,000 in today's dollars. A private university or out-of-state public college will run you a total of $100,000 in today's dollars.
- *Retirement.* If you're in your mid-30s to 40s, you'll need a taxable nest egg of at least $1 million in today's dollars by the time you retire. That will provide you with about $40,000 to $45,000 a year in income after taxes.

Ask yourself which goal takes priority. Reaching both goals will be difficult. But which one is more important if push comes to shove?

Some people save first for retirement and then deposit whatever is left into their kids' education accounts. They assume that their children can always borrow what they need and then work to pay it back, whereas they won't be able to do so in retirement.

Others feel that providing for their children's education is more important and plan to work past age 65 to fund both.

Knowing which one is important up front will help you make smarter planning decisions.

Start saving for college early. If your child is a newborn, you have plenty of tax-free options under the new law, including the 529 plan and the Education IRA.

But if you didn't start saving until your child was 10 years old, you'll need to save about $500 a month for a public college and $1,200 a month for a private university.

Start saving for retirement early. If you're in your 30s, you need to save 10% to 15% of your annual gross income in a taxable or tax-deferred account—or both. If you start saving later in life, you'll have to put away more each month to reach your goal.

(continued)

Shift assets as you near your goals. You want to move assets into safer investments as you near your goals. By doing so, you'll lock in the value of your portfolio and keep it from being ravaged by sudden shifts in the markets.

- *College.* Follow the allocations used by 529 college savings plans. One plan, for example, starts with an allocation of 80% stocks and 20% bonds for newborns. Then it shifts to 60% bonds and 40% stocks for 10-year-olds. When a child is 18 years old, the allocation moves to 10% stocks and 90% bonds.
- *Retirement.* As you grow older, shift more of your assets out of stocks and into bonds. For example, in your 40s, you might have 90% of assets in stocks and 10% in bonds. In your 50s, that allocation should shift to 80% stocks and 20% bonds.

  By the time you're in your 60s, your allocation could be 60% stocks and 40% bonds. In addition, as you age, your stock and bond choices should become less risky.

Discuss your plans with your financial planner. As you grow older and the value of your assets rises, it's wise to discuss your savings strategies with a financial planner. Regular discussions are especially important in light of the new tax law and the many changes that take effect over the next 10 years.

THE THIRD CHANGE

The student-loan interest deduction rises starting in 2002.

Do You Qualify for This?

Yes. If your AGI does not exceed $130,000 (married) and $65,000 (single).

BACKGROUND

If you pay interest on a student loan, the interest is deductible up to a level set by the law.

Under the old law, the maximum deduction was $2,500 if your level of adjusted gross income (AGI) was low enough that you qualified for the full or partial deduction. Under the old law, the full deduction was available to you if your AGI was not higher than $60,000 (married filing jointly) and $40,000 (single). Once your AGI broke through these thresholds, the deduction started to decline. And once your AGI reached $75,000 (married) and $55,000 (single), you were no longer eligible to claim the deduction.

Under the new law, the deduction is higher—and so is the level of AGI you need to qualify for all or part of the deduction. Put simply, more taxpayers will have a better shot at taking a larger deduction for borrowing money for college costs.

> **Don't forget:** The IRS views this deduction as an adjustment to your gross income, so it is available to you whether or not you itemize your deductions.

The deduction is allowed only on interest paid on a qualified education loan. Under the old law, you could take a deduction on the interest paid over the first 60 months of the repayment of the loan. The new law repeals this qualification and generously makes the term the life of the loan.

Also, the child for whom you borrowed the money is a dependent on your tax return. So, you cannot claim the deduction if you borrowed money for a child who lives with your divorced spouse and the child is claimed on his or her tax return.

THE NEW LAW

Higher deductions. In 2002 and 2003, the maximum deduction for paying interest on a college loan is $3,000. In 2004 and 2005, the maximum deduction will be $4,000.

Higher AGI limits. You can claim the full deduction if your AGI is below $100,000 (married) and $50,000 (single). Your deduction will start to decline as your AGI rises above those levels. You will no longer be eligible for the deduction when your AGI exceeds $130,000 (married) and $65,000 (single).

New time frame. You can claim the deduction for the full term of the loan—not just for the first 60 months under the old law.

WHAT YOU NEED TO KNOW

Run the numbers if you risk triggering the AMT

Taking the deduction for student-loan interest payments may make you a victim of the alternative minimum tax, which uses a harsher set of rules than the regular income tax to determine your tax liability.

Have your tax planner determine in advance whether this deduction will force you to pay taxes under the AMT's rules. If so, ask your planner to tell you about steps you can take to minimize the odds of this happening or how to make the most of the AMT's rules.

Take out a home-equity loan and deduct the interest payments

The IRS allows you to deduct interest payments on a home-equity line of credit up to $100,000. There is no rule that the loan has to be used to upgrade your house. The money could be used to pay for college costs, and you can deduct the interest payments.

But watch out for the alternative minimum tax (AMT). A home-equity loan could trigger this much-hated tax, which requires you to use a different set of rules to calculate your tax liability than the regular tax rules. There's no way to know if you will owe taxes under the AMT until you calculate your taxes both ways. You wind up owing the larger amount.

What's more, the AMT's rules do not allow you to deduct interest payments at all on a home-equity loan if the amount you borrowed is not used for repairs or upgrades to your home.

Recent interest-rate cuts make some loans more attractive

College loans are tied to short-term interest rates—the ones the Federal Reserve has cut throughout 2001. As a result of the Fed's recent cuts, interest rates on two college-loan programs haven't been this low since the early 1980s. The two attractive loan programs are:

1. *Stafford Loan Program.* Under this one, undergraduate or graduate students can borrow a limited amount of money for college from the federal government.

    How much can an undergrad borrow? Up to $2,625 the first year, $3,500 the second year, and $5,500 in the third and fourth

years. Graduate students can borrow up to $8,500 a year. Part of the loan can be subsidized by the federal government, which pays the interest while the student is in school. The student doesn't start making loan payments until six months after graduating.
2. *Parent Loans for Undergraduate Students (PLUS).* A parent is the one who borrows the money under this program. The parent can borrow as much as needed for college tuition but the loan must be repaid starting immediately.

Interest rates on both loans are set each July 1 based on the auction of the 91-Day Treasury bill in May. As a result, the new variable rates on a Stafford loan dropped to 5.39% (for students still in school) or 5.99% (for students in graduate school making payments). The new variable rate a parent must pay for a PLUS loan is 6.79%.

Taxpayers who already have borrowed under these plans can lock in the new lower rates by consolidating their loans with the federal government. Consolidating is, in effect, refinancing, which takes all of your variable-rate loans for college costs and gives you a fixed-rate loan with a longer repayment schedule. You can consolidate online at *www.loanconsolidation.ed.gov* (800-557-7392).

Bonus: Under the new law, the interest payments on the PLUS loans and the Stafford loans are fully deductible up to $2,500 (in 2001)—if your AGI is low enough that you qualify for the deduction.

THE FOURTH CHANGE

New deduction for college expenses.

Do You Qualify for This?

Yes. If you pay college expenses in 2002 and have AGI below the required levels.

BACKGROUND

Under the old law, there was no such thing as deducting your college costs. If you took college courses, you could deduct them only if the classes were necessary for your trade or business. The classes had to have a direct bearing on your skill or craft or had to be required as part of your employment.

If you wanted to switch careers and decided to take courses to satisfy potential employers, you were on your own. Those expenses were admirable but not deductible.

And in cases where you had deductible educational expenses you were able to deduct them only when they and your other miscellaneous deductions exceeded 2% of your AGI.

In 2001, if your AGI exceeds $132,950 (for both married filing jointly and single taxpayers), limitations on itemized deductions might reduce the deductible amount.

Keep in mind, this deduction as well as the many other deductions available to taxpayers who qualify aren't meant to cover the cost of college. They are simply available to lower the amount you have to pay in taxes.

THE NEW LAW

Deduction in 2002 and 2003. In these years, you can claim an annual deduction up to $3,000 for qualified college education expenses.

AGI limits. You qualify for the full $3,000 deduction if your AGI does not exceed $130,000 (married filing jointly) and $65,000 (single). If your AGI does exceed these levels, you are not eligible for the deduction.

This is one of those rare situations in which the deduction does not phase out as your AGI rises. If you're over the line, you don't qualify, period. The deduction is available whether or not you itemize.

The deduction rises again in 2004 and 2005. In these years, the maximum deduction is $4,000.

So does the AGI limit. You qualify for the full $4,000 deduction if your AGI does not exceed $130,000 (married) and $65,000 (single). Once your AGI rises above these levels, the size of your deduction drops to $2,000. You are not eligible for the deduction if your AGI exceeds $160,000 (married) and $80,000 (single).

WHAT YOU NEED TO KNOW

Keep an eye on the calendar

If the new law that relates to college expenses deducted is not extended after 2005, the old rules will spring back into action. While it's impossible to predict the future, it is likely that Congress will extend the law or adjust the amounts higher. But you never know.

Consider the impact on the HOPE or Lifetime Learning credits

If you deduct tuition, you can't claim your Hope or Lifetime Learning tax credit for the same student in the same year.

Only your dependent's education expenses can be claimed

So if your child is a dependent of your divorced spouse, you cannot claim the deduction even if you pay for half the child's college tuition and fees.

Time your college payments carefully

The new law lets you take the deduction for expenses paid during a tax year. So if you can hold off on paying for the 2002 spring semester until January 2002 instead of paying in the fall, the tuition payment would be eligible for the deduction if you qualify. However, if you pay for the spring in 2001, it would not qualify.

In future years, determine whether it pays to write a check for the spring tuition bill in the fall or whether it's more beneficial to wait until early the following year just before the spring semester begins.

Forget the "business purpose" paperwork

Under the old law, to deduct the education expense, you had to prove that the training was a necessary part of your employment or current occupation.

Under the new law, the deduction is available in all cases where you can meet the adjusted gross income eligibility. The only caveat is that you can't use an expense for more than one deduction.

Cut college expenses with a scholarship

If your child qualifies for a scholarship, the size of your college bill and your loans will be lower.

How can you improve the odds that your child will receive an academic scholarship? Here's what your child can do in each grade of high school to become a standout student:

9th grade

■ *Spot the passions.* It's so important to develop a four-year plan with your child. The key isn't to make your child a well-rounded person. Most Ivy Leaguers received excellent grades, excelled in sports, performed community service, and worked on the school newspaper.

> **More important:** Your child must have a special interest or major talent. Schools want your child to be a great addition to a well-rounded freshman class.

■ *Identify your child's passions and develop them.* Don't push him or her to play the violin or study butterflies. The topic is less important than your child's drive to develop a high level of competence.
■ *Participate in class.* Colleges look for students who have shown a demonstrated ability to speak up. If your child hesitates to participate in class, he or she can overcome these hurdles by taking a speech class or participating in the debate team. Your child needs to show that he or she stimulated discussion in high school.
■ *Take SAT II subject tests.* SAT I grades are important. But admission officers also look hard at whether your child took the SAT II tests.

The SAT II is a one-hour subject-specific exam. There are SAT II tests in over 20 areas, such as math, writing, biology, chemistry, etc.

Your child can study for the SAT II and focus on his or her natural strengths. Most top schools require that applicants take three SAT II subject tests. Have your child take five or six SAT II tests starting in the 9th grade.

These tests also can boost your child's competency on the critical SAT I.

10th grade

- *Take on an extracurricular activity.* Colleges like to see that a candidate has made a long-term commitment to an activity that leads to expertise and a leadership role.

  Touching on a bunch of interests creates the impression that your child was more interested in making an impression and fitting in than doing what truly excited him or her.
- *Take the PSAT for practice.* The more comfortable your child is with the PSAT, the better he or she will do on the SAT.

  If your child scores well on the PSAT (given in the 11th grade), he or she may qualify as a National Merit semi-finalist or finalist.
- *Get a challenging summer job.* Working as a camp counselor is acceptable, but a less cushy job, such as working as a volunteer in an organization that helps unfortunate people is better. It builds character, kindness, and emotional strength. Even a rank-and-file job such as a supermarket cashier or warehouse clerk shows strength.

  But if your child has a particular talent, line up a job that suits his skills.

11th grade

- *Take tough courses.* Focus on honors, advanced placement (AP), and international baccalaureate (IB) classes offered by the high school. If the high school offers none, have your child get permission to take them at a local college after school or on weekends.

  Have your child take the AP or IB exams. A score of 3 or better on at least three of the exams (5 is the highest score) will designate your child as a "College Board AP Scholar." On the IB exams, 7 is the highest, while scores from 5 to 7 are considered exceptional. These exams are highly regarded by admissions committees.
- *Take the SAT II for practice.* If your child's score is below 600 on any subject test, you can improve it with a prep course or self-study. If your child already is scoring over 600, he probably just needs to brush up on a few areas, practice the test more, and become intimately familiar with the test.

(continued)

The best colleges generally only consider students with SAT scores of over 750.

■ *Don't take the SAT more than twice.* It's doubtful your child can beat his score by taking it a third time or more. Admissions officers see all of the scores. And showing minimal improvement after each test is particularly unimpressive.

■ *Take intensive summer classes.* You want your child to take two months of classes—even if your child has to go on weekends or evenings. This indicates that the student is truly serious about learning and acquiring knowledge.

12th grade

■ *When applying, avoid e-mail applications.* Most admissions officers dislike them. They often are in a format that's different from what officers expect. E-applications work against candidates when officers have to wade through 30 a day.

■ *Modify the essay.* The experience in the essay needs to come alive. Avoid common themes, such as the mountain climbing or volunteer experience. These may seem singular, but they are so common that they won't seem special.

■ *Tell teachers to focus on academics.* Most letters of recommendation foolishly detail a student's personal side and character. You want the letters to focus on your child's intellectual potential.

■ *Keep grades up.* Colleges can and do withdraw scholarships if a student's work ethic goes off a cliff. Even if the admissions office accepts your child's reasons for the poor grades, your child's academic performance will be carefully monitored freshman year.

THE FIFTH CHANGE

More liberal Hope and Lifetime Learning credit rules start in 2002.

Do You Qualify for This?

Yes. If your AGI does not exceed $100,000 (married filing jointly) and $50,000 (single).

BACKGROUND

The Hope Scholarship credit and the Lifetime Learning credit were created by the Taxpayer Relief Act of 1997 to reduce the tax liability of middle-income taxpayers who pay college tuition and fees.

- *The Hope credit* lets you take a credit for the first $1,000 you spend on college tuition and fees plus 50% of the next $1,000— bringing the total maximum credit to $1,500.

   The Hope credit is good only for the first two years of college. Are there two children in your family attending college? No problem. You can claim the Hope credit for each one.

- *The Lifetime Learning credit* is $1,000 in 2001 and 2002 but rises to $2,000 in 2003 and beyond. The credit was created to give parents a break when their child was in higher education beyond the first two years and for continuing education.

   Unlike the Hope credit, however, the Lifetime Learning credit is the same, regardless of how many children you have in college at the same time.

Like most tax credits, the Hope and Lifetime Learning credits have income restrictions. Fortunately, for the sake of simplicity, they share the same rule:

AGI limit: You can claim the full credit on your tax return if your adjusted gross income (AGI) does not exceed $80,000 (married filing jointly) and $40,000 (single). The size of your credit starts to decline as your AGI rises above this level. If your AGI exceeds $100,000 (married) and $50,000 (single), you are no longer eligible for either credit.

The credits are available if anyone in your family is attending college—you, your spouse, or your children.

Under the old law, you could not claim a Hope or Lifetime Learning credit if you withdrew assets from an Education IRA to cover tuition or fees and elected to exclude the withdrawal from income. This rule changes under the new law.

THE NEW LAW

A higher credit. Starting in 2003, the annual Lifetime Learning credit will rise to $2,000. The Hope credit will remain at its $1,500 level.

New twist. Starting in 2002, the Hope and Lifetime Learning credits can be claimed in the same year that you withdraw assets from an Education IRA.

Catch: You cannot claim the credits for the same expenses covered by your Education IRA withdrawal.

WHAT YOU NEED TO KNOW

Get around the AGI limits by putting money in your child's name

Higher income taxpayers who aren't eligible for the Hope or Lifetime Learning credit can have the child claim the credit on the child's tax return. In order to do this, the parents have to waive their personal exemption deduction for that child. It's important to remember that if you're a higher-income taxpayer, you probably don't get a benefit from claiming your child as a personal exemption.

As a result, it's smarter for your college-age child to file his or her own tax return and claim the credit. Your child probably has income from a summer job between semesters. Because your child's income is below the AGI threshold, your child can use the Hope or Lifetime Learning credit to reduce his or her tax hit.

Use the credit and Education IRA withdrawals for different purposes

Under the new law, you cannot claim the credit for the same expense as the money withdrawn from the Education IRA. So be sure that you use the sizable Education IRA withdrawal for tuition and, if you qualify, apply room and board or administrative fees for the credit.

Take the Hope or Lifetime Learning credit or the education deduction—but not both

A deduction for education expenses is not allowed for an individual student if a HOPE or Lifetime Learning credit is claimed in the same year.

If Congress extends the law that applies to the deduction beyond 2005, inflation adjustments for the Hope and Lifetime Learning credits could make them more broadly available than the education expense deduction.

Don't try to score a double

If you deduct an expense under any other part of the new tax law, the same expense can't be used toward the education expense deduction.

You can take a Hope or Lifetime Learning credit for a college expense only if money used for that expense isn't otherwise non-taxable. You must reduce the total amount of qualified education costs by the amount you excluded for 529 plan withdrawals, education IRA, or U.S. savings bond interest used to pay for college.

> *Example:* Let's assume your child goes to an inexpensive state school, where tuition is $3,000 a year. If you're paying that sum with assets from other non-taxable education plans, you're not entitled to the Hope or Lifetime Learning credit. Why? Because tuition expenses have been covered by those other assets.

How to improve your financial aid package

The new tax law makes it easier for middle- and lower-income tax-payers to pay for college.

But competition among colleges trying to attract bright students is heating up. That means you have more leverage when negotiating financial aid packages. Consider these strategies:

■ *Maximize grant and scholarship money.* The financial aid officer at your college of choice has wide latitude when extending gifts or loans.

— *Grants and scholarships* awarded by the college are almost always tax-free and never have to be repaid.

— *Student loans.* While the terms of these loans are fixed, you may be able to qualify for more if the school re-examines your financial situation.

The most popular loans include the federal Perkins loan (up to $4,000 a year at 5% interest), the unsubsized federal Stafford loans (up to $2,625 for freshmen at a variable interest rate), and the subsidized Stafford loan, which is based on need.

(continued)

- *Compare aid packages.* Weigh the different schools' packages, not just the lump sum each one has promised. The key is to see what you're expected to pay under the package vs. how much your child is expected to borrow.
- *Call financial aid officers.* There's nothing to lose by trying to cut a more favorable deal. The college cannot take back its original offer of admission or its aid package.

  Ideally, you want to have a more attractive number in mind when you call. You want to be ready if the financial aid officer asks you how much you can afford.
- *Prove you can get a better deal.* If you send a letter asking for a better deal, include a copy of other schools' more attractive packages.

  Outline your argument in a precise letter that runs no longer than a page. And use dollar amounts.
- *Don't goof up on your income.* Show in your letter that the financial aid officer misjudged your financial situation.

  For example, if you can show that there was a real reason why your income was unusually high last year, your aid package may be adjusted.

  How could your income be unusually high? See if you did any of the following:

  — *Convert a Traditional IRA to a Roth IRA?* The conversion may have boosted your taxable income.

  — *Roll over a pension to an IRA?* Financial aid formulas don't include rollovers as untaxed income. But the school may incorrectly assume that you failed to include the untaxed pension as part of your income.

  — *Receive a bonanza?* Retroactive pay increases, casino winnings and an inheritance can significantly boost income.

  — *Filed a joint return even though you separated from your spouse?* On the financial aid forms, report only the financial information of the parent who spent the most time with the child over the past 12 months.
- *Include unreimbursed medical expenses.* Most people aren't aware that many schools use a formula that's different than the one used by the IRS for calculating the eligibility of such expenses. You may have had large, unreimbursed medical expenses that you couldn't deduct on your tax returns.

Legitimate deductions include unreimbursed expenses for braces and other orthodontist work, doctors, eyeglasses, contact lenses, therapy, and any prescription drugs paid out-of-pocket.

Don't forget health-insurance premiums deducted from your pay or that you paid for personally, transportation to and from the doctors' offices, and the cost of lodging when the purpose is to receive treatment at a medical institution.

9

Estate, Gift, and GST Tax

THE BIG NEWS

Starting in 2002:

- The unified credit rises, the top estate tax rate declines, and the surcharge on the superrich is repealed.
- The gift-tax exemption rises to $1 million.
- The state death-tax credit begins to phase out (replaced by a deduction).
- The generation-skipping transfer (GST) tax exemption rises.

THE FIRST CHANGE

Starting in 2002, the unified credit rises, the top tax rate declines, and the surcharge on the superrich is repealed.

Do You Qualify for This?

Yes. If your taxable estate exceeds $1 million in 2002 and beyond.

BACKGROUND

The "death tax" is dying. Starting in 2002, the estate tax will begin to fade away. In 2010, it will disappear completely. No more estate tax— provided Congress extends the estate tax's repeal beyond 2010.

If Congress doesn't act, the "sunset" provision that was built into the new law will cause the estate tax to spring back to life in all its glory. Should Congress not extend the law, the estate tax in 2011 would be exactly the same as it was in 2001.

The dark humor here, of course, is that individuals with large estates who want to leave all of their assets to heirs and not a dime to the government have to kick the bucket in 2010, when the law is repealed.

But if the past is any guide, Congress will likely act to keep some form of estate tax on the books. While Congress probably won't allow the old estate tax rules to return in 2011—that would be too cruel—it also won't likely let the law be repealed either. Revenue received from the estate tax is easy money for Washington. The government only runs into trouble when too many estates on the low end of the law are affected and their owners become angry.

But if Congress decides to keep part of the estate tax in place before it is repealed or the old laws return, it will need a solid reason for doing so. By now, most people are convinced that the tax is unfair—even if their own estates aren't affected by it.

Much of what happens will depend on the economy over the next 10 years and on which party controls Congress. If the economy is in bad shape and the government needs revenue, keeping the estate tax around may pay a few bills. As for Congress, Republicans are on record as wanting to do away with the estate tax while Democrats tend to favor it as a way to fund government programs they feel are necessary.

If history is any guide, there would need to be a real or perceived crisis of special proportions to retain a law that most people feel is unnecessary and unjust. While the estate tax currently affects just 2% of the population, it could affect many more people as individuals' estates climb in value over the next 10 years. Tax-deferred retirement savings plans will likely appreciate significantly in value depending, of course, on the fate of the stock market.

But the estate tax not only affects what you want to leave your heirs but also what you stand to inherit. Over the next 10 years, baby boomers will begin inheriting the estimated $10 trillion that their parents intend to leave them.

Taxing the assets that an individual accumulates over a lifetime and leaves to heirs isn't a new way for the federal government to cover its costs. But using the tax for reasons other than war is a relatively modern concept that the post-Depression public has adjusted to over time.

In the past, the estate tax was used only in times when the government had to raise significant sums to mobilize, feed, and supply an army. In fact, all of the early estate-tax rates were rather modest and affected estates of only extremely wealthy individuals.

When the first estate tax was enacted in 1797, the government needed to re-arm in anticipation of war with France. Expected to last five years, this estate tax was repealed one year later because the revenue was no longer needed.

The second estate tax was passed in 1862, when the Union needed capital to fight the Civil War and didn't have the South to tax. But in 1870, five years after the war ended, the estate tax was repealed.

The Spanish-American War led to the third estate tax in 1898, but the tax was repealed in 1902.

The fourth estate tax, in 1916, was used to foot the bill for World War I. But unlike earlier estate taxes, it was not repealed after World War I. The tax was used by the government to help cover the debts left behind by Europe, which was decimated after the war. Besides, an uncertain Congress liked having it around.

But in 1932, the government decided to raise the estate tax and change its image. The Depression had arrived, and the government decided a higher estate tax was needed to raise revenue. It also decided that the tax would help redistribute the nation's wealth, shifting it away from the rich and giving it to lower-income taxpayers in the form of government assistance programs.

Back then, only one out of every four Americans was working. Fewer workers meant fewer taxes. To help support the government assistance programs of the time, the estate tax rate was increased to 60% in 1934 and to 70% in 1935. After World War II, the estate tax continued to be used to help pay for peacetime government programs.

While the modern estate tax can be traced back to 1916, the law has been tinkered with many times over the years. Since 1976, there have been 10 major pieces of legislation that have modified or enhanced the estate and gift tax.

Today, there are two schools of thought about the estate tax. And the interesting thing about the debate is that middle-income taxpayers tend to disparage the estate tax, while the superwealthy love it.

Taxpayers who are most upset about the estate tax tend to argue that it's unfair for assets to be taxed twice—once as income when it was earned and again when the assets are passed to heirs upon death. Ironically many of these taxpayers are not the ones who end up owing the estate tax.

The rich do—and many superwealthy taxpayers don't mind the estate tax. Why? Because they fear that unless their wealth is taxed or donated, it will wind up in the hands of their heirs. Such a free-wheeling transfer of massive wealth, they believe, would create a class of young, idle rich who will become chronically unmotivated to work or make a meaningful contribution to society. In fact, the people who are most in favor of the estate tax are members of some of the country's wealthiest families.

Under the new tax law, as estate taxes ease, many of the super-wealthy will be seeking guidance from estate planners. They will want to find ways to further limit their children's access to their wealth as the law relaxes and their heirs begin to kick back and wait.

As a result, charities will likely benefit most from the estate tax's decline as the rich give more of their assets away during their life-time and leave even more to charities in their wills.

The other oddity of the estate tax is that because it is so misun-derstood by taxpayers, the people who are most concerned about it won't even have to pay it. Before the new law was passed, most tax-payers automatically assumed that their estates or their parents' es-tates would qualify for the estate tax. In some cases, they were right, especially as certain assets such as life insurance payouts and re-tirement savings pour into estates at death.

But most people aren't aware of the calculation that takes place to determine the estate tax. This calculation, which includes special exemptions and credits, often reduces or eliminates the part of their estate that is taxable. Nevertheless, when politicians call for the estate tax to be repealed, few taxpayers will stand in their way.

To popularize the need to repeal the estate tax, candidate George W. Bush made a point during the presidential campaign of saying that countless family farms would be lost if the estate tax were left in place. The argument was that a low-income family that inherited Dad and Mom's dear old farm would have to sell it against their wishes just to meet their estate tax obligation on the inherited prop-erty. The image was sad and sentimental.

However, it turned out that the colorful family farm illustration was a bit of a stretch. In April 2001, *The New York Times* reported that the American Farm Bureau Foundation could not cite a single case of a family farm lost due to the estate tax.

Nevertheless, most Americans like the idea that the estate tax will soon be dead. It means they will inherit more of their parents' assets. It's also comforting for most people to know that if they work hard and do well, their estate will easily clear the tax hurdle and they will be able to pass most of it on, enabling their children to have a better—and hopefully productive—life.

How is the estate tax calculated?

To understand the changes in the new law, you first have to understand the basics of how the estate tax is calculated.

There are four simple steps to determine how much estate tax— if any—an estate will owe:

- Step 1: Figure out the estate's gross value.
- Step 2: Subtract the allowable deductions.
- Step 3: Calculate the estate tax.
- Step 4: Subtract the allowable credits.

Let's take a look at how the estate tax is calculated in greater detail.

Step 1: Figure out an estate's gross value. When an individual dies, everything the person owned fully or partially is considered part of his or her estate. As a result, the value of your assets needs to be added up. What assets are included?

- *Cash* held in bank accounts and money market accounts
- *Securities* in taxable and retirement accounts
- *Real estate* that you own, including second homes
- *Personal property*, such as furniture, jewelry, artwork, etc.
- *Gifts* given to others that exceeded $10,000 a year
- *Gift tax* paid within three years of the person's death
- *Jointly held property* owned by you and another person
- *Life insurance benefits* on policies in your name

Why life insurance benefits—considering you never see them while you're alive? Because if you are considered the owner of the policy, the benefits of the policy are considered to belong to your estate regardless of who actually gets the proceeds. Many people overlook this fact and are surprised when an estate that was assumed to be under the estate-tax limit suddenly jumps into taxable territory after a huge life insurance policy is paid out.

How are the assets in an estate valued? Under the law, there are two ways to determine the value of assets in an estate. Which one you use depends on the method that produces the most favorable outcome for you. You either can determine the assets' fair market value on the date the owner died or you can use their value exactly six months later. The only rule is that all of the assets must be valued using the same date and that using the six month date results in a lower tax.

Obviously, it makes the most sense to wait until six months pass before sizing up the estate for estate-tax purposes. Just remember that the estate's executor and heirs have to carefully determine how all of the estate's assets have appreciated or depreciated over this six-month period.

This six-month grace period gives heirs wiggle room should the market for one or more assets fall dramatically.

> **Example:** If the value of a person's stocks and bonds falls rapidly over that six-month period, all of the estate's assets can be valued six months after the person's death to hold down the size of the estate.

Add up all of these assets and you have what is known as the estate's "gross value"—or the value before allowable deductions and credits are subtracted.

Step 2: Subtracting the allowable deductions. Once you know the estate's gross value, you reduce the total by subtracting the deductions that the government allows you to take.

These deductions include:

- *Funeral expenses*, including burial costs, tombstone, burial lot, gravesite management and care, etc.
- *Estate administration expenses*, such as estate attorney's fees, court costs, commissions paid to an executor, accounting fees, and other costs related to settling an estate.
- *Debts* can range from outstanding credit-card balances to amounts left unpaid on college loans and home-equity loans. Deductible debts also include unpaid bills for services such as cable TV, utilities, cell phones, etc.

- *Unpaid mortgages* include amounts still owed to lenders on a primary or secondary residence, or any other property in the deceased's name.
- *Charitable deduction* includes the value of any property given by the estate to a charitable organization.
- *Unlimited marital deduction.* The tax law allows a spouse who is a U.S. citizen to inherit an unlimited amount of assets from his or her spouse with no estate tax. When calculating the estate tax, an estate takes a deduction that equals the value of assets transferred to a surviving spouse. This means that whatever assets are left to a spouse escape estate tax.

  This deduction is available only when a surviving spouse inherits his or her spouse's assets.

When you subtract all of these deductions from the estate's gross value, you will be left with the "taxable estate."

The third and final step is to take the taxable estate and calculate the "tentative tax" and, ultimately, the estate tax.

Step 3: Calculating the estate tax. Now that you've calculated the "taxable estate," it's time to hit the tables to find the "tentative tax"—or the amount owed before you begin subtracting allowable credits.

The estate tax, like the regular tax, is progressive—meaning that different tax rates apply to different levels of an estate's taxable value. As you can see in Table 9.1, there are 18 rates, each applying to a different range or bracket.

Once you have arrived at the tentative tax, the next step is to subtract any allowable credits.

Step 4: Subtracting the allowable credits. The federal government lets you subtract the following credits from your tentative tax:
- *Unified estate and gift tax credit.* No estate or gift taxes are assessed on the first $675,000 of assets in 2001. This is accomplished by allowing a credit which covers the tax on that amount of assets. However, the unified credit will rise significantly in 2002 and in future years.

  As the amount rises, the number of estates that will owe estate taxes will shrink.
- *State death tax credit.* Estate or inheritance taxes that are paid to a state are allowed as a credit. The credit in 2001 is calculated by applying a rate that corresponds to the taxable estate minus

Table 9.1   Calculating the Tentative Estate Tax (2001)

Amount		Tentative Tax			
Over	But not over	Tax		%	On excess over
0	$10,000	0	plus	18	0
$10,000	$20,000	$1,800		20	$10,000
$20,000	$40,000	$3,800		22	$20,000
$40,000	$60,000	$8,200		24	$40,000
$60,000	$80,000	$13,000		26	$60,000
$80,000	$100,000	$18,200		28	$80,000
$100,000	$150,000	$23,800		30	$100,000
$150,000	$250,000	$38,800		32	$150,000
$250,000	$500,000	$70,800		34	$250,000
$500,000	$750,000	$155,800		37	$500,000
$750,000	$1 million	$248,300		39	$750,000
$1 million	$1.25 million	$345,800		41	$1 million
$1.25 million	$1.5 million	$448,300		43	$1.25 million
$1.5 million	$2 million	$555,800		45	$1.5 million
$2 million	$2.5 million	$780,800		49	$2 million
$2.5 million	$3 million	$1.0258 million		53	$2.5 million
$3 million	$10 million	$1.2908 million		55	$3 million
$10 million	$21.04 million	$5.1408 million		60	$10 million
$21.04 million		$11.7648 million		55	$21.04 million

$60,000. Under the new law, the state death tax credit will be phased out starting in 2002 (and state death taxes will instead be allowed as a deduction from the gross estate).

- *Credit for prior transfers.* There's a credit for estate taxes paid on assets transferred to the deceased person or the person's estate 10 years before the person's death or two years afterward. This lets the estate avoid double taxation—once when estate taxes were paid upon inheritance and again when the owner dies.
- *Foreign death tax credit.* Estate taxes paid to a foreign country can be claimed as a credit when the assets that were taxed are subject to the federal estate tax.
- *Gift tax on gifts included in gross estate.* Since you add prior gifts over $10,000 to your gross estate, you get a credit for any gift tax paid.

When you subtract these credits from the "tentative tax," you're left with the estate tax owed to the federal government.

Now you see why so few Americans owe the estate tax. The value of their gross estate may be large but once the allowed deductions and credits are subtracted, no estate tax will likely be owed.

Let's see how this four-step calculation works in the real world. Table 9.2 shows three different estates for three different people—Joe, Mary, and Rich—and how they would be taxed in 2002.

As you can see in Table 9.2, each person has a different size estate.

Table 9.2 Three Estate-Tax Scenarios

Step 1: Figuring an estate's gross value			
	Joe	*Mary*	*Rich*
Cash	$25,000	$60,000	$500,000
Personal property	$20,000	$40,000	$200,000
Taxable securities	$105,000	$500,000	$2.9 million
401(k) plan	$100,000	$300,000	$700,000
IRA	0	$50,000	$200,000
Life insurance	$500,000	$600,000	$3 million
Primary home	$250,000	$450,000	$1.2 million
Second home	0	0	$800,000
Business equity	0	0	$500,000
Gross estate	$1 million	$2 million	$10 million

Step 2: Figuring the taxable estate			
	Joe	*Mary*	*Rich*
Gross estate	$1 million	$2 million	$10 million
Funeral expenses	$4,000	$6,000	$10,000
Estate administration	$1,000	$10,000	$60,000
Debts	$15,000	$5,000	$30,000
Unpaid mortgages	$35,000	0	$200,000
Marital deduction	$750,000	0	$5 million
Charitable deduction	0	0	$50,000
Total deductions	$805,000	$21,000	$5.35 million
Taxable estate	$195,000	$1.979 million	$4.65 million

Step 3: Figuring the estate tax			
	Joe	*Mary*	*Rich*
Gross estate	$1 million	$2 million	$10 million
Total deductions	$805,000	$21,000	$5.35 million
Taxable estate	$195,000	$1,979,000	$4.65 million
Tentative tax	$53,200	$771,350	$2,100,800
Unified credit	$53,200	$345,800	$345,800
State tax credit	0	$73,586	$264,300
Federal estate tax	0	$351,984	$1,490,700

*Doesn't consider deduction of state estate tax.

Joe. Most of his assets are being left to his wife, so if he were to die in 2002, his taxable estate would be $195,000, which is well below the $1 million that escapes estate tax under the new law.

Mary is a different story. She is a widow and inherited her husband's assets when he died many years ago. As a result, she cannot take the marital deduction. She didn't do much estate planning, so his assets plus her assets will wind up being added together to form her taxable estate.

If she were to die in 2002, she would owe $351,984 in federal estate taxes, on the amount that exceeds the $1 million threshold.

Rich is, well, rich. He left a large portion of his estate to his wife. His children received the rest and some went to charity. Because Rich used a portion of his marital deduction and all of his unified credit, he was able to reduce his federal estate tax to $1,490,700.

However, Rich could have avoided federal estate tax entirely on his death if he left all of his estate in excess of $1 million to his wife. In that case, estate tax would not be due until the death of the surviving spouse.

What's the gift tax?

The gift tax is the federal government's way of discouraging people with sizable estates from giving away all of their assets before they die to help their estates escape taxation.

How does the gift tax work? Each individual is allowed to give another individual up to $10,000 a year. This is called the "gift tax exclusion." Amounts that exceed $10,000 in a single year are reported by filing IRS Form 709 and may be subject to gift tax. You get a unified credit for gift taxes also.

If you're giving an asset instead of cash, you pay tax on the fair market value of the asset. The rates are graduated depending on the amount over $10,000.

The rule does not apply to gifts exchanged between spouses, which are exempt from gift tax. Because the gift tax functions as a back-up to the estate tax—they both have the same goal, not letting you give away too much without facing taxes—the rates are the same, at least until 2010.

Many people whose estates will face the estate tax can reduce the size of their taxable estates by giving $10,000 a year to each heir, tax-free, or by putting part of their assets into trusts.

Under the new law, there are tax breaks starting in 2002 that apply to estates close to being subject to the estate tax, estates of the well-to-do that definitely are subject to the estate tax, and estates of the super wealthy that paid a surcharge in addition to the estate tax.

THE NEW LAW

1. *Higher unified credit.* The unified credit rises in 2002 to $1 million, increasing to $3.5 million in 2009.

    Simply put, you will be able to leave $1 million to an heir in 2002 estate-tax-free. As a result of the law, estates whose assets were on the border in 2001 won't likely have to worry about the estate tax in 2002 (see Table 9.3).

Table 9.3   Top Unified Credit (2001–2011)

Year	The most you can leave to heirs, estate-tax-free
2001	$675,000
2002–2003	$1 million
2004–2005	$1.5 million
2006–2008	$2 million
2009	$3.5 million
2010	0
2011	$1 million

2. *Lower top tax rate.* The top rate for estate and gift taxes drops to 50% in 2002 and applies to estates that exceed $2.5 million.

    Simply put, this a break for well-to-do taxpayers. The amount they can give to heirs will be higher over the years leading up to repeal, while the top tax rate is lower.

    Under the old law, the top rate was 55% on amounts that exceeded $3 million. The lower rates all remain the same.

    The top estate-tax rate is further reduced in the years after 2002 leading up to repeal in 2010 (see Table 9.4).

Table 9.4 Top Estate Tax Rate (2001–2010)

Year	The top tax rate	On taxable assets that exceed
2001	55%	$3 million
2002	50%	$2.5 million
2003	49%	$2.5 million
2004	48%	$2.5 million
2005	47%	$2.5 million
2006	46%	$2 million
2007	45%	$1.5 million
2008	45%	$1.5 million
2009	45%	$1.5 million
2010	0%	0
2011	55%	$3 million*

*If Congress does not extend the estate tax's repeal beyond 2010, the law will return to the 2001 level.

3. *The Superrich get a break.* Starting in 2002, the 5% surtax on estates valued between $10 million and $17,184,000 million is repealed. In other words, the wealthy catch a big break here.

   After 2003, the credit for gift taxes stays at $1,000,000.

WHAT YOU NEED TO KNOW

Know the size of your estate now

Many people don't bother assessing the size of their estate, either because they don't know how or they don't like to think of their own mortality. Others prefer to leave the math and the complications to those who will inherit their assets. But a failure to plan now can leave those you love with a tremendous labor-intensive burden and perhaps a costly estate-tax bill.

And don't just assume estate-tax will be owed because your assets are above the unified credit—the amount you can leave to heirs tax-free. It might turn out that your estate won't owe any tax once the deductions and other credits are subtracted from the gross estate.

Example: Bob Smith dies in 2007. His taxable estate is $2 million. Under the old law, after subtracting the allowable deductions, he would have had a tentative tax of almost $800,000. After subtracting the allowable credits, the estate tax would be almost $350,000 in federal estate taxes. But under the new

law, his estate will owe no federal estate tax. That's because the unified credit in 2007 is $2 million.

Meet with your estate planner annually

As your assets rise, you should meet with your estate planner on an annual basis. You want to update the value of your estate and be sure your estate is under the estate-tax limit as the unified credit rises and top tax rate declines. Otherwise, you'll need to discuss estate-planning strategies to help you reduce the size of your estate while ensuring that the heirs you want to benefit from your estate are sufficiently protected.

Don't forget to include in your total estate the big three items that most people forget:

- Retirement plan assets
- The value of your home
- Life insurance payouts

If your taxable estate is under $1 million in 2002, you're safe

If this is the case, the fastest way to transfer assets is to own them jointly with your spouse. That's why most spouses choose to own homes and financial accounts together. When one spouse dies, the other spouse inherits them instantly, estate-tax-free. Talk to your tax planner if you own assets jointly with a non-spouse. There could be gift taxes on such assets.

Think about the future of your assets

While the value of your taxable estate may be lower than $1 million in 2002, think about how your estate may grow over the next 10 years as the estate tax phases out. It's also critical from an estate-planning viewpoint to monitor the estate tax carefully. If it doesn't look like the repeal is going to be extended beyond 2010, you will need to put in place trusts and other planning strategies to be sure your assets pass to heirs with as few taxes as possible.

Lower your taxable estate by gifting

The most you can give to each person gift-tax free is $10,000 a year. But you can lower your taxable estate even more by doing the following:

- Deposit up to $50,000 a year ($100,000 per couple) into a 529 college savings plan. Under the new law, such a gift is viewed as five gifts of $10,000 over five years.
- Pay a grandchild's school tuition or medical bill. There is no gift tax if the check is sent directly to the institution or health care provider. If your estate makes such a payment upon death, it won't lower the size of your estate.

Pull life insurance policies out of your estate

If the value of your life insurance policy benefits is significant—$2 million or more—and will likely push your estate over the line when you die, remove the policy from your estate.

All you have to do is set up a life insurance trust. The trust, not you, owns the policy, and your spouse can use the assets in coordination with the trustee to pay for key expenses for your children. Upon your spouse's death, your children would inherit the assets, tax-free. Another way to accomplish this is simply to give the policy to your heirs outright.

However, for this planning opportunity to work, you must have transferred an existing insurance policy to the trust at least three years before your death. In addition, if the life insurance policy that you transfer into the trust has a cash surrender value (typically true of whole-life type policies), you may trigger a gift tax. All the more reason why you should speak with your financial planner before you implement this strategy.

Give away assets that will appreciate in value

If you give $10,000 worth of stock to a child in a single year, the transfer will reduce your estate. When the assets increase in value, your estate will not owe any tax because the assets are not part of your estate.

In some cases it may even pay to give appreciable assets that exceed $10,000 and pay the gift tax. Why? The tax you pay now will be much lower than the tax that will be due when the assets grow significantly in value—unless you die in 2010, when the estate tax is repealed—and the gift tax you pay is removed from your estate.

This move will also allow your estate to avoid the change in stepped-up basis when the estate tax law is repealed in 2010. Under the new law, when the estate tax is repealed, the person who inher-

its the asset will carry over the basis of the asset's value when it was originally purchased. That could be costly, because the asset had so many years in which to appreciate.

For now, and up until 2010 at least, an asset's value is stepped up, meaning that you owe income tax only on any appreciation that exceeds the inherited asset's market value at the time of death. That's a much more attractive rule and will limit how much tax is owed, if any.

Consider tapping into taxable accounts first

If you've established that your estate will owe estate tax and you're older than age 59½, it may be wiser to withdraw assets from a taxable account first rather than dipping into your tax-deferred ones, such as a 401(k) or Traditional IRA.

While tax-deferred assets become part of your estate and are taxed accordingly, heirs can delay the income tax they will owe. Instead of withdrawing the entire ingeritence at once, heirs can choose to take smaller distributions over their life expectancy and cut down on the income tax owed.

If you are concerned that your assets will be stuck in tax-deferred accounts and heirs won't have sufficient liquid assets to cover the costs and taxes your estate will generate, consider buying an inexpensive term life insurance policy. The payout upon death would help cover these expenses and taxes.

If you are survived by your spouse, he or she can roll over the tax-deferred assets into his or her IRA and maintain the tax-deferred status.

Roll tax-deferred assets into a Roth IRA

Rolling over your tax-deferred accounts into a tax-free Roth IRA—if you qualify to open one—will benefit your heirs greatly. Remember, you could have a high net worth but a low annual adjusted growth income, which would qualify you for a Roth IRA. Then the estate tax that your heirs will have to pay can come from your after-tax taxable accounts.

By shifting tax-deferred assets to a Roth IRA, you also shelter your tax-deferred accounts for life from income taxes. Even though minimum distribution rules apply to a Roth IRA after your death, the use of a young heir's life expectancy will allow Roth IRA assets to grow on a tax-free basis over a very long period.

Transfer assets in retirement accounts to heirs

Another option once you turn age 59½ is to transfer $10,000 in retirement account assets per year to each heir. As you know, starting at this age, you can withdraw assets from a 401(k), Rollover IRA, or Traditional IRA penalty free.

You will owe income tax on the withdrawals in the case of these accounts. But the gifted assets will be out of your estate. This strategy makes sense when you have a significant retirement-plan portfolio as well as a high level of assets in taxable accounts.

Obviously, if you own a Roth IRA, these assets can be withdrawn free of income tax.

Keep careful cost-basis records

When you purchase an asset such as stocks, bonds, or a mutual fund, the price you paid for the asset is known as the cost basis. You owe tax on the amount your sold asset earned above the cost basis.

Under the current law, when you inherit an asset, its basis is determined on a "stepped up" formula. This means that the basis of the asset is determined based on its worth when you inherit it. As a result, the asset's taxable appreciated value over time is erased—a huge benefit to the person who inherits the asset.

But when the estate tax is repealed in 2010, the rules that govern the basis of inherited assets will change. Instead of the current value, you will have to know the price when the deceased person bought them.

As a result, you or your broker need to keep careful records of when you bought assets and the price you paid for them. This will make your heirs' lives much easier.

It's just as important that you or your parents organize their paperwork so that the cost basis for their assets is easy to find when it's needed.

But there is some good news. Under the new law, the executor will have the power to step up the basis of a portion of the estate's assets—up to $1.3 million. The executor also will be responsible for determining which assets are being stepped up and for reporting the information to the IRS. Assets left to a spouse can have the basis stepped up by an additional $3 million.

Friction-free ways to pass along the family house

The family home is often a financial, legal, and tax nightmare just waiting to happen. When parents die, their house becomes a battleground among heirs who want it and those who would rather sell it to raise cash.

Here are strategies that can help:

- *Leave the house to the estate.* Parents often assume that leaving their house to one child or to the children will keep the house in the family. In reality, most children would rather have the cash value of the house to meet their financial needs.

    By leaving the house to your estate, your children will decide whether they want to keep it or sell it. In most cases, the house is sold and the assets are divided up evenly among the heirs.

- *Put a real price on the house now.* Nostalgia is nice, but it has little to do with the real value of a home. In truth, the home may be more run down than you think or be in need of major repairs.

    Or the child to whom you left the house may not want to live in the neighborhood, may not be able to afford it upon inheritance, or for psychological reasons might not want to live there.

    If you get the home appraised now, all family members will know its current value. The knowledge will help intended heirs decide whether or not they want the house and whether it's smart to fix it up now.

- *Ask if your children want to buy it.* Rather than go through the hassle needed to avoid gift-tax and estate-tax issues if you give your children your home, sell it to them—if they want it.

    The first $500,000 in capital gains on the sale of a house is tax-free—if the owners have lived there for two of the past five years.

    So, up to $500,000 of your capital gains on the sale will escape taxation. The child who moves in will have the $500,000 exemption from taxation on future gains when the house is sold.

- *Be careful if you have more than one child.* Children who are friendly toward each other now may wind up fighting when there's a major asset such as house at stake. This is especially true in situations where one child is well off and the other is not. If you still want to leave the house to one child because he or she is the only one who lives in the area, ask yourself these questions:

(continued)

— What will the house be worth when inherited?

— Is that the child's fair share of the total estate?

— How will the other children feel about one child inheriting the house? Are they likely to sue to gain a fair share?

— Is the neighborhood changing for the better or worse? The value of the house may be declining and you may not even realize it.

— Can the child afford to own the home?

■ *Pick a picky executor.* When your home passes to your estate, your will's executor will have a critical role in making sure heirs get their fair share.

You can make all your children executors of your will. Then they can figure out how to sell the home and how the assets will be divided.

If the children don't get along, name an executor who is neutral, fair, and understands the personality issues at hand.

■ *Work in a clause.* Include a clause in the provision outlining the disposition of the home that sets conditions if one child wants to sell while the other wants to own. Your estate planner can help you with the wording.

If one child wants to live in the home, an appraiser could determine its fair value. That's the amount the home-buying child would divide among other siblings.

If more than one child wants to own the house, they could be required to submit a sealed bid to the executor. Then, the child who bids the highest would own the house.

Q&A

Q. Who pays the estate tax, me or my heirs?

A. Your heirs will pay the estate tax on your estate when you die— if there is any estate tax to pay. The money to pay the tax bill will come out of your estate. Neither you nor your spouse will owe any estate tax on your assets during your lifetime or your spouse's lifetime.

In fact, you can leave an unlimited amount of assets to your spouse, and neither your spouse nor your children will owe any current estate or gift tax. Your children may owe tax on your estate after you die and your surviving spouse dies. These events typically occur in old age. But if you and your spouse die suddenly, your heirs will have to scramble to calculate the value of your estate and the estate tax owed.

Q. Is estate planning only appropriate for older rich people?

A. Not at all. A young couple with a new child could suffer a tragic accident. Without a will and estate plans, the custody of their children and their assets could be in limbo. In general, if you are married or have children, estate plans are a must, no matter how old or wealthy you are.

Q. What key issues should my estate planner review under the new law?

A. Review the following with your estate planner:
- Calculate the value of your estate.
- Calculate your estate tax now. Your estate may not owe anything.
- See whether your estate is likely to owe tax as the law changes.
- Review your will and whether you want the same assets to pass to the same heirs.
- Review existing trusts to be sure that they accomplish what they were set up to do.
- Consider setting up trusts in cases where they are advised.

Q. What trusts may no longer be necessary?

A. Setting up an irrevocable trust, such as a life insurance trust, may not be necessary once the estate tax is repealed—and stays repealed. However, any irrevocable trust that you've already set up cannot be changed. You're stuck with it. By law, an irrevocable trust only terminates in accordance with its terms.

Q. Do I still need a will?

A. Just because the estate tax is phasing out, the unified credit is rising and other rules that affect estate taxes are changing, a will is still essential. You need a will for four basic reasons:
1. To legally describe how you want your assets distributed after death.
2. To name the person or persons you want to be in charge of your estate.
3. To name the guardian of your minor children. A court will make this decision if there is no will and could rule that your

children be placed with a relative who has the most money but not necessarily the kindest heart or best judgment.

4. To set up tax-planning trusts so that designated heirs receive what you want them to inherit and pay only the taxes necessary based on their status under the trust.

Ideally, you want to update your will after any major life event, such as marriage, divorce, birth of a child, or relocation.

And given the new law's twists and turns regarding the estate tax, it may make sense to update your will annually if your estate's assets grow significantly.

Q. How should the will be modified?

A. Wills that use a formula to distribute assets upon the death of the owner between the surviving spouse and children need particular attention. Changes under the new law for estate-tax exemptions as well as repeal in 2010 may overreward or shortchange heirs.

> **Example:** Let's assume at the time the will was drafted 20 years ago, a father bequeathed the family house to one of his two children because it was equal to 25% of the estate's value at the time. Today, the house may be worth many times what it was worth back then, making up 50% of the estate. As a result of the formula used in the original will, one child may wind up with a much larger share of the estate than the other child.

While you may say that this inequity will probably have been changed over the years during regular reviews, you'd be surprised how many people use such a formula in their original document and forget about it as the years go on.

Q. When do I need to name a guardian?

A. Even though a larger part of an estate's assets will avoid taxation under the new law, you still need someone to raise minor children. There are two rules to remember here:

1. *Name one person instead of a couple.* Even if the couple you have in mind are the most loving people in the world, they could wind up divorced. A long and messy custody battle over your child could follow. That's why naming one person as a guardian makes more sense. It's also smart to name backup

guardians in case that first person you named dies or does not want the responsibility at the time care must begin.

2. *Name someone else to handle the money.* Ideally, you want someone who is loving to raise your child and someone who is financially savvy to manage your child's inheritance. You may even want to name your child's guardian a co-trustee, so that he or she has a say in how the money is being managed.

As you can see, both situations are highly sensitive and should involve the consultation of an estate planner.

Q. Who should I name as my executor?

A. The executor of your will is the person who carries out its provisions and settles your estate. The person you select holds this position until those tasks are completed. Then there is no longer a need for the position. The person you choose should be:

- Someone you trust and has good, solid judgment.
- Someone who's responsible and has some financial knowledge. While the person doesn't have to be a financial planner, you want someone who knows enough to hire someone who is.
- Someone other than your attorney or accountant. There could be a conflict of interest or judgment and sensitivity issues. The person you name can always hire an attorney or accountant to consult, especially if you urge the executor to do so in your will or leave them with the name of an attorney you trust in a letter.

Q. Should I name more than one executor?

A. Yes. The first person you name may not be healthy or up to the job for a variety of reasons by the time you die. If your surviving family members believe that the executor isn't capable, they could go to court to force the person to give up the position, which could be costly and stressful for everyone.

In your will, be sure to specify that if the person named as executor isn't up to the task or isn't healthy, they must resign. You also may want to write a letter to the executor and leave it with your estate planner to be opened upon your death. This will give your executor a clear set of your wishes regarding when you want the person to perform the tasks and when you don't.

The rule of thumb is be as specific about your wishes as possible in your will and in letters left for the executor, guardian, and anyone else who will play a major role in executing your estate or raising your children. Most disagreements emerge when the executor makes decisions based on what he or she thinks you would want while your heirs think you would act differently. If your instructions are clear, the odds of a prolonged, unfriendly battle are minimized.

Q. What if I'm named as a trustee?

A. Before you agree to become a trustee, make sure you understand the responsibility. Here's what a trustee has to do:

■ *Translate the trust documents.* As trustee, you are a fiduciary. That means you must behave in a responsible manner, just as an attorney or bank would do. As a result, you can be held liable for your actions. Ignorance of trust documents is not an excuse.

Action: Read over important trust documents now and have the grantor's lawyer clarify in writing sections you don't understand.

■ *Size up the beneficiaries.* Trust beneficiaries often know how they want to spend their trust money. But their plans may differ from rules set up by the trust. Your mission as trustee is likely to be to preserve the trust for the life of the beneficiary. This may require you to make hard decisions when granting or denying a beneficiary's request for funds.

Example: If Freddy asks for $120,000 to buy an exotic motorboat, you may need to say, "no can do." However, if Freddy asks for $20,000 to buy a more reasonable boat, you may likely be able to say "yes."

As you can see, what's important to consider is the current lifestyle of the beneficiary and how reasonable his or her request is in light of that lifestyle. That's why it probably pays to meet with Freddy annually, so that you both remain on friendly terms.

■ *Do you know enough about money?* Most trusts hold cash, life insurance benefits and proceeds from the sale of a house and/ or personal property. Before you agree to become a trustee, make sure you know enough about managing money or know advisors to turn to if you need help. Fortunately, all costs of managing a trust come out of the trust's piggy bank, not yours.

- *Know the other regular duties.* Trustees need to perform a series of regular duties. Here's a list of the basics.
  - Keep beneficiaries informed. Send them copies of investment statements or prepare quarterly reports that outline your actions.
  - File papers with the IRS. A trust is a taxable entity, so you'll need to file a tax return for the trust annually.
- *Expect to put in time.* All of the duties of a trustee take time. The good news is that you should expect to be compensated. A reasonable amount each year for a trust up to $1 million is 1% of the principal. For example, if a trust were worth $2 million, your yearly fee would be $20,000.

THE SECOND CHANGE

Starting in 2002, the lifetime gift-tax exclusion rises to $1 million.

Do You Qualify for This?

Yes. *Everyone qualifies for this one.*

BACKGROUND

While you can give away up to $10,000 a year gift-tax-free while you're alive, the law places a different cap on the total amount you can give away free of tax over your entire lifetime.

Under the old law—and in 2001—$675,000 of your assets escape under the lifetime gift-tax exclusion. This total is the same amount as the estate-tax exclusion because the two have been unified, working hand-in-hand. So if the total amount of gifts a person made over the course of his or her lifetime did not exceed $675,000 and that person died in 2001, that person's estate can exclude the remaining unused portion of the $675,000 exclusion.

But if the value of that person's lifetime gifts exceeded $675,000, there would be no estate-tax exclusion available upon death in 2001.

As you can see, you take either one exclusion or the other, but not both.

Wondering whether you can get around these exclusions with the unlimited marital deduction? Absolutely. You can leave your spouse an unlimited amount of assets, estate-tax-free, and avoid the lifetime gift tax exclusion and estate tax exclusion. The only hitch is that your spouse must be a U.S. citizen.

But remember, your individual lifetime gift-tax and estate-tax exclusions disappear when your spouse inherits your assets. In effect, your individual lifetime gift-tax and estate-tax exclusions are folded into your unlimited marital deduction.

When your surviving spouse dies, the only amount that will be excluded from his or her estate is his or her own estate-tax exclusion. Your exclusion and your surviving spouse's exclusion are not combined (although your heirs would find it much more beneficial if they were).

> **Example:** Jack and Jill had an estate worth $5 million. When Jack died in 2000, Jill inherited everything estate-tax-free, so Jack's gift and estate-tax exclusion of $675,000 was not needed and was lost permanently.
>
> When Jill died in 2001, only her exclusion of $675,000 was subtracted from her taxable estate—not the combined amount of $1.35 million. So her heirs owed estate tax on the amount that was left after subtracting the allowed deductions and credits.

Clearly, the higher gift tax exclusion under the new law is beneficial for people who give family members or friends large amounts of money or assets.

THE NEW LAW

Higher lifetime gift-tax exclusion. The lifetime gift-tax exclusion rises to $1 million in 2002—up from $675,000.

The $1 million level will remain fixed through 2009. This means that between 2002 and 2009 an individual will be able to exempt $1 million of gifts given over a lifetime (see Table 9.5).

As you can see, under the old law, the lifetime gift-tax exclusion and the estate-tax exclusion were unified—meaning they were exactly the same.

Table 9.5   Top Lifetime Gift-Tax Exclusion v. Estate-Tax Exclusion (2001–2010)

Year	Gift-tax exclusion	Estate-tax exclusion
2001	$675,000	$675,000
2002	$1 million	$1 million
2003	$1 million	$1 million
2004	$1 million	$1.5 million
2005	$1 million	$1.5 million
2006	$1 million	$2 million
2007	$1 million	$2 million
2008	$1 million	$2 million
2009	$1 million	$3.5 million
2010	$1 million	0
2011	$1 million	$1 million*

*Amount that would have been available under the old law.

Under the new law, the lifetime gift-tax exclusion is frozen at $1 million through 2009, while the estate-tax exemption continues to rise to $3.5 million. And after 2009, when the estate-tax is repealed, the gift-tax rate will be 35%.

What does this mean in practical terms? Your estate-tax exclusion is reduced by the amount of any gift-tax exclusion used.

Example: A person who dies in 2009 gave away $1 million in taxable gifts over the course of his lifetime. The person's estate would then subtract the $1 million from the $3.5 million estate-tax exclusion. The resulting $2.5 million is the amount that the person's estate can use as the estate-tax exclusion.

WHAT YOU NEED TO KNOW

The law has a big impact on your parents

Given the complexity of the law and the fact that your parents probably have more assets than you do but aren't as familiar with the new law's twists and turns, you should encourage them to consult with an estate planner.

Rework wills carefully if expensive art is involved

Under the old law, a superwealthy couple could donate their Picassos to a museum to reduce their estate while leaving their children the other assets.

The charitable gift would lower the parents' estate, which would allow their children to keep more of the estate's balance. But when the estate tax is repealed in 2010, there will be no financial incentive to leave the Picassos to the museum. The kids could hang onto them as well as the cash.

If you want to limit your children's inheritance, your will have to specifically outline how your want gifts to charity handled. You may want to give the Picassos away during your lifetime if the estate tax is repealed and take the income tax deduction while you're still around.

Give your spouse top priority in your will

When the estate tax is repealed in 2010, the new law will allow you to pass along up to $3 million of investment gains to your spouse and up to $1.3 million in investment gains to heirs without forcing them to pay capital gains taxes at the assets' original cost basis. As a result, you should leave your spouse assets that have grown significantly in value.

Example: Leave your spouse the General Electric stock that you bought for $48 a share and that has tripled in value since that time or the second house you bought on the quiet lake that is now a hot vacation destination.

Divide IRAs into several accounts

IRAs often make up one of the largest portions of a person's estate. That's because after a lifetime of rollovers, contributions, and appreciation, the amount can be significant at death.

But heirs who inherit the assets in a Traditional IRA will owe income taxes as they withdraw the assets. Withdrawals from an inherited Roth IRA, however, would be tax-free.

Solution: Create separate Traditional IRAs for each heir. Then name a different beneficiary for each IRA. Under the new law, assets in your IRAs can be moved around tax-free provided they remain under your name. This means you can tweak each of these IRAs as you age so that an equal amount is in each IRA designated for heirs. You'll need to keep an eye on the allocations as the estate-tax exclusion rises during the span of the new law.

Choose your second beneficiaries carefully

The tax law allows a spouse to decline his or her share of the inheritance within nine months of your death. When that occurs, the assets will pass to the people named as contingent beneficiaries. These beneficiaries may owe income tax, however.

> *Strategy:* Your spouse may want to decline the inheritance of your retirement assets. If he or she declines them, the assets can be passed on to the second beneficiary. If the second beneficiary were a child, the assets would pay out over the course of the child's lifetime, which would be much longer than your spouse. As a result, more of the assets would be left in the inherited retirement plan to continue growing tax-deferred.

Be sure your will outlines your retirement plan wishes

When you opened a retirement plan such as an IRA, you filled out paperwork and named your beneficiaries. By law, your spouse must be the primary beneficiary. After that you are allowed to name whomever you wished, as well as the allocation you want them to receive upon your death.

But while the beneficiary designation that you made for your retirement plan dictates who inherits what, your will can dictate how much you want an heir to inherit to minimize their tax hit. You can do this by creating a trust for each beneficiary that outlines when withdrawals can be taken and how much can be withdrawn. That's why it's important to coordinate estate planning with retirement plan assets.

How much you gift depends on your age

The way the new law is set up, it pays to live until 2010, when the estate tax is repealed. If you are older and not in good health, then it makes sense to gift as much as possible early on. If you are young and in good shape, it makes more sense to postpone transferring assets to heirs, since you will be able to give more and more as the years go on until 2010, when your estate won't owe any tax. Just be aware that in 2011, the old nasty estate-tax rules from 2001 may bounce back into play unless congress extends the repeal.

Keep an eye on the law and consult your estate planner as you age. Your health and the size of the estate are key considerations.

Be sure to leave your new spouse something

If you leave all of your money to your kids from a first marriage and nothing to your new wife, your new wife is almost certainly going to sue them. She will likely claim that you forgot to change the will to have it comply with the new tax law. Most states have laws ensuring that a surviving spouse inherits at least one-third of an estate. But going to court to force the estate to comply could be costly for your current surviving spouse.

Q&A

Q. I'm confused—what's the difference between the annual gift-tax exemption and the lifetime gift-tax exclusion?

A. The annual amount you can give to any individual is $10,000. Amounts that exceed this level face taxation. Over the course of your lifetime, the total amount you can give away gift-tax-free is $675,000 in 2001 and $1 million in 2002–2009.

Q. How can I keep angry relatives from challenging my new will?

A. Under the new law, a greater amount of assets will be able to pass to heirs estate-tax-free. The higher the amount of assets at stake, the greater the risk that an ex-spouse or children from a first or second marriage will contest the will—even though the person who signed the will knew exactly what he or she was doing.

So, whenever you create a new will, draw up a similar one a few months later. To differentiate the two wills, bequeath a small charitable gift—such as a few thousand dollars to the local museum—in the newer will. This addition will prove to a court that you reconsidered your will but remained consistent in your intentions concerning the children.

Several similar wills over a long time period with slight changes will show a court that you did not write up a new will or change your intentions on a whim.

If you have several similar wills, disgruntled relatives will have a hard time invalidating them. Even if the court invalidates your most recent will, the relatives would have to go through the legal process again to challenge the previous one and the one before that. This could be a lengthy and costly process.

The more time there is between the wills, the more difficult it is for the court to determine that you were incompetent to make rational decisions.

Q. Should I create a living will?

A. Under the new tax law, the rules are changing in many cases on an annual basis. As a result, you want to be sure your family is aware of your wishes. Here's an example that may seem far-fetched, but exaggeration always has a way of making a point crystal clear:

> **Example:** Let's say Larry never ever wants to be kept on a life-support system. He tells his oldest son it's just not how he wants to live out his last days—and he doesn't want to subject his family to that kind of anguish.
>
> But Larry never draws up a living will.
>
> Unfortunate circumstances occur and Larry is indeed put on a life-support system. All members of Larry's family and the hospital aren't aware of his wishes. So some members of Larry's family insist that he be kept on the system.
>
> Larry left a large life insurance policy to take care of his family. But they cannot dispose of his estate or inherit assets while he's alive.
>
> Now let's assume the year of this tragedy is 2010, and the estate tax has been repealed. Larry's family should be able to inherit everything estate-tax free if Larry's wishes were carried out. But they can't because Larry is on a life-support system and there's disagreement about whether to remove him from it. When Larry dies in 2011, the estate

tax is back in full force and his heirs owe estate taxes under the old law.

Of course, this is an extreme example. But it does help to illustrate the importance of a living will and what impact not having one could have on your family.

A living will ensures that you receive the medical care you want if you're too sick to articulate your decisions. This document lets your family know how you want to be treated if you're chronically sick or terminally ill. The document outlines:
- Who should make your healthcare decisions if you can't.
- What kind of medical treatment you want and don't want.

It also makes sense to discuss living wills with aging parents before they encounter any major health problems. It's far less stressful to discuss a living will with your healthy family than at the hospital.

Give copies of your living will to your legal surrogate, your doctors, your family, and your religious advisors. Don't store this document in a safe-deposit box. Place it in an accessible place where it can be easily located in case of an emergency.

Which trusts to trust in tricky situations

Under the new tax law, trusts will become even more powerful estate planning tools. With new rules coming and going, the right trust ensures that:
— Heirs receive the assets you want them to receive.
— Heirs receive the assets under the conditions you outline.
— The size of your estate is reduced, easing estate tax liability.
— Future tax law changes won't leave your assets or estate vulnerable.

With that said, here is a list of tricky situations and which trusts likely make the most sense…
- *Problem:* Spouses want to preserve their unlimited marital deductions.
- *Solution:* Set up a bypass trust.

As you know, the unlimited marital deduction allows one spouse to pass an unlimited amount of assets to his or her spouse free of estate taxes. But that means the surviving spouse will be left with a larger estate. As a result, heirs will be exposed to greater estate tax risk when he or she dies.

With a bypass trust (also known as a "credit shelter trust"), your first $675,000 (2001) or $1 million (2002) goes into a trust for the surviving spouse's benefit. The surviving spouse receives income from the trust. And everything above the amount in the trust passes to the surviving spouse, tax-free, thanks to the unlimited marital deduction. Keep in mind, though, that the unlimited marital exclusion only applies to spouses who are U.S. citizens.

> **Example:** Robert owns assets of $2 million—double the amount covered under the new law in 2002. He leaves all of his assets to his wife, Joan, when he dies in 2002. No estate tax is owed because of the unlimited marital deduction.
>
> But when Joan dies, her heirs will owe significant estate taxes on her estate of $2 million. In effect, Robert's unified credit was wasted when he left his assets outright to Joan.
>
> If Robert instead had placed $1 million in a bypass trust for Joan's benefit, it would not have qualified for the marital deduction and Joan would inherit the balance of his estate outright. No tax would be owed at Robert's death because the remaining amount in his estate would be sheltered by his unified credit.
>
> Meanwhile, Joan would receive income for life from the bypass trust. Upon her death, Robert and Joan's children would receive the property in the trust estate-tax-free. The balance of her estate—the $1 million Robert gave her outright—would be sheltered by her unified credit.

- *Problem:* You are divorced and have two families.
- *Solution:* Set up a Qualified Terminal Interest Property (QTIP) trust.

A QTIP trust comes in handy when you want to protect the assets you left to a spouse from nasty creditors or a greedy new spouse. It's also used for people in second marriages.

The trust allows you to control how assets are distributed among heirs from your first marriage and second marriage.

(continued)

Example: Let's say you want to provide for the spouse from your second marriage and your children from a second marriage when you die. The QTIP would provide income on an annual basis to your second spouse. When he or she dies, the assets would then pass to the children of your first marriage.

- *Problem:* You own a valuable home.
- *Solution:* Use a Qualified Personal Residence Trust (QPRT).

This trust is ideal when your estate will face estate taxes and your family home makes a big part of your assets.

By putting your home into this trust, the value of your home and any subsequent appreciation in value are removed from your taxable estate. You also retain the right to live there for a set number of years—usually 10 to 15 years—depending on your life expectancy.

Then the real estate becomes the property of your children or another beneficiary. You would be responsible for the expenses of maintaining the residence as if you owned it.

Caution: Choose a period of years that you reasonably expect to outlive. If you die before the period stated in the trust, the property will automatically be included in your taxable estate.

If you want to continue living in the property after the term expires, direct that the property can remain in trust for the benefit of your children or another beneficiary. You then will have to pay fair market-value rent to the trustee to live in the house. The trustee will pay the real estate taxes and expenses.

Big benefit: By paying rent to the trustee, you can transfer more money to your children or other beneficiaries. Why? Because your rent payments serve to fund the trust and maintain the property that will eventually pass outright to them.

- *Problem:* You have a large life insurance policy.
- *Solution:* Set up a life insurance trust.

As you know, the cash benefits paid out by a life insurance policy that you own is included as part of your taxable estate. That's not a problem unless your insurance policy is significant enough that its benefits will push you into taxable territory.

With a life insurance trust, the policy's benefits pour into a trust and are used to facilitate the payment of whatever estate taxes are owed.

Even if your insurance policy's benefit is to be paid to a surviving spouse and avoids taxation under the marital deduction, you still will have a problem. When the surviving spouse dies, the amount in the estate that exceeds $675,000 in 2001 and $1 million in 2002 will be subject to taxes.

What to do: Set up an irrevocable life insurance trust with Crummey powers. The trust owns your life insurance policy. When you die, the insurance benefit pours into the trust. Your spouse can receive annual income for life, and the trust proceeds will pass to your children when your spouse dies. No estate taxes are owed on the life insurance payout.

Adding "Crummey powers" to this trust allows the annual insurance policy payments to qualify for the $10,000-per-year gift tax exclusion. As a result, transfers to the trust will qualify for the annual gift tax exclusion and won't be considered taxable gifts.

The trust recipient must have the right to withdraw money from the trust each year that's equal to 5% of the value of the trust principal or $5,000, whichever amount is greater.

Remember, if you transfer existing insurance policies into the trust, you have to survive three years beyond the transfer date for the insurance to be excluded from your taxable estate. You can avoid the delay by setting up the trust and letting the trustee buy a new life insurance policy.

■ *Problem:* You want young kids to have your investment assets.
■ *Solution:* Set up a custodial account or a Minor's Trust.

Stocks that increase dramatically in value are part of your estate at death. The current market value is what's taken into consideration for estate taxes, not the low price you paid for them.

What to do: If you want to pass assets directly to your children who are under age 21, a "custodial account" or a "Minor's Trust" should be set up for each of them. Accounts set up under a Uniform Gifts or Transfers to Minors Act will be owned by your children and taxed at their lower rates (as long as they're 14 years old or older).

(continued)

Unlike custodial accounts, which terminate at age 18 or 21, assets can be left in a Minor's Trust after a child turns age 18 or 21. But there's a catch: With a Minor's Trust, the child must be permitted to withdraw the entire amount of the trust when he or she reaches age 21.

Talk to your children to minimize the risk that they will terminate the trust when they reach that age. You can give the trustee as much discretion as you'd like to pay out income to your children during their minority. You also can direct partial payments of the trust principal outright at various ages—often ages 25, 30, 35, and 40.

- *Problem:* You don't want children to go wild with an inheritance.
- *Solution:* Set up a Crummey Trust.

With a Crummey Trust, all gifts paid into the trust will be excluded from estate tax. While a child could always remove these assets, in theory the child is supposed to leave the money in the trust.

However, for a special-needs child, you will generally establish a trust under your will, not a Crummey Trust. The trust would kick in at your death and fund whatever special care the disabled child needs, beyond what available government programs would pay for.

- *Problem:* You want to control assets but pass on the gains.
- *Solution:* A Grantor Retained Annuity Trust (GRAT).

A GRAT allows you to control an asset for a certain term but pass on the future appreciation free of estate tax to heirs when the term expires. This trust is especially helpful if the estate tax returns in 2011—or sooner following an amendment to the law. Ideally, you want to include an asset that will likely appreciate significantly over the trust's lifetime or term.

There are many complex issues related to the establishment of a GRAT and you should consult with your estate planner if you are considering establishing one.

THE THIRD CHANGE

The state death-tax credit for federal estate tax starts to phase out in 2002 and is repealed in 2005.

Do You Qualify for This?

Yes. *Everyone does. If your estate is subject to federal estate taxes, it is likely subject to state death taxes as well.*

BACKGROUND

Unless you've settled an estate or have already done some estate planning, you probably aren't aware that an estate must not only pay a federal estate tax but also a state estate tax. Many state death taxes were set up in an unusual way so that you weren't paying an amount in addition to the federal tax. Instead, states took what the federal government said you could claim as a credit. This is going to change under the new tax law.

Under the old law and in 2001, an estate is entitled to a federal credit for state death taxes paid. The amount of the credit is based on the decendent's "adjusted taxable estate," which is the taxable estate minus $60,000. The maximum credit an estate could take was calculated using a rate table.

Since 1926, nearly all states subject estates to some type of death and/or inheritance tax. Today, most of them impose a tax on an estate that equals the credit allowable under the federal tax system. In other words, whatever amount the federal government says you don't owe under this credit must be handed over to the state.

As of July 1, 2001, 38 states and the District of Columbia have this so-called "pick up" tax—picking up what the federal government forgives. Two other states—Louisiana and Connecticut—just passed pick-up tax laws starting in 2004 and 2006, respectively. The remaining 10 states use a different method to calculate estate taxes.

Most of these states are expected to lose $50 billion to $100 billion in revenue over the next 10 years as the federal estate tax phases out. The 38 states that use the pick-up method are expected to lose the most. But the 10 states with separate structures are expected to lose money as well.

The new law phases out the federal government's state death-tax credit starting in 2002. In 2005, the state death tax credit will be repealed. That will all but eliminate the state death tax, given that states had used the federal credit as the amount they picked up for their estate tax.

THE NEW LAW

Lower credit for state death taxes. Starting in 2002, the state death tax credit is reduced by 25% annually starting in 2002. In 2005, the credit will be repealed (see Table 9.6). Instead the state death tax, if any, will be allowed as a deduction.

Table 9.6 Amount the Federal Government's State Death-Tax Credit Will be Reduced

2002	25%
2003	50%
2004	75%
2005	0

Table 9.7 is used to calculate the federal government's state death tax credit in 2001.

To find out how the credit will be reduced in 2002–2004, simply:

- Multiply the middle two columns by the percentage for that year.
- Subtract the result from the 2001 number.
- The result will be the new, lower state tax credit.

Example: In 2002, when the rate is reduced by 25%, if your adjusted taxable estate is over $2.54 million (the highest level), the maximum tax credit will be $110,000 (0.75 × 146,800).

Table 9.7 The Federal State Death Tax Credit (2001)

Adjusted taxable estate	The tax credit will be	Plus	Of the excess over
$40,000–$90,000	$0	8%	$ 40,000
$90,000–$140,000	$400	1.6%	$ 90,000
$140,000–$240,000	$1,200	2.4%	$140,000
$240,000–$440,000	$3,600	3.2%	$240,000
$440,000–$640,000	$10,000	4%	$440,000
$640,000–$840,000	$18,000	4.8%	$640,000

Table 9.7 *(Continued)*

Adjusted taxable estate	The tax credit will be	Plus	Of the excess over
$840,000–$1.04 million	$27,600	5.6%	$840,000
$1.04 million–$1.54 million	$38,800	6.4%	$1.04 million
$1.54 million–$2.04 million	$70,800	7.2%	$1.54 million
$2.04 million–$2.54 million	$106,800	8%	$2.04 million
$2.54 million–$3.04 million	$146,800	8.8%	$2.54 million
$3.04 million–$3.54 million	$190,800	9.6%	$3.04 million
$3.54 million–$4.04 million	$238,800	10.4%	$3.54 million
$4.04 million–$5.04 million	$290,800	11.2%	$4.04 million
$5.04 million–$6.04 million	$402,800	12%	$5.04 million
$6.04 million–$7.04 million	$522,800	12.8%	$6.04 million
$7.04 million–$8.04 million	$650,800	13.6%	$7.04 million
$8.04 million–$9.04 million	$786,800	14.4%	$8.04 million
$9.04 million–$10.04 million	$930,800	15.2%	$9.04 million
Over $10.04 million	$1,082,800	16%	$10.04 million

WHAT YOU NEED TO KNOW

Run the numbers on your state's death-tax rates

Estates that are worth more than $3 million could face higher estate taxes if the person who died lived in a state with high death taxes. Why? The new tax law phases out and then repeals in 2005 the credit that coordinated state and federal estate taxes.

Most states charged a death tax that was equal to the amount the federal government lets you claim as a credit. Because the two are linked, as the state credit declines so will the amount of tax that the states will collect. In 2005, there no longer will be a credit, which may force your state to enact its own estate tax to make up the difference.

By 2005, states may begin to charge an estate tax—but there will no longer be a federal credit. Consult your estate planner for advice.

Moving to a new state?

Have your estate planner review your will and other estate planning documents such as trusts. Estate-tax rules could be different from state to state, depending on which states pass death tax laws to make up for revenue lost on the repeal of the federal government's state death tax credit.

THE FOURTH CHANGE

The generation-skipping transfer (GST) tax exemption starts to rise in 2002 and is repealed in 2010.

Do You Qualify for This?

Yes. If you plan to give a grandchild more than $1 million in cash or assets during your lifetime or when you die.

BACKGROUND

The estate tax limits how much of your assets can be left to heirs when you die. The gift tax limits how much you can pass along while you're alive. The GST tax limits how much you can pass along to grandchildren.

Back in the early 1980s, the GST didn't exist. You were able to pass along assets to your grandchildren without paying any taxes. That's because there was a big loophole in the estate tax law that said taxes were owed only at your death and when your grandchildren died. Hence, you could transfer an unlimited amount of wealth to them, reduce the size of your estate, and minimize estate taxes at a single gift-tax cost.

The Tax Reform Act of 1986 closed the loophole by creating the GST tax. It kicks in when the assets being passed along exceed a certain level set by the law. Back then, the amount was $1 million per grandparent but that number has since climbed with inflation.

How the GST works

In 2001, every grandparent is allowed to exempt from the GST tax up to $1.06 million of assets from his or her estate when those assets pass to grandchildren. The amount can be divided among the grandchildren any way the grandparent wishes. Amounts that exceed the limit face the GST tax, which isn't pretty. In 2001, assets in excess of the limit are taxed at a rate of 55%. Remember, the GST tax is payable in *addition* to any estate or gift tax owed.

Many wealthy grandparents escape paying the GST. Why? Because there are several ways to transfer a large amount of assets without triggering the tax, and any generous grandparent transferring more than $1.06 million to a grandchild is likely to use a trust to minimize the tax impact on their estate.

THE NEW LAW

1. *Lower GST rate.* The rate used to calculate the generation-skipping transfer (GST) tax will start to decline in 2002 and disappear in 2010, when the tax is repealed.
2. *Higher transfer amount.* The maximum amount that can be transferred and escape the GST tax will start to rise in 2002 and will be unlimited in 2010.

Like the estate tax, there is a seesaw effect at work with the new law—and both favor the taxpayer. As you can see in Table 9.8, the tax rate will decline while the amount that will escape taxation will rise.

Put simply, you'll be able to transfer a greater amount of your assets to your grandchildren without facing taxes, and the tax on the amount that exceeds the lower limit won't be as much.

Most people do not face the GST tax because most grandparents do not have that kind of money to pass along to grandchildren. They give their grandchildren money around the holidays or give them larger assets such as a car or furniture when they feel generous or want to make their grandchildren happy.

Table 9.8   Generation-Skipping Transfer Tax Rate (2001–2011)

Year	Rate	Taxed on amount that exceeds
2001	55%	$1.06 million
2002	50%	$1.06 million, plus an inflation adjustment
2003	49%	$1.06 million, plus an inflation adjustment
2004	48%	$1.5 million
2005	47%	$1.5 million
2006	46%	$2 million
2007	45%	$2 million
2008	45%	$2 million
2009	45%	$3.5 million
2010	0%	0
2011	55%	$1.06 million*

*If the GST tax's repeal is not extended by Congress beyond 2010, the law will return to its 2001 levels.

And a grandparent who wants to pay for a grandchild's tuition or for medical treatment can pay the bill directly to the institution and avoid taxation, no matter how large the tab.

But there are plenty of wealthy, generous grandparents who know how important it is to reduce the size of their estate while they're alive. They become heroes to grandchildren without going over the GST limit.

Example: Let's say that grandmother and grandfather want to write junior a huge check or transfer that summer house down at the shore to him. They can do either one without paying the GST tax—provided the cash or the house is worth no more than $2.12 million ($1.06 million per grandparent).

WHAT YOU NEED TO KNOW

If you transfer wealth, do it with appreciating assets

You can give your grandchildren up to $1.06 million in 2001, and more in 2002 and beyond. Cash is nice but assets such as stock and real estate are even nicer. Why? Because assets such as securities and real estate tend to appreciate in value over time. The value of your gift for the GST is assessed at the time you give it, so you wouldn't face the GST if the asset you gave away doubled in value in three years, for example. But those appreciating assets could face the estate tax if they are left in your possession at the time of death.

Set up a generation-skipping trust

Assets would go into this trust when you die and would avoid taxation if they did not exceed the gift-tax exclusion and generation-skipping transfer limits. Then the assets would transfer to your grandchildren when your own adult children die.

As a result, the assets would not be included as part of your estate or of your children's estate. The trust could be set up so that part of the sheltered assets passes to grandchildren annually. Many wealthy families use this trust to reduce the size of their taxable estate and provide grandchildren with a steady stream of income when they are older and more mature.

Age and health will play a big role in planning

If you're older and not likely to live until the GST tax is repealed in 2010, take steps to pass along wealth to grandchildren either directly or through trusts. Otherwise the assets will become part of your taxable estate.

However, if you are younger and in good health, postpone transfers to grandchildren until the maximum amount rises high enough to allow for a tax-free transfer. Or if amounts are significant, wait until the tax declines in the coming years. Or wait until the GST tax is repealed in 2010.

Because it is impossible to know whether the law will be extended, it's probably smart to set up trusts for grandchildren. Your tax and estate planners can help.

10

Sunset Provision

Think of Cinderella at the ball when the clock strikes 12 and you'll have some sense of what is due to happen to the new tax law at midnight of December 31, 2010.

All of those dream changes in the new tax law—the repeal of the estate tax, lower regular income tax rates, no more limits on itemized deductions, enhanced education incentives, etc.—will disappear. They'll be replaced by the harsher rules that were in place in 2001, before the new tax law was enacted.

Most people think that the sunset provision was put there by a vindictive Congress seeking to take back the tax breaks the law provides between 2001 and 2010. Not quite. When Congress passed the new tax law in May 2001, the House and Senate had to include the sunset provision to comply with the Congressional Budget Act of 1974.

In short, the act says that any time Congress passes legislation that affects the budget, it needs at least a two-thirds vote to make the law permanent. Otherwise, the law must include a sunset provision, which requires Congress to revisit the legislation by a specific date or else the new law expires.

As you can see, the sunset provision acts as a safety valve. It's meant to keep the politics of the moment from forcing the government to live with bad laws that affect the budget. In the case of the new tax law, the Republicans in Congress did not have enough votes to make the new legislation permanent. As a result, taxpayers must live with the prospect of the new law being replaced with the old law starting January 1, 2011.

In short, the sunset provision says to taxpayers, "You know all those tax breaks we gave you in the new law? We're taking them back in 2010 unless we decide to extend them."

That's what the sunset provision means on paper. In practical terms, however, the provision will function as a giant timer between now and the end of 2010. The timer will tick away, reminding Congress and politicians running for office that the law needs to be addressed if the expiration date is to be extended.

What are the odds of nothing happening to extend the tax law between now and 2010? Pretty slim. Congress has made significant changes to nearly ever major tax law it has passed since 1981. And sunset provisions are not foreign to past tax legislation, when the laws passed by a slim margin.

How significant newer tax-law changes will be in the coming years is another matter. The magnitude of the tax law amendments rests largely on:

- *The economy.* If it falters, expect more tax cuts to stimulate growth.
- *The budget surplus.* If it shrinks, look for tax increases.
- *The party that controls Congress.* Republicans and Democrats often have different policy agendas. Agendas cost money.
- *The person running for President.* Promises of tax cuts are a frequent favorite during national campaigns.
- *The sacred programs that need funding.* Tax cuts remain in place until Washington needs money for programs it considers essential.

While everyone fully expects Congress to fiddle with the current tax law and extend its timetable for extinction, you should plan as if the sunset provision will take effect. Remember, no one expected a presidential election tie. As we now know, strange things happen when results are assumed and the heavy lifting is left to fate.

Key: Review the current schedule of tax law changes over the next nine years and assess the impact on your finances now. Then take the appropriate steps to take advantage of the new law and minimize your tax liability. Then make additional changes to your plan as the law is amended in the coming years. The trick is to stay flexible.

WHAT YOU NEED TO KNOW

Keep a sharp eye on 2004 and 2008

These are presidential election years, when candidates traditionally call for lower taxes and modifications to the tax law, while incumbents tend to avoid touching the tax law at all in the year leading up to the election campaign.

Keep a sharp eye on the other years, too

Congressional elections will be held in 2002, 2004, 2006, 2008, and 2010. That's when the balance of power in the House and Senate can shift, creating new agendas and unexpected alterations to the tax law as we know it today.

Hire a sharp tax planner

If your assets are significant, you need someone you can turn to for tax advice on a regular basis, especially as the law changes. Tax planners charge for their advice, but it's money well spent, especially as your assets grow. If you have a family and a significant number of assets, the do-it-yourself approach could be costly in the long run.

In addition to planning advice, a good personal tax planner can help you reduce your tax bill under the current law, take advantage of deductions you may not know about, and help you minimize the likelihood of paying taxes under the alternative minimum tax rules.

Meet with your financial planner at the start of each year

Under the new law, your regular income-tax rate has dropped, your risk of paying tax under the alternative minimum tax rules are greater, and the size of your estate may qualify for estate taxes—even though the amount you can pass on to heirs is higher.

And that's just for starters. There are dozens of other changes that likely affect you and your finances. Planning isn't about figuring out how to beat the IRS at its own game. Its about fully taking advantage of the rules so that you don't have to write a check for more than you are required to pay.

These are key questions to ask your financial planner:

■ How close am I to owing taxes under the AMT rules?

- If my spouse and I died today, would my heirs owe estate taxes?
- What's my net worth?
- Do I have enough life insurance?
- What's the most tax-efficient way for me to save for my child's education?
- What deductions can I take?
- What can I do to reduce my tax hit?
- Am I saving enough for retirement?
- Based on my spending pattern, how can I save more?
- Are my investment assets well diversified?
- Are they allocated correctly?

Call for quarterly updates

In the past, most taxpayers could sail through the tax year without a hitch. Now, with the tax law changing and your assets growing in value, you need to do more planning throughout the year. The days of being surprised by the amount you owe in April are over.

Ask your financial planner for quarterly updates of your financial and tax position. When you have a firm fix on your tax situation throughout the year, you can take steps early enough to minimize your tax hit in April.

Examples of questions to ask on a quarterly basis:

- How much will I owe next April?
- What can I do this year to reduce the bill?
- How can I reduce the risk of paying the AMT?
- If I have to pay the AMT, how can I take advantage of it?
- Is my AGI too high to qualify for credits?
- Is my AGI too high to qualify for an Education IRA or Roth IRA?
- How can I reduce my AGI?
- How can I reduce my taxable capital gains this year?
- Should I rebalance my investment portfolios?
- Have I paid in enough to avoid an underpayment penalty?
- Should I own tax-exempt securities?
- Should I shift assets to my children?

If nothing changes, 2010 will be quite a tax year

If it looks like parts of the new tax law are not extended beyond 2010, many taxpayers will be taking major steps to preserve their wealth and protect their estates. To take advantage of the lower tax rates and full deductibility of itemized deductions, you may need to accelerate income and deductions in 2010 and limit them from landing in 2011, when the tax law of 2001 will be restored. But this kind of planning will have to be carefully balanced with the need to include major deductions in 2011 to reduce the higher income tax and estate tax liability of that year.

Index